STUDY GUIDE

STUDY GUIDE

Stephanie Stolarz-Fantino
University of California, San Diego

to accompany

Cole, Cole, and Lightfoot

The Development of Children

Fifth Edition

WORTH PUBLISHERS

Study Guide
by Stephanie Stolarz-Fantino
to accompany
Cole, Cole, and Lightfoot: **The Development of Children,** Fifth Edition

ISBN: 0-7167-8673-7 (EAN: 9780716786733)

First Printing, 2004

Worth Publishers
41 Madison Avenue
New York, NY 10010
www.worthpublishers.com

Contents

To the Student

This Study Guide was designed for use with *The Development of Children,* Fifth Edition, by Michael Cole, Sheila R. Cole, and Cynthia Lightfoot. It is intended to help you understand and remember the ideas and facts presented in the textbook. The guide has 16 chapters corresponding to the 16 chapters of the textbook; each chapter has the following sections:

- The introduction will orient you to the ideas presented. You may want to read it before reading the text chapter.
- The **Learning Objectives** are questions to keep in mind while studying each chapter.
- The detailed **Chapter Summary** can be read before the textbook chapter, as preparation, or afterward, as a review; it will also be useful when studying for quizzes and exams. Reading the outline cannot, however, substitute for reading the text; while it contains the basic ideas, it leaves out many important examples and illustrations that will help you understand and remember these ideas.
- The **Key Terms** listed at the end of each textbook chapter are reproduced. The matching exercise will give you the opportunity to test your understanding by identifying examples that illustrate key terms.
- **Multiple-Choice Practice Questions** cover material that is especially likely to appear on exams.
- **Short-Answer Practice Questions** are intended to make you think about important topics introduced in the chapter. Sometimes you will need to utilize ideas presented in different sections of the chapter to answer these questions.
- **Putting It All Together** appears in some, but not all, chapters of the guide. It contains exercises that require you to combine material from the chapter you are currently studying with information from previous chapters to help you gain a better overall view of development.
- **Sources of More Information** supplement the additional readings listed at the end of each text chapter.
- An **Answer Key** in each chapter lists the correct answers for the key terms matching exercise, the multiple-choice questions, and, where appropriate, for the putting it all together section.

It is hoped that by using this Study Guide, you will find your study of child development to be interesting and enjoyable.

STUDY GUIDE

The Study of Human Development

For centuries, philosophers have asked, "What is human nature?" Within this question are others, about how individual humans become what they are, and about how the events of their lives help or hinder their development.

Today, developmentalists from a variety of academic disciplines bring the techniques of scientific research to bear on these questions. Using interviews, observations, and experiments, they gather information on human development and interpret it within various theoretical frameworks.

This research is not of interest solely to philosophers. It helps all of us to make informed decisions in diverse areas; for example: public policy, by asking questions about what kinds of programs for children should receive public support; education, by asking under what conditions children learn best; and child rearing, by asking about what practices are most likely to help children grow up happy and well-adjusted.

Developmental science does not yet have answers to all our questions. But each year developmental research adds something to our understanding of human nature and to our appreciation of the development of individual children.

Learning Objectives

Keep these questions in mind while studying Chapter 1.

1. How did developmental science become an area of scientific study?
2. What are the four central questions that inform research in the area of human development?
3. All scientific research must conform to certain standards in order for its results to be accepted by other scientists. What are these criteria of scientific description and how can we tell if they have been met?
4. Which methods of data collection are commonly used by developmental scientists? What are the advantages and disadvantages of each?
5. What must researchers do to protect the rights and privacy of children who participate in developmental studies?
6. What are the strengths and weaknesses of longitudinal and cross-sectional research designs for understanding how behavior changes over time?

7. Why is it useful to devise theories to explain particular aspects of development?
8. What are the four broad frameworks into which we can organize most work in developmental science? How does each perspective explain developmental change?
9. What is a "bio-social-behavioral shift"? How does this concept help us to understand the interacting roles of biological, social, behavioral, and cultural factors in development?

Chapter Summary

Victor, the "Wild Boy of Aveyron," remains something of a mystery two centuries after his discovery. Was he, as believed by many authorities of his time, abandoned by his parents because of innate mental deficiency? Or, as his benefactor Jean-Marc Itard believed, was his development stunted by years of isolation in the forest?

I. THE STUDY OF CHILD DEVELOPMENT

In Itard's time, philosophers, social reformers, and scientists were already expressing interest in children and their development. Eventually, this interest grew into the study of child development—the physical, cognitive, social, and emotional changes that children undergo from conception onward.

A. The Rise of a New Discipline

In the beginning, the study of child development was influenced by philosophical questions; later, practical questions related to child welfare issues became important.

- The English philosopher John Locke viewed the infant's mind as a blank slate ("tabula rasa"); he believed in the importance of early experiences, especially adult guidance, for shaping children's characteristics. The French philosopher Jean-Jacques Rousseau, conceived of children as "born pure" and later corrupted by the influences of society; he believed that children passed through a series of qualitatively distinct stages as they developed. The ideas of these philosophers continue to influence our ideas about the nature of children and society's responsibilities toward them.
- Interest in children and their development grew as the industrial revolution in Europe and America brought large numbers of children into factories, working long hours in unhealthy conditions.
- Charles Darwin's Origin of Species also focused interest on children, as their development was thought to provide clues to the ways that humans are related to other species. Scientists began to ask how the abilities and behaviors of today's humans are influenced by our evolutionary past. Wilhelm Preyer, a 19th century embryologist, wrote the first textbook on child development and developed a set of rules for observing children's be-

havior (described in Table 1.1 of the textbook). Mark Baldwin contributed the first notable stage theory; he believed that children's abilities progress through a series of specific, systematic changes on the way to their adult forms. According to Baldwin, in order to understand the adult mind one must understand the child mind that precedes it. By the late 19th century, U.S. universities had taken up the study of development. Government agencies and philanthropic organizations began to support developmental research and to make publications devoted to child rearing available to parents. The same philosophical and practical questions that influenced the earliest research continue to motivate research today.

B. Modern Developmental Science

Once established as a discipline, the study of child development was pursued mainly by psychologists. In recent years, however, developmental science has become more interdisciplinary in nature. It has also become more international, reflecting the importance of cultural context in development. Developmentalists seek to organize their observations of development into theories—broad frameworks that guide the collection and interpretation of facts—in order to further our understanding of the principles of human development.

II. THE CENTRAL QUESTIONS OF DEVELOPMENTAL SCIENCE

Developmentalists share an interest in four fundamental questions:

- Is development a gradual process of change or do periodic sudden, rapid changes result in new forms of thought and behavior? This is a question about continuity.
- What are the contributions to development of the body's genetic program and of forces in the environment? This is a question about the sources of development.
- To what extent does the course of development change, through accident or through intervention? This is a question about plasticity.
- How do individual differences develop, making each human being unique?

A. Questions about Continuity

Within the question about continuity are two basic issues:

- Are the principles of human development distinctive?

Are human beings distinctive? This is a question about phylogeny, the evolutionary history of a species. Charles Darwin, for example, believed in continuity among species—that differences between humans and other life forms are "of degree, not of kind." Certainly, humans have much in common with other animals; for example, we share 99% of our genetic material with chimpanzees. We also have distinctive characteristics. One factor that contributes to the distinctiveness of humans is culture, the "man-made" part of the environment. Culture is a people's design for living, as expressed in their language and visible in their artifacts, knowledge, beliefs, values and customs. Language, through which culture is passed from one generation to the next, is also viewed as a distinctively human characteristic. Certainly, humans' capacity for using language and culture is greater than that of any other species.

- Is individual development continuous?

  This is a question about ontogeny—the course of development during an individual person's lifetime. Some developmentalists view development as quantitative—a gradual accumulation of small changes. Others emphasize the appearance of more abrupt, qualitative changes at particular points of development. These qualitatively new patterns are called developmental stages. Stage theories have had a great deal of influence throughout the 20th century. However, while observations of discontinuities in behavior support the existence of stages, there is also evidence to support the view that young children and adults experience the world quite similarly. Of particular difficulty for stage theories are observations that, at a given time, children often exhibit behaviors associated with more than one stage.

B. Questions about the Sources of Development

The question about the roles of genes and environment in development is often thought of as a debate about the relative importance of nature (an individual's inherited biological predispositions) and nurture (the influences of the social and cultural environments on the individual). This debate is illustrated by the argument over Victor, the Wild Boy of Aveyron. What were the sources of his disabilities of speech and social interaction? Modern developmentalists continue to debate the roles of nature and nurture, but they recognize that development cannot be adequately explained by either factor in isolation.

C. Questions about Plasticity

Are there times during development when behavior is especially open to influence by the environment? In some nonhuman species, critical periods are times during which particular events must occur in order for development to proceed normally. An example is the period after hatching during which chicks or ducklings become attached to their mothers. In humans, true critical periods seem only to occur during embryonic development. Therefore, when observing human development, researchers look for sensitive periods—times that are optimal for certain events to occur, and when environmental influences are likely to be most effective in fostering their occurrence. An example would be the period in childhood during which children acquire language. However, sensitive periods do not have to involve biological readiness; for example, Yasuko Minoura found evidence for a "cultural sensitive period" for children's adjustment to certain aspects of Japanese culture.

D. Questions about Individual Differences

The question about individual differences is really two questions: 1) What makes people different from one another (really the same as the question about sources of development)? and 2) Do people's characteristics remain stable over their lifetimes—for example, can you predict their behavior as adults from their traits in infancy? Apparently, the stability of characteristics over time depends, to some degree, on how they are measured. If different testing measures are used at different ages—as they often must be—characteristics may appear unstable over time. Stability of characteristics is also influenced by the stability of a person's environment; if the environment changes, personal characteristics may change as well.

III. THE DISCIPLINE OF DEVELOPMENTAL SCIENCE

Developmentalists want to be able to understand the behavior of the individual person and also to be able to draw conclusions about people in general. Balancing these two goals can be challenging.

A. The Goals of Scientific Description

Research in development can be described as belonging to one of several categories, depending on its goals:

- Basic research is carried out in order to advance scientific knowledge of human development; this research often explores major theoretical issues.
- Applied research is carried out in order to answer practical questions so as to help solve specific problems.
- Action research, also known as "mission-oriented" research, is carried out in order to provide data that can be used for making decisions about social policy.

B. Criteria of Scientific Description

Researchers judge their findings according to specific scientific criteria:

- Observations should have objectivity—that is, they should not be biased by the investigator's preconceived ideas.
- Observations should have reliability—they should be consistent when observed on more than one occasion, and particular observations should be agreed on by independent observers.
- Observations should have replicability—that is, when others perform the same study using the same procedures, they should obtain the same results.
- The measures used should have validity—the data being collected should actually reflect the underlying process the researcher is studying.

C. Methods of Data Collection

There are a variety of ways in which developmentalists collect data:

- Naturalistic observation is a method in which behavior is observed in the context of everyday life. Naturalistic observation is important in the discipline of ethology, the study of the biological, evolutionary basis of behavior. Ethologists believe that it is important to study behavior in the settings in which it naturally occurs. The accounts of ethnographers—scholars who study ethnography, the cultural organization of behavior—are also based on naturalistic observation and can be valuable in the study of development.

Observation can take place in a single context or in many contexts. Behavior is observed in many contexts in the study of children's ecology. Ecology is a term that refers to the range of situations in which people act, the roles they play, the problems they encounter and the consequences of those encounters. From an ecological standpoint, a child's place in the community—the physical and social context in which the child lives—can be thought of as a developmental niche. Barker and Wright's detailed study of a day in the life of a 7-year-old boy is an example of an ecological study.

For practical reasons, it is more usual to observe children in more narrow contexts. An example is Susan Gaskins' study of the activities of Mayan children living in rural Mexico.

A limitation on the usefulness of naturalistic observation is that behavior may change when people know that they are being observed. Also, because it is difficult for observers to record everything, their preconceived ideas may influence what actually is recorded.

- In a psychological experiment, investigators introduce a change into the experience of a person or group of people; their behavior in response to that change is compared with that of randomly-assigned people who do not receive the experimental treatment. If done properly, this allows the investigators to confirm or disconfirm a scientific hypothesis—an assumption that is precise enough to be tested and potentially shown to be true or false. An example in Chapter 1 is the study of "kangaroo care" for infants carried out by Nathalie Charpak and her colleagues. In an experiment with children, the group of children whose experience is changed is called the experimental group. Their behavior is compared with that of the control group, who are treated as much as possible like the experimental group except for not undergoing the experimental manipulation. An important advantage of using experimental methods is that experiments can demonstrate causation, in which the occurrence of an event depends upon the occurrence of a previous event. Many of the factors of interest to developmentalists cannot be experimentally controlled (for example, a child cannot be randomly assigned to be male, 5 years of age, or from a middle-income family). Therefore, researchers are also interested in the correlation between these factors and various measures of development. Correlation is a measure of the strength of association between two factors, but does not tell whether Factor A causes Factor B, whether Factor B causes Factor A, or whether some other factor causes both. The issue of correlation and causation is discussed in the box in Chapter 1 titled "Correlation and Causation."

  A limitation of experiments, according to some researchers, is that they may lack ecological validity; this term refers to the extent to which children's behavior studied in one environment—the laboratory, for example—is characteristic of their behavior across a range of settings.

- In the clinical method, researchers tailor questions to the individual subject. The answers to questions determine the direction the questioning will take. Jean Piaget made effective use of this method in his studies of children's thinking at different ages. The clinical method can reveal a great deal about individual behavior; however, it may be difficult to arrive at general conclusions using this technique. This method also relies a great deal on verbal expression and therefore may underestimate children's cognitive abilities.

D. Research Designs

Before beginning a study, researchers need to develop an overall plan describing how the study is put together—a research design. Developmentalists use several types of research designs:

- In a longitudinal design, data are collected from the same group of people as they grow older over an extended period of time. Carrying out a longitudinal study is costly and time-consuming; in addition, they may suffer selective dropout—that is, subjects may drop out during the course of the study, changing the sample from its original composition. Longitudinal designs also may confound age changes in behavior with changes due to other influences relating to the subjects' cohort—the group of people born at about the same time who share particular experiences unique to those growing up during that era. Using a cohort sequential design, in which the longitudinal study is replicated with several cohorts, helps researchers to separate cohort-related factors from changes due to age.
- The cross-sectional design, in which different groups of subjects of different ages are each studied once, is the most commonly used design in developmental research. This type of design is less expensive and time-consuming, and requires less commitment from subjects. However, it is important, when carrying out a cross-sectional study, to be sure that subjects in each age group are comparable in many characteristics besides age, such as sex, ethnicity, education, and socioeconomic status. It is also possible for cohort-related confounding to occur, so this must be taken into account when interpreting the results. Also, because of the way a cross-sectional study "slices up" development, it does not allow researchers to see how behavior actually changes over time and they must fill in the gaps through extrapolation and guesswork.
- To get around this problem, researchers can use microgenetic methods, which focus on development over the course of a relatively short time interval, allowing them to observe developmental mechanisms in action. Such methods are usually used with children who are thought to be on the threshold of an important developmental change.

The advantages and disadvantages of each type of design are discussed in the textbook in Table 1.2.

E. Ethical Standards

Today, research is evaluated for its ethical soundness as much as for its scientific accuracy. Most of the ethical guidelines for the treatment of human research participants are based on the Nuremberg Code and share several main concerns:

- Freedom from harm, both physical and psychological
- Informed consent, including parental consent for research with children
- Confidentiality of the information collected

Each university or agency at which research with children is conducted reviews research plans before they are carried out in order to ensure that the appropriate guidelines are followed.

F. The Role of Theory

The information psychologists obtain about children's behavior is only meaningful in the context of theory. At present, there is no single theory that unifies knowledge about development. However, the main theoretical perspectives can be grouped into four frameworks, according to their positions on the important questions about development that were introduced earlier in the chapter; each provides a distinctive and useful way of looking at the process of development.

- The biological-maturation framework

  According to the "biological-maturation" framework, the changes characterizing development have endogenous causes—that is, they arise as a consequence of the organism's biological heritage. According to this view, therefore, maturation—genetically determined patterns of change that occur with age—is the most important mechanism of development. Arnold Gesell was an influential biological-maturation theorist; another was Sigmund Freud, whose work is discussed in Chapter 1 in the box titled "Psychodynamic Theory: Freud and Erikson." Biological-maturation theorizing has received greater attention recently due to interest in evolutionary developmental psychology and to the availability of new technologies that allow researchers to measure biological processes more directly than was possible before. The new technological advances are discussed in the box "High-Tech Research on Brain Development and Disorders."

- The environmental-learning framework

  According to the "environmental-learning" framework, biological factors provide a foundation but much developmental change has exogenous causes—that is, causes that come from the environment. In this way of viewing development, learning—the process in which behavior is modified as a result of experience—is the most important mechanism of developmental change. B. F. Skinner was an important environmental-learning theorist.

- The constructivist framework

  According to the "constructivist" framework, nature and nurture both play important roles in development, and the influence of the environment may differ depending on the child's current stage of development. Constructivist theorists emphasize children's roles in actively shaping their own development. They believe that culture may affect the rate of development by varying children's environments, but expect all children to go through the same sequence of developmental changes. Jean Piaget was the most influential constructivist theorist.

- The cultural-context framework

  According to the "cultural-context" framework, children and their caretakers are viewed as coconstructors of children's development. This approach is similar to the constructive framework; however, it emphasizes the role of cultural groups in organizing children's experiences. Also, this perspective places less emphasis on stage-like consistency across tasks. It is expected that children's performance will vary on different tasks and that the existence or nonexistence of stages may depend on children's cultural-historical circumstances. Lev Vygotsky was an important cultural-context theorist.

IV. THIS BOOK AND THE FIELD OF DEVELOPMENTAL SCIENCE

It is difficult to know how best to divide development into different periods and also how to keep track of the many aspects of development as they combine and recombine at different times of life. One way of looking at these things is suggested by Robert Emde and his colleagues; this is the idea of bio-behavioral shifts, points at which biological maturation and behavioral changes combine to result in a reorganization of a child's functioning. Bio-behavioral shift also involves changes in the children's social worlds; therefore, the textbook organizes its discussion of developmental change from conception through adulthood around a series of bio-social-behavioral shifts. These shifts are points at which converging changes in children's biological characteristics and their behavior—which, in turn, lead them to experience the social environment differently and cause them to be treated differently by other people—lead to the emergence of distinctively new forms of behavior. The series of bio-social-behavioral shifts that characterize development from conception to adulthood are shown in Table 1.3. The bio-social-behavioral framework provides a way to keep in mind the constantly interacting forces that bear on human development.

It will be useful, in reading the text, to keep in mind the questions introduced in this chapter about the nature of development and what it means to be human. The questions that motivated Itard and other early developmentalists still drive today's research in developmental science.

Key Terms I

Following are important terms introduced in Chapter 1. Match each term with the letter of the example that best illustrates the term.

1. ______ causation
2. ______ clinical method
3. ______ cohort
4. ______ cohort sequential design
5. ______ control group
6. ______ correlation
7. ______ cross-sectional design
8. ______ ecological validity
9. ______ experiment
10. ______ experimental group
11. ______ longitudinal design
12. ______ microgenetic design
13. ______ naturalistic observation
14. ______ objectivity
15. ______ reliability
16. ______ replicability
17. ______ research design
18. ______ scientific hypothesis
19. ______ triangulation
20. ______ validity

a. The use of several different research methods to determine the cause of a particular behavior.
b. Watching children interact on the playground at recess is a form of this.
c. This describes research designs that are not biased by preconceived ideas.
d. A measure has this characteristic when it reflects what it is purported to. (For example, in order to have this characteristic, a written memory test would need to be given to subjects who could read.)
e. A group of subjects in an experiment who undergo a manipulation of their environment.
f. A psychologist who is comparing a group of 8-year-olds, a group of 10-year-olds, and a group of 12-year-olds on a problem-solving task is conducting this type of study.
g. In order to be useful, this must be capable of being disconfirmed.
h. Subjects in an experiment who do not receive the experimental manipulation, but are otherwise treated the same as those who do.
i. A measure has this if subjects, when tested on more than one occasion, earn nearly the same scores.
j. An example is "American children beginning kindergarten in 1992."
k. In this way of studying development, questions are tailored to the person being interviewed.
l. An example is the relationship between age and height in children.
m. A researcher needs to put this plan together before beginning a project.

n. This characterizes a study that yields the same results when carried out by another set of researchers using the same method.
o. Some laboratory experiments are criticized as lacking this characteristic.
p. A researcher studying adolescence follows several groups of children from 10 through 15 years, adding a new group of 10-year-olds to the study every five years.
q. Researchers are doing this when they test the effectiveness of a new way to teach math by teaching one group with the new method and compare the results to those from a group taught by the previous method.
r. A psychologist who studies one group of children's social relationships from kindergarten through sixth grade is conducting this type of study.
s. This is most often used when children are on the verge of a significant developmental change.
t. This is demonstrated when the occurrence of an event depends upon some other event that has already occurred.

Key Terms II

Following are important terms introduced in Chapter 1. Match each term with the letter of the example that best illustrates the term.

1. ______ bio-social-behavioral shift
2. ______ child development
3. ______ critical period
4. ______ culture
5. ______ developmental niche
6. ______ developmental stage
7. ______ ecology
8. ______ endogenous
9. ______ ethnography
10. ______ ethology
11. ______ exogenous
12. ______ learning
13. ______ maturation
14. ______ nature
15. ______ nurture
16. ______ ontogeny
17. ______ phylogeny
18. ______ plasticity
19. ______ sensitive period
20. ______ theory

a. The developmental history of an individual organism.
b. A broad conceptual framework within which facts can be interpreted.
c. The process by which new behaviors arise when behavior is modified by experience.
d. The knowledge and beliefs of a group of people are an example of this.
e. The sequence of physical and behavioral changes that occur from conception to maturity.
f. This describes influences on development that come from "inside"—from the child's biological heritage.
g. A species' evolutionary history.
h. Genetically determined patterns of change that occur during development.
i. This describes influences on development that come from "outside"—from the child's interaction with the environment.
j. This term refers to the range of situations in which behavior occurs, the roles people play, and the results of their encounters with the environment.
k. A distinctive period of development marked by discontinuity from the periods occurring before and after.
l. This represents the influence of the environment on the individual.
m. A reorganization of behavior, such as the one that occurs at the end of infancy, which comes about as a result of changes in several different areas of development.
n. A time in an organism's life when certain experiences are necessary if normal development is to occur.
o. This refers to the individual's inborn, biologically based capacities.
p. A term used by ecologists to refer to the child's place within the community.
q. This involves observing behavior in the settings in which it ordinarily occurs, rather than in the laboratory.
r. For children's language development, this occurs during the first several years of life.
s. The study of the cultural organization of behavior.
t. A behavior has this characteristic if it is possible to change it through intervention.

Multiple-Choice Practice Questions

Circle the letter of the word or phrase that corr ectly completes each statement.

1. John Locke, the 17th-century English philosopher, believed that most differences between people were
   a. caused by genetic differences.
   b. unimportant.
   c. due to the way they were brought up.
   d. due more to influences in later life than to influences during childhood.

2. Jean-Jacques Rousseau's ideas about ____________ remain influential today.
   a. the child's mind as a "blank slate"
   b. the importance of original sin
   c. the importance of beginning formal education at an early age
   d. the stagelike character of development

3. The work of Charles Darwin stimulated interest in the study of children's development for which of the following reasons?
   a. Economic and social changes led to concern about children's health and welfare.
   b. Scientists thought that children's behavior might shed light on our evolutionary past.
   c. Educators were searching for the causes of learning difficulties.
   d. Darwin's work highlighted the vast differences between the development of humans and that of other species.

4. The history of a species over thousands or millions of years is called
   a. ontogeny.
   b. continuity.
   c. phylogeny.
   d. development.

5. Knowledge about how to live is passed from one generation of humans to another through
   a. culture.
   b. the genetic code.
   c. mutations.
   d. unknown means.

6. According to John Flavell, reaching a new stage of development is characterized by
   a. quantitative change (for example, the ability to remember more words).
   b. slow, steady improvement (for example, being able to walk more quickly).
   c. simultaneous change in several areas of behavior.
   d. the appearance of new behaviors with no obvious input from the environment.

7. We say that observations have ____________ when they are agreed on by independent observers.
   a. validity
   b. plasticity
   c. objectivity
   d. reliability

8. In general, as children's shoe sizes increase, so do their vocabularies. This is an example of
   a. a positive correlation.
   b. a negative correlation.
   c. a causal relationship.
   d. a zero correlation.

9. A teacher who keeps track of preschool children's cooperative play during recess is participating in which form of data collection?
   a. naturalistic observation
   b. experimental
   c. ethnographic
   d. clinical interview

10. When conducting an experiment, researchers usually compare the performance of the experimental group with that of a control group that
    a. is assigned to the same experimental treatment.
    b. undergoes no experience at all.
    c. is composed of people who did not volunteer to be in the experimental group.
    d. is treated like the experimental group except for not receiving the experimental treatment.

11. A problem with the experimental method is that experiments
    a. cannot uncover causal influences on behavior.
    b. take place in artificial environments.
    c. are difficult and expensive to carry out.
    d. are harmful to the participants.

12. A scientific hypothesis has little value
    a. unless an experiment shows it to be true.
    b. unless it is precise enough to be able to be found true or false.
    c. once it has been tested.
    d. if it is disprovable.

13. In using the clinical method, investigators
    a. ask each subject the same set of questions in the same way.
    b. introduce a change into each subject's experience and measure the effect on behavior.
    c. tailor questions to the individual subject.
    d. restrict their questions to those aimed at uncovering psychological problems.

14. When researchers compare the performance of three groups of children—3-year-olds, 5-year-olds, and 7-year-olds—on a test of picture recognition, they are conducting
    a. a cross-sectional study.
    b. a cohort-sequential study.
    c. a longitudinal study.
    d. a microgenetic study.

15. Compared to other research methods, __________ give the clearest picture of the actual process of development.
    a. experiments
    b. microgenetic designs
    c. naturalistic observations
    d. clinical interviews

16. A(n) ________ provides a framework for investigating and interpreting facts.
    a. theory
    b. experiment
    c. observation
    d. cohort

17. The _________ framework views development as being due mainly to factors "inside" the child.
    a. environmental-learning
    b. cultural-context
    c. constructivist
    d. biological-maturation

18. The work of which researcher reflects an environmental-learning approach to the study of development?
    a. Jean Piaget
    b. Arnold Gesell
    c. Sigmund Freud
    d. B. F. Skinner

19. The cultural-context framework is similar to the ________ framework, but also emphasizes the effect on development of the society into which a child is born.
    a. biological-maturation
    b. environmental-learning
    c. constructivist
    d. sociobiological

20. Bio-social-behavioral shifts
    a. are transition points at which biological, social, and behavioral changes converge.
    b. are the same as developmental stages.
    c. occur at the same ages in all children, regardless of culture.
    d. are best explained by the biological-maturation framework.

Short-Answer Practice Questions

Write a brief answer in the space below each question.

1. What might be some reasons why Victor, the Wild Boy of Aveyron, never developed completely normal behavior, despite Itard's educational efforts?

2. In what ways do the ideas of philosophers John Locke and Jean-Jacques Rousseau influence the study of human development?

3. What is “culture” as developmentalists use the term? Why is it important to consider the role of culture in development?

4. Compare the advantages and disadvantages of naturalistic observation and experiments for studying children’s behavior.

5. Describe how researchers might use a longitudinal design or a cross-sectional design to gather information on the same aspect of development. What are the advantages and disadvantages of each?

6. Discuss what developmental scientists need to do in order to be certain that their studies meet the ethical standards for developmental research.

Sources of More Information

Azar, B. (1997, May). Nature, nurture: not mutually exclusive. APA Monitor, 1, 28.
In this article, published in the news bulletin of the American Psychological Association, the author shows how genes affect our experience of the environment and how the environment influences the effects of our genes.

Barker, R. G., & Wright, H. F. (1951). One boy’s day: A specimen record of behavior. New York: Harper & Row.
This book, which records in detail a day in the life of a 7-year-old boy, illustrates one method of naturalistic observation.

Cole, M. (1999). Culture in development. In M. H. Bornstein & M. E. Lamb (Eds.), Developmental psychology: An advanced textbook (4th ed.). Mahwah, NJ: Lawrence Erlbaum.
This chapter gives the reader an overview of the cultural-context framework and presents examples of research on the role of culture in development.

Elkind, D. (1981). Children and adolescents: Interpretive essays on Jean Piaget (3rd ed.). New York: Oxford University Press.
Although most of the material has been inspired by Piaget, this book also contains sections comparing the Piagetian and psychometric approaches to development and comparing the work and goals of Piaget and Maria Montessori.

Gesell, A., Ilg, F. L., & Ames, L. B. (1995). The infant and child in the culture of today: The guidance of development in home and nursery school. Northvale: Jason Aronson Publishers.
This book presents Gesell's maturational approach to infancy and early childhood, with an emphasis on the child's increasing abilities of self-regulation.

Horvat, J., & Davis, S. (1998). Doing Psychological Research. Upper Saddle River, NJ: Prentice Hall.
This discussion of psychological research techniques includes many examples from published studies and effectively explains the logic of research design.

Jones, N. B. (Ed.) (1972). Ethological studies of child behaviour. New York: Cambridge University Press.
This book contains many different ethological studies, including examples of child-child and mother-child interaction.

Miller, S. A. (1998). Developmental research methods (2nd ed.). Upper Saddle River, NJ: Prentice Hall.
This book on research methods is tailored to students of developmental psychology.

Patterson, G. (1976). Living with children: New methods for parents and teachers. Champaign, IL: Research Press.
In this book, parents and teachers are shown how to change children's behavior for the better by arranging environmental contingencies to encourage desired behaviors and eliminate undesired ones. This book illustrates the environmental-learning approach to development.

Smuts, A. B., & Hagen, J. W. (Eds.). (1985). History and research in child development. Monographs of the Society for Research in Child Development, 50(4–5, Serial No. 211).
This monograph, published for the fiftieth anniversary of the Society for Research in Child Development, contains chapters on the history of the family and on scientific developments within the field of child development, set within their social contexts.

Answer Key

Answers to Key Terms I: 1.t, 2.k, 3.j, 4.p, 5.h, 6.l, 7.f, 8.o, 9.q, 10.e, 11.r, 12.s, 13.b, 14.c, 15.i, 16.n, 17.m, 18.g, 19.a, 20.d.

Answers to Key Terms II: 1.m, 2.e, 3.n, 4.d, 5.p, 6.k, 7.j, 8.f, 9.s, 10.q, 11.i, 12.c, 13.h, 14.o, 15.l, 16.a, 17.g, 18.t, 19.r, 20b.

Answers to Multiple-Choice Questions: 1.c, 2.d, 3.b, 4.c, 5.a, 6.c, 7.d, 8.a, 9.a, 10.d, 11.b, 12.b, 13.c, 14.a, 15.b, 16.a, 17.d, 18.d, 19.c, 20.a.

The Human Heritage: Genes and the Environment

In many ways, all human beings seem very much alike. Yet within that basic similarity, the details of appearance and behavior vary a great deal. In fact, people exhibit an amazing diversity of both talents and troubles.

How do genes and the environment combine to create our unique characteristics as human beings? If we were all raised in identical environments, would we behave completely alike? Nearly all developmentalists would say "No." Human development is an interaction between biologically based tendencies and the environmental circumstances in which people live. Nearly all of us are genetically unique, so a hypothetical universal environment would affect each person in a different way. On the other hand, under ordinary circumstances, even genetically identical individuals—monozygotic twins—develop individual interests, abilities, and characters.

Some of the differences among people are shaped systematically by the cultures in which they live. Human beings can adapt to changing conditions through cultural evolution, building upon the expertise of countless generations.

Because biological and cultural evolution have occurred together for so long, it is not easy to distinguish their separate influences on development. But by comparing members of the same families and by studying the effects on development of mutations—mistakes in gene replication—and inherited genetic disorders, psychologists can learn more about how genes and environment interact to produce each unique person.

Learning Objectives

Keep these questions in mind while studying Chapter 2.

1. In what ways do the processes of reproduction ensure that, except for monozygotic twins, all people inherit a unique combination of genes?
2. How is a person's genetic sex determined? What are the implications of this process for the transmission of sex-linked genetic defects?
3. How are a person's observable characteristics produced through the interaction of genes and environment?
4. In what ways do researchers use kinship studies to help them estimate the degree to which characteristics are influenced by heredity and environment?

5. What are the effects on development of genetic mutations and abnormalities?
6. In what ways does culture influence the transmission of adaptive behaviors from one generation to the next?

Chapter Summary

The similarities and differences among people result from the interaction of the environments in which they develop and the genes they inherit from their parents.

I. SEXUAL REPRODUCTION AND GENETIC TRANSMISSION

Each person's *genes* are found on 46 threadlike *chromosomes,* each a single molecule of *deoxyribonucleic acid (DNA)* in the shape of a double helix. There are thousands of genes on each chromosome; each contains a set of instructions for making some substance that is necessary for building or maintaining the body. The father's sperm and mother's ovum each contain 23 chromosomes; they fuse to form the *zygote,* a single cell containing 46 chromosomes from which all the child's cells will develop.

A. Mitosis: A Process of Cell Replication

The zygote creates these new cells through *mitosis,* a process of duplication and division. This is also the way new *somatic (body) cells* are created and replaced throughout a person's lifetime. Under ordinary circumstances, the genetic information in the new cells is an exact copy of that in the original.

B. Meiosis: A Source of Variability

Meiosis is the cell-division process by which *germ cells* (sperm and ova) are formed. It results in cells with 23 unpaired chromosomes—half the original set from the parent cell. When a sperm cell fertilizes an ovum, the resulting zygote will have 46 chromosomes.

The mixing of genes from both parents during sexual reproduction and the process of *crossing over* (an exchange of genetic material between two chromosomes) during meiosis make each human being, with the exception of *monozygotic twins,* genetically unique.

Occasionally (1 of every 250 conceptions) the daughter cells separate during one of the early mitotic divisions to form two genetically alike individuals: monozygotic twins. Monozygotic twins are called "identical twins"; however, they are not really identical, in appearance or in behavior. *Dizygotic twins,* or fraternal twins, result from the fertilization of two ova by two sperm; these twins are no more alike genetically than any brothers or sisters.

C. Sexual Determination: A Case of Variability

The twenty-third pair of chromosomes in normal females are both *X chromosomes;* normal males have one X chromosome and one much smaller *Y chromosome*. While an ovum always contains an X chromosome, a sperm may contain an X or a Y; thus, the sperm cell determines the genetic sex of the resulting child.

II. GENOTYPE AND PHENOTYPE

An individual's *genotype* represents that person's genetic endowment and is constant over the person's lifetime. The individual's *phenotype,* or observable characteristics, develops as a result of the interaction between that person's inherited traits and the *environment*—the totality of the conditions and circumstances surrounding the person.

A. The Laws of Genetic Inheritance

Some characteristics are inherited through a simple type of genetic transmission in which a pair of genes, one from each parent, contributes to a trait. The genes that influence the trait may have alternative forms, or *alleles.* People who have inherited the same allele from both parents are *homozygous* for the trait; those who have inherited a different allele from each parent are *heterozygous.* How an allelic form of a trait is expressed in a heterozygous person depends on whether the allele is *dominant* (in which case it will be expressed), *recessive* (in which case it will not be expressed), or whether the two alleles have *codominance* (in which case a distinctively different outcome will result). In some instances, both alleles have some influence and an intermediate outcome will occur. Some characteristics—for example, blood type—are *discrete traits;* that is, they are "either-or" traits involving a single gene. However, most human characteristics are polygenic; a *polygenic trait* involves interactions among several genes—in some cases more than 100.

- *Sex-linked characteristics* are affected by genes found only on the X or Y chromosome; because the X chromosome carries more genes, the phenotypic expression of these traits is seen more often in males, who have only one X chromosome, than in females, whose second X chromosome may contain an allele that will prevent expression. Because of this, certain harmful recessive traits, including red-green color blindness, hemophilia, and muscular dystrophy, are far more common among males.

B. Genes, the Person, and the Environment

It is only through the interaction of genes with their environments that a person's actual characteristics develop.

- Genes are in constant interaction with cell material, and the individual—the system of cells—is in constant interaction with the environment. According to *behavioral geneticists*—researchers who study how genetic and environmental influences lead to individual differences in behavior—several principles apply to gene-environment interactions:
  1. Because environmental variations at any level can have large effects on an individual's phenotype, interactions between organisms and their environments should be

studied in a broad, ecological framework. An example is work demonstrating the influence of family circumstances on the expression of infant temperament.

2. When speaking of gene-environment interaction, it should be remembered that interaction works in two directions. For example, parents of irritable infants may change their behavior in response to the infants' irritability; in turn, this may make the infants even more irritable.
3. Children's genetic characteristics (for example, a liking for high levels of stimulation) may influence the environments they select for themselves.

- Researchers studying such organisms as plants, fruit flies, and mice use two approaches to study gene-environment interactions: holding the environment constant to see what variations in phenotype are due to genes; and keeping genotype constant while varying the environment. This second approach demonstrates the *range of reaction* for a particular genotype.
- Some genetically determined traits are not easily influenced by the environment; this is called *canalization.* The tendency for children to learn language is a highly canalized process; only severe and prolonged deprivation would prevent it from occurring. Highly canalized processes tend to self-correct after deprivation or other unusual experiences; for processes that are not highly canalized, variability in the environment results in greater variability among individuals and self-correction is less likely to occur.

C. The Study of Genetic Influences on Human Behavior

We usually speak of human characteristics as being "genetically influenced" or "heritable" rather than "genetically caused."

- Behavioral geneticists study the influence of genetic traits on behavior by estimating *heritability*—the degree to which variations in a particular characteristic among individuals is related to genetic differences among those individuals. One way of representing this is as the *heritability coefficient,* which is the proportion of variance in a trait within a population that can be attributed to genetic variation in that population. Heritability can be estimated by comparing people who have different degrees of genetic relationship to one another. There is no "true" heritability for any given trait. Instead, estimates of heritability apply to a particular population at a particular time, and under the environmental conditions that are present at the time of the estimate. A high heritability estimate for a trait (height, for example) does not mean that the environment has no influence (for example, nutrition has an influence on height). There are a number of other common misconceptions surrounding the idea of heritability. The box "The Concept of Heritability and Myths about Genetic Influences" presents useful explanations and corrections by Michael Rutter and Robert Plomin:
  1. High heritability for a trait within a population does not mean that differences between populations are also due to heredity. Between-group differences are likely to be associated with differences in environment.

2. It is rare to find a one-to-one correspondence between a gene and a disorder. Most disorders, such as diabetes, asthma, and depression, are determined by many genes interacting with a number of environmental influences.
3. The same genetic influence may have "bad" and "good" effects. For example, shyness is a risk factor for anxiety disorder; however, it also acts as a protective factor against anti-social behavior.
4. *Eugenics,* the policy of attempting to eliminate "undesirable" genes by preventing people who carry them from mating or by selectively aborting fetuses that are affected, is based on a misunderstanding of how heritability works. Many genetically-related disorders are not inherited, but result from mutations and others anomalies. Also, all people carry some genes that would put them at risk for problems, but only in the presence of certain other genes or environmental influences.
5. It is unlikely that gene therapy will play an important role in treating most disorders, since they are caused by the interaction of many genes with the environment.

Kinship studies allow behavioral geneticists to estimate the genetic and environmental contributions to a phenotypic trait by examining the similarity among relatives who vary in their degree of genetic closeness.

In a *family study,* comparisons among members of the same household show how similar people with varying degrees of genetic relationship are with respect to a specific characteristic. Of course, people who are biologically related also share similar environments; therefore, similarities can be due to environmental as well as genetic similarity.

In a *twin study,* monozygotic twins and same-sex dizygotic twins are compared to one another and to other kin relationships for similarity on a trait. Monozygotic twins should resemble one another more than dizygotic twins with respect to a heritable trait.

An *adoption study* is another strategy for estimating the contribution of genes and environment to particular traits.

Studies have shown the pattern of greater similarity with closer genetic relationships for a number of characteristics, including intelligence, some personality traits, and susceptibility to schizophrenia. However, researchers studying individual differences have pointed out problems with kinship studies. For example, monozygotic twins may be treated more similarly than dizygotic twins because they look more similar. It is also true interestingly that family members are often quite different from one another, despite their close genetic relationship (see Table 2.1 in the textbook). Besides having different combinations of genes, individuals in a family experience unique environments, having their own particular teachers, friends, and sibling relationships.

III. MUTATIONS AND GENETIC ABNORMALITIES

Changes in the human *gene pool*—the total genetic information possessed by a sexually reproducing population—can occur through *mutation,* an error in gene replication that results in a change in the molecular structure of genetic material. Mutations in somatic cells affect only the person in whom they occur, while mutations in the germ cells may result in changed genetic information being passed on to the next generation. Mutations are a natural part of life; as many as half of all human conceptions have a genetic or chromosomal abnormality. However, the majority of mutations are lethal, resulting in miscarriage early in pregnancy. About 3.5 percent of babies born have some kind of genetic aberration. When the abnormal gene is recessive, as is often the case, it may be counteracted by a normal gene from the other parent. Otherwise, it may lead to a disorder. Table 2.2 describes some common diseases and conditions relating to genetic abnormalities. Researchers study mutations and genetic abnormalities for several reasons: to understand how heredity and environment interact; to find ways to prevent defects; and to lessen the impact of defects on children and their families.

A. Down Syndrome: A Chromosomal Error

Down syndrome is caused by a chromosomal error; an affected person has an extra copy of chromosome 21 (this is called *trisomy 21*). The disorder results in mental retardation as well as a number of distinctive physical characteristics. However, the severity of the disorder varies and supportive intervention can improve the functioning of Down syndrome children. Down syndrome affects about 1 of every 1000 children born in the United States. The older a woman is when she conceives, the greater her chance of producing a child with this disorder, suggesting that environmental agents may damage the genetic material or interfere with the process of meiosis.

B. Phenylketonuria: A Treatable Genetic Disease

Phenylketonuria (PKU) is an inherited metabolic disorder that results in brain damage leading to mental retardation. However, by altering the environment of children with this disorder—specifically, by removing from their diets foods high in the amino acid phenylalanine—the effects of the disorder can be mainly prevented. A blood test given to newborn babies can detect most cases of PKU, so that dietary intervention can begin immediately. PKU can also be detected prenatally, and a test to identify carriers of the recessive gene for the disorder is also available. The box titled "Genetic Counseling" discusses options available to those who are carriers of genes for genetically-based disorder.

C. Sickle-Cell Anemia: An Example of Gene-Environmental Interaction

Sickle-cell anemia, a serious blood disorder, occurs in people who are homozygous for the sickle-cell trait—they inherit it from both parents. People who are heterozygous for the gene have the sickle-cell trait but do not suffer from severe symptoms of the disease. The sickle-cell trait is found primarily among people of African descent; heterozygous carriers have the advantage of greater resistance to malaria than those without the trait. This provides a good example of gene-environment interaction. In West Africa, the area from which the ancestors of most African Americans came, and where malaria is still a serious problem, more than 20 percent of people carry the sickle cell trait. In contrast, in the United States, where malaria is rare, the trait no longer provides an advantage and is gradually being eliminated from the gene pool; it is carried by only 8 to 9 percent of Americans of African descent.

D. Klinefelter Syndrome: A Sex-Linked Chromosomal Abnormality

Half of all chromosomal abnormalities in newborns involve the 23rd pair of chromosomes—those that determine the baby's sex. The most common sex-linked chromosomal abnormality is Klinefelter syndrome, in which a boy has an extra X chromosome (XXY). This disorder occurs in 1 of every 900 males. They develop normally until adolescence, at which point they fail to develop the characteristics of sexual maturity; they may also have speech and language problems leading to difficulties in school. Testosterone replacement therapy, beginning at age 11 or 12, has beneficial effects on physical development and sexual functioning; however, men affected by this disorder are sterile.

IV. BIOLOGY AND CULTURE

During the 19th and early 20th centuries, biologists did not know how hereditary transmission was accomplished. They hypothesized that characteristics acquired by people during their lifetimes (for example, engaging in criminal activity) were passed on in the same way as physical characteristics such as hair and eye color. Today, we know that acquired characteristics are not inherited biologically; however, cultural evolution allows people to benefit from the experiences of those before them. Developmentalists use the term *meme* (the cultural counterpart to the gene) to describe how innovative forms of behavior are passed from one generation to the next.

A. Biology, Culture, and Survival Strategies

Individuals who have access to knowledge that enhances survival—for example, how to build shelters, prepare food, and heal illness—are more likely to live long enough to reproduce and pass their knowledge on to their children. Cultures also have "hazard prevention strategies" that optimize the chances that their children will survive; for example, cultures whose post-weaning diet is low in protein may breastfeed their children for a relatively long period.

B. Coevolution

Rudimentary forms of culture were already present during early phases of human evolution. Humans' biological evolution did not end with the appearance of culture. Instead, the two forms of evolution, biological and cultural, have interacted with each other in a process called *coevolution*. Because of coevolution, it is difficult, when comparing people from different parts of the world, to determine the extent to which the differences between them are due to genetically transmitted characteristics and to differences in the cultures in which they have been raised. During the course of human development, we repeatedly see instances of gene-environment interaction, with culture playing a mediating role.

Key Terms I

Following are important terms introduced in Chapter 2. Match each term with the letter of the example that best illustrates the term.

1. ______ allele
2. ______ canalization
3. ______ chromosome
4. ______ codominance
5. ______ crossing over
6. ______ deoxyribonucleic acid (DNA)
7. ______ dominant allele
8. ______ environment
9. ______ eugenics
10. ______ gene pool
11. ______ genes
12. ______ genotype
13. ______ heterozygous
14. ______ homozygous
15. ______ kinship studies
16. ______ phenotype
17. ______ recessive allele
18. ______ X chromosome
19. ______ Y chromosome

a. There are 46 of these threadlike structures in the nucleus of each cell.
b. This sex-determining chromosome can be inherited only from the father.
c. These molecules, found on chromosomes, contain "blueprints" for development.
d. The cells of normal females contain two of these.
e. This exchange of material between chromosomes helps to increase genetic diversity.
f. This term expresses the tendency for some characteristics, such as children's ability to learn language, to follow the same developmental path, despite most environmental variations.
g. An alternative form of a gene; for example, the O form of the gene for blood type.
h. This term refers to a person's genetic endowment.
i. A person's observable characteristics, developing through interaction between genes and environment.
j. The genetic information available in a whole reproducing population.
k. When a child inherits an allele for type A blood from his mother and an allele for type O blood from his father, we use this term to describe his genotype for blood type.
l. A child inherits an allele for type O blood from each parent; this term describes her genotype for blood type.
m. A less powerful allele—for example, the allele for type O blood—that is not expressed when a more powerful allele is present.

n. An allele whose effects show up phenotypically—in type A blood, for example—even in the presence of another allele (such as the O allele).
o. Children's development results from the interaction of this with their genetic inheritance.
p. A trait is contributed to by two different alleles; for example, Type AB blood.
q. Each chromosome is made of a single, double-stranded molecule of this substance.
r. This term refers to policies designed to reduce the incidence of undesirable genes in the population by restricting reproduction of affected individuals.
s. These are useful in estimating the genetic and environmental contributions to a trait.

Key Terms II

Following are important terms introduced in Chapter 2. Match each term with the letter of the example that best illustrates the term.

1. ______ adoption study
2. ______ behavioral geneticist
3. ______ coevolution
4. ______ discrete traits
5. ______ dizygotic twins
6. ______ family study
7. ______ germ cells
8. ______ heritability
9. ______ meiosis
10. ______ meme
11. ______ mitosis
12. ______ monozygotic twins
13. ______ mutation
14. ______ polygenic trait
15. ______ range of reaction
16. ______ sex-linked characteristics
17. ______ somatic (body) cells
18. ______ twin study
19. ______ zygote

a. These come in two varieties: sperm and ova.
b. This expresses the degree to which genetic factors influence the amount of variability in a trait.
c. Nearly all the body's cells are produced by this process of duplication and division.
d. All the cells in the body with the exception of the sperm and ova.
e. These result from the fertilization of two ova by two sperm.
f. Exposure to radiation can cause this change in the structure of the genetic material.

g. This allows researchers to estimate the degree to which a particular trait is influenced by genes and environment.
h. The process through which sperm and ova contain 23 chromosomes, rather than 46.
i. Members of the same family are compared to assess their similarity for a particular trait.
j. Characteristics influenced by the interaction of several genes, as in the case of height and many other human characteristics.
k. This single cell results from the joining of sperm and ovum at conception.
l. Red-green color blindness is one of these.
m. The fact that this occurs makes it difficult to pinpoint the source of differences between people who have grown up in very different parts of the world.
n. We can determine this by varying the environment of a particular genotype and charting the changes that occur in the phenotype.
o. This researcher studies the effects of genes and environment on individual differences.
p. These two individuals have exactly the same genotype.
q. This may involve studying genetically related individuals who are raised in different environments or genetically unrelated individuals who are raised in the same environment.
r. This is involved in passing on acquired characteristics.
s. Blood type is one of these; height is not.

Multiple-Choice Practice Questions

Circle the letter of the word or phrase that correctly completes each statement.

1. The somatic cells of the body each contain
   a. 23 chromosomes.
   b. 23 pairs of chromosomes.
   c. 46 pairs of chromosomes
   d. 50 pairs of chromosomes.

2. Crossing over during meiosis
   a. increases genetic diversity.
   b. determines the sex of the embryo.
   c. is the main cause of sex-linked genetic defects.
   d. makes inherited characteristics more resistant to environmental influences.

3. A person who is genetically male receives, at conception,
   a. an X chromosome from his mother and a Y chromosome from his father.
   b. a Y chromosome from his mother and an X chromosome from his father.
   c. an X chromosome from each parent.
   d. a Y chromosome from each parent.

4. Sex-linked characteristics are
   a. passed from one generation to the next on the Y chromosome.
   b. phenotypically expressed more often in females than in males.
   c. limited to characteristics that determine a person's physical and psychological sex.
   d. phenotypically expressed more often in males than in females.

5. When two alleles for a trait are present but only one is expressed, we call the one that is not expressed
   a. dominant.
   b. codominant.
   c. complementary.
   d. recessive.

6. Which characteristic is an example of codominance of alleles?
   a. type O blood
   b. female sex
   c. type AB blood
   d. red-green color blindness

7. People who are heterozygous for the sickle-cell trait
   a. do not develop sickle-cell anemia.
   b. may have some symptoms under conditions of low oxygen.
   c. are more resistant to malaria than those without the gene.
   d. all of the above

8. Errors in gene replication, called ______ , often have lethal results.
   a. meioses
   b. canalizations
   c. mutations
   d. recessive traits

9. ______ is a genetic disorder caused by an extra chromosome.
   a. Down syndrome
   b. Sickle-cell anemia
   c. Phenylketonuria
   d. Klinefelter syndrome

10. Which is an example of a polygenic trait?
    a. height
    b. blood type
    c. hemophilia
    d. Tay-Sachs disease

11. The total genetic material in a reproducing population is called the
    a. genotype.
    b. phenotype.
    c. range of reaction.
    d. gene pool.

12. ______ traits are resistant to environmental influence.
    a. Learned
    b. Canalized
    c. Physical
    d. Psychological

13. If a child receives an allele for type A blood from her mother and an allele for type B blood from her father, she is ______ with respect to blood type.
    a. heterozygous
    b. recessive
    c. homozygous
    d. complementary

14. Meiosis is
    a. the process by which the body's cells reproduce.
    b. the process by which the germ cells come to contain fewer chromosomes than the somatic cells.
    c. an error in gene replication.
    d. a polygenic trait.

15. Which of the following would indicate that the environment had an effect on a particular characteristic?
    a. Identical twins are more similar than fraternal twins with respect to this characteristic.
    b. Siblings are more similar than unrelated people with respect to this characteristic.
    c. Adopted children are more similar to their adoptive siblings than to their biological siblings with respect to this characteristic.
    d. Fraternal twins and ordinary siblings are equally similar with respect to this characteristic.

16. ______ is an inherited disorder that can be treated through dietary intervention.
    a. Tay-Sachs disease
    b. Klinefelter syndrome
    c. Thalassemia
    d. Phenylketonuria (PKU)

17. When a characteristic has high heritability, this means that
    a. the amount of variability due to genetic factors is the same in any environment.
    b. a large amount of the variability in the population for this characteristic can be attributed to genetic factors.
    c. environmental interventions will have no effect on this characteristic.
    d. differences in this characteristic between different groups in the population are due entirely to genetic factors.

18. Behaviors such as reading, writing, and numeric calculation are passed from one generation of people to the next through
    a. evolution.
    b. mutation.
    c. culture.
    d. genetic transmission.

19. _________ make(s) it difficult to tell whether differences between groups of people are genetically transmitted or are environmentally caused.
   a. Recent research in genetics
   b. The existence of mutations
   c. Recessive traits
   d. Coevolution of physical and culture characteristics

Short-Answer Practice Questions

Write a brief answer in the space below each question.

1. What is a sex-linked genetic effect, and how is it transmitted from one generation to the next? Describe two examples of such an effect.

2. Sometimes, genes for disorders remain in the gene pool despite the adverse consequences to those who carry them. Explain why the sickle-cell gene remains in the population despite its cost in illness and premature death.

3. Describe how family studies are used to separate genetic and environmental contributions to behavior. What are some problems with such studies?

4. How does the Himalayan rabbit provide an example of gene-environment interaction? Give an example of gene-environment interaction in humans.

5. What are some reasons why siblings raised in the same family can be quite different from one another?

6. In what ways do children's genetic characteristics influence the kind of environments they inhabit? Give examples.

7. What does it mean to say that a characteristic is heritable? What are some examples of heritable psychological characteristics?

8. How does coevolution affect attempts to separate the contributions of nature and nurture to human differences? Describe an example of a human characteristic shaped by coevolution.

Sources of More Information

Asimov, I. (1962). *The genetic code.* New York: New American Library of World Literature.
This book traces the research that led to the discovery of DNA.

Darwin, C. (1958). *The origin of species.* New York: New American Library of World Literature.
Charles Darwin's classic evolutionary account of the origin of human beings.

Carson, R. A., & Rothstein, M. A. (Eds.). (1999). *Behavioral genetics: The clash of culture and biology.* Baltimore, MD: Johns Hopkins University Press.
In this edited volume, the authors focus on the science behind behavioral genetics and the ethical, legal, and social issues raised by work in this area.

Dunn, J., & Plomin, R. (1990). *Separate lives: Why siblings are so different.* New York: Basic Books.
The authors tackle the question of how siblings, who share a great deal of genetic heritage, develop into quite different individuals.

Hamer, D., & Copeland, P. (1998). *Living with our genes: Why they matter more than you think.* New York: Doubleday.
This book examines links between DNA and behavior and highlights the complex interactions between hereditary tendencies and environmental effects, as they influence such characteristics as body size, aging, addiction, and temperament.

Hassold, T. J., & Patterson, D. (Eds.) (1999). *Down syndrome: A promising future, together.* New York: Wiley.
Medical, educational, developmental, and vocational issues are addressed in this book, which is aimed at giving the latest information to parents and others who work with children affected by Down syndrome.

Hawley, R. S., & Mori, C. A. (1999). *The human genome: A user's guide.* San Diego, CA: Harcourt Academic Press.
The authors—a professor of genetics and a health education writer—explore discoveries of modern genetics and their relevance to such topics as cloning, inherited health problems, gene therapy, and mental illness.

Kitcher, P. (1996). *The lives to come: The genetic revolution and human possibilities.* New York: Simon & Schuster.
This book gives readers a philosopher's view of the ethical dilemmas that accompany new discoveries in the field of genetics.

Stockton, W. (1979). *Altered destinies: Lives changed by genetic flaws.* New York: Doubleday.
A medical reporter follows the lives and experiences of families affected by genetically based disorders.

What we learn from twins: The mirror of your soul. *The Economist,* January 3, 1998, 74–76.
This magazine article provides some interesting information about the history of twin studies and some of the political issues involved in research on the relative contributions of heredity and environment.

Answer Key

Answers to Key Terms I: 1.g, 2.f, 3.a, 4.p, 5.e, 6.q, 7.n, 8.o, 9.r, 10.j, 11.c, 12.h, 13.k, 14.l, 15.s, 16.i, 17.m, 18.d, 19.b.

Answers to Key Terms II: 1.q, 2.o, 3.m, 4.s, 5.e, 6.i, 7.a, 8.b, 9.h, 10.r, 11.c, 12.p, 13.f, 14.j, 15.n, 16.l, 17.d, 18.g, 19.k.

Answers to Multiple-Choice Questions: 1.b, 2.a, 3.a, 4.d, 5.d, 6.c, 7.d, 8.c, 9.a, 10.a, 11.d, 12.b, 13.a, 14.b, 15.c, 16.d, 17.b 18.c, 19.d.

Prenatal Development and Birth

During the 9 months between conception and birth, rapid development transforms the human organism from a single cell to a baby capable of life outside the mother's body. Development proceeds through the processes of differentiation and integration: differentiation of one type of cell into many, and integration of bodily systems into a smoothly functioning whole.

At no time during the course of prenatal development is the developing organism completely buffered from the outside world. On the one hand, while still in the womb, the fetus registers signals from its sense organs, particularly those of balance and hearing. It may even learn to recognize familiar experiences. On the other hand, outside influences such as malnutrition, chemicals, and disease organisms may interfere with normal development.

Birth is a dramatic transition, both physically and behaviorally. It also marks the beginning of children's first social relationships, starting with their first face-to-face encounters with their parents. And finally, at birth, the beliefs and customs of the cultural groups into which children are born begin to shape their development in more direct ways. The influence of culture can be seen in how preparations for childbirth are carried out—whether in a hut or a hospital—in the rituals surrounding the process, and in the expectations with which the infant is greeted by parents and other members of the community.

Learning Objectives

Keep these questions in mind while studying Chapter 3.

1. Why do developmentalists consider it important to understand prenatal development?
2. What transformations occur as the one-celled zygote develops into a baby capable of surviving outside the mother's body?
3. How might the developing sensory abilities and motor capabilities of the fetus help to prepare it for postnatal life?

4. In what ways do environmental factors, for example, nutrition and maternal emotions, affect prenatal development?
5. How do teratogenic substances act to cause deviations from normal prenatal development?
   - What occurs during the birth process and how does it affect the newborn?
   - What are the risks to babies born prematurely or with low birth weight?
   - Why is birth the first "bio-social-behavioral shift?"

Chapter Summary

Birth is the culmination of a crucial period of development that begins at conception. Many developmental theorists consider development during the prenatal period to be a model for development during later periods, from birth to death. For example, stagelike changes occur, each associated with distinct kinds of interaction between the developing organism and its environment. Understanding prenatal development is important for this reason; in addition, it is important in helping to promote the birth of healthier babies.

I. THE PERIODS OF PRENATAL DEVELOPMENT

The fertilized ovum, or zygote, containing genetic material in its nucleus and surrounded by a thin envelope—the *zona pellucida*—divides many times to form many different kinds of cells. During the approximately 266 days necessary for the zygote to develop from a one-celled organism to a newborn baby, it passes through three broad periods of development: the *germinal period,* the *embryonic period,* and the *fetal period.* Each period is characterized by distinctive patterns of growth and interaction with the environment.

A. The Germinal Period

The germinal period begins at conception and lasts until, 8 to 10 days later, the organism is attached to the wall of the uterus.

- During its journey through the fallopian tube, the zygote divides, through the process of mitosis. These initial mitotic divisions, called *cleavage,* begin about 24 hours after conception. In this process, cells divide at different times, rather than all together (*heterochrony*), which results in different parts of the organism developing at different rates (*heterogeneity*).
- After the first few cleavages occur, a cluster of identical cells—the *morula*—takes shape. Each of its cells—called *stem cells*—has the potential to grow into an embryo and develop into a baby. They are *totipotent;* that is, they have the flexibility to become any kind of cell. This is discussed in the box "Stem Cells." When the cluster of cells reaches the uterus, fluid collects between the cells and the morula separates into two parts with two different kinds of cells. The organism is now a *blastocyst* consisting of the *inner cell mass,* which will become the organism itself, and the *trophoblast,* which

will become the membranes that will supply it with nourishment and protection. What causes the undifferentiated cells of the zygote to become the differentiated cells of the blastocyst and, eventually, all the cells present in the newborn baby? It is thought that undifferentiated cells are transformed into the many different kinds of cells present at birth through a process of *epigenesis*—interactions between cells and their environments. A cell's environment depends on the location of the cell. Therefore, changes occur in a cell's environment as the organism grows, leading to further cell differentiation and new forms of organism–environment interaction.

- *Implantation* occurs when the blastocyst, having moved further into the uterus, puts out tiny branches which burrow into the uterine wall and contact maternal blood vessels. If attachment is successful, this marks the transition between the germinal and embryonic periods of development.

B. The Embryonic Period

The embryonic period begins at implantation and continues for about 6 weeks. During this period, the basic organs take shape and the embryo begins to respond to direct stimulation. The nutrition and protection it receives from the mother allow it to grow rapidly.

- The membranes that will protect and nourish the developing embryo are: the *amnion,* holder of the fluid that surrounds the embryo; and the *chorion,* which becomes the fetal portion of the *placenta,* an organ made from both maternal and embryonic tissue. The placenta is linked to the embryo by the *umbilical cord.* The placenta acts as a barrier between mother and embryo and as a filter that allows nutrients and oxygen to be delivered to the embryo and waste products to be carried away to the mother's blood stream to be eliminated through her kidneys.
- The inner cell mass differentiates into three cell layers: the first to develop are the outermost, or *ectoderm,* from which the skin and nervous system, among other things, develop; and the innermost, or *endoderm,* which develops into the digestive system and lungs. Next, the *mesoderm,* which becomes the bones, muscles, and circulatory system, appears between these layers. Beginning during the prenatal period and continuing through adolescence, development occurs in *cephalocaudal* (from the head down) and *proximodistal* (from the midline outward) patterns. Table 3.1 shows the timetable of development during the embryonic period. The pattern of development for all but the sexual organs is the same for all human embryos.
- For the first six weeks after conception there is no structural difference between genetically male and genetically female embryos; both have *gonadal ridges* from which the male and female sex organs will develop. Sexual differentiation for genetically male (XY) embryos begins in the seventh week of gestation with the formation of the testes, while sexual differentiation in genetically female (XX) embryos will not begin until several weeks later, when ovaries begin to form. The rest of the process of sexual differentiation is controlled by hormones: in the presence of the male hormone testosterone, the external genitalia will be male; in the absence of testosterone, female genitalia will

develop and a cyclical pattern of hormonal secretion will be established by the pituitary gland. Because an embryo can develop male or female characteristics, it sometimes happens that a baby has sex organs with characteristics of both sexes; these babies are called *hermaphrodites*.

C. The Fetal Period

The fetal period lasts from the eighth or ninth week of gestation until birth. At the start of the fetal period, all of the basic tissues and organs exist in some form. The skeleton has begun to ossify. In the months that follow, the fetus increases in length from 1 1/4 inches to 20 inches and in weight from about .02 lb. to about 7.1 lb. Important changes take place in the digestive, respiratory, and nervous systems during this time.

Even though it is protected and nourished by the mother's body, the fetus interacts with both the uterine environment and the outside world. Some influences are beneficial, while others are potentially harmful.

- Understanding the fetus's sensory capacities helps researchers determine how the environment affects its development.

  About 5 months after conception, the fetus begins to develop a sense of balance and can sense changes in its mother's posture as it floats in the fluid-filled amniotic sac. The sense of motion is fully mature at birth.

  At 26 weeks, fetuses respond to light. Toward the end of pregnancy, they may actually see light through the stretched wall of the mother's abdomen.

  Fetuses are able to respond to sound at 5 to 6 months of gestation. The sound level inside the uterus has been measured at about 75 decibels. Fetuses can hear and discriminate between sounds originating outside the mother's body. The mother's voice is heard best, because it is transmitted from outside and also as vibrations inside the body. The fetus's heart rate may change in response to its mother's voice.
- As the fetus develops it also becomes more active, engaging in more varied and coordinated movements. At 15 weeks, it performs all the movements observed in newborn infants. At 24 to 32 weeks, activity alternates with quiet periods, and breathing movements increase. This decrease in activity is thought to result from inhibition by maturing higher brain regions.

  Research with other species suggests that fetal movement may be necessary for normal development to take place; for example, chick embryos paralyzed with drugs fail to eliminate excess neurons, a process that ordinarily accompanies neuromuscular development. As a result, their joints become fused. The human fetus makes breathing motions that are unnecessary for obtaining oxygen; however, they help to develop the muscles that will be necessary for respiration after birth.
- There is evidence that some learning takes place during the prenatal period. For example, one study showed that newborns appeared to recognize a story read to them repeatedly before birth and would modify their rates of sucking in order to produce the story. Newborns also prefer the sounds of their native language and are sensitive to differences between musical notes.

II. MATERNAL CONDITIONS AND PRENATAL DEVELOPMENT

Fetuses are indirectly affected, through biochemical changes, by events affecting their mothers.

A. Maternal Attitudes and Stress

Research by Henry David, based on a study carried out in Czechoslovakia in the 1960s and 1970s, lends support to the idea that a woman's attitude toward her pregnancy can affect development of the fetus. Negative feelings, such as lack of acceptance of the pregnancy on the part of the mother, are associated with lower birth weight and more medical complications. Mothers who are under stress or emotionally upset secrete hormones (adrenaline and cortisol) that pass through the placenta and affect the fetus's motor activity. This is associated with premature delivery and with *low birth weight* (weight of less than 5 pounds).

B. Nutritional Influences

Adequate maternal nutrition during pregnancy is necessary for normal fetal development. Pregnant women need to consume between 2000 and 2800 calories per day in a diet that contains an adequate supply of vitamins (including folic acid) and minerals (including calcium and iron). A woman's culture influences her view of which foods are beneficial during pregnancy.

As demonstrated by the effects of severe famine—for example, the siege of Leningrad during World War II—extreme malnutrition in early pregnancy results in greater numbers of central nervous system abnormalities, preterm birth, stillbirth, and death at birth. Deprivation later in pregnancy leads to low birth weight and fetal growth retardation.

Less severe nutritional malnourishment can lead to low birth weight and miscarriage. There is also some evidence that people who were undernourished as fetuses are at greater risk in later life for heart disease, strokes, and other illnesses. In addition, malnourished mothers are likely to live in impoverished environments and to have less access to education, sanitation, and medical care. Studies of the WIC program—a supplemental food program for low-income women, infants, and children—showed that women receiving supplemental food had fewer infants who died during infancy. Infants whose mothers received food supplements during late pregnancy did better on intellectual measures than those who did not receive supplements until after the infants were born. Similar results have been found in studies carried out in rural Guatemala and in Zanzibar.

III. TERATOGENS: ENVIRONMENTAL SOURCES OF BIRTH DEFECTS

Teratogens are environmental agents—for example, drugs, radiation, infections, and chemical pollutants—that can kill the developing embryo or fetus or cause serious abnormalities.

Several principles apply to teratogenic effects:

- The impact of teratogens on the developing organism depends on when exposure occurs. Exposure during the first 2 weeks may destroy the organism; after that time, exposure will affect whatever system is in the process of developing.

- Each teratogen causes a particular pattern of abnormal development.
- Not every developing organism will be equally affected by the same exposure to a teratogen.
- Factors such as the mother's age and health can intensify or decrease the risk from exposure to a teratogen.
- The greater the concentration of a teratogen to which the organism is exposed, the greater the risk.
- Levels of a teratogen that can harm the developing organism may produce little or no effect on the mother.

A. Drugs

Most U.S. women take some medications during their pregnancies and a sizable minority use nonmedical drugs of some kind.

- Prescription drugs can cross the placenta to affect the developing child. Some, like thalidomide, cause major deformities; other common drugs have also been found to cause abnormalities in the developing fetus.
- Caffeine, found in coffee, tea, and soft drinks, is not associated with malformations of the fetus; however, in large doses, it is associated with spontaneous abortion and low birth weight.
- Tobacco smoking is associated with spontaneous abortion, stillbirth, and neonatal death; there is evidence that exposure to smoke is associated with lower levels of oxygen and higher levels of carbon monoxide in the blood of mother and fetus.
- Heavy consumption of alcohol during pregnancy can lead to serious abnormalities in infants, for example, *fetal alcohol syndrome,* which is associated with abnormalities of the brain, eyes, heart, and joints and with facial malformation. The effects of more moderate drinking can vary according to the amount and timing of exposure.
- Marijuana use during pregnancy is associated with low birth weight and possibly with preterm delivery. However, in the United States, women who use marijuana during pregnancy have other risk factors, for example, being less educated and using other drugs; they also gain less weight and have less prenatal care than nonusers.
- Cocaine use during pregnancy puts the mother at risk for heart attack, stroke, and seizures. The baby is at risk for prematurity, low birth weight, stroke, birth defects, postnatal irritability, lack of motor coordination, and learning problems.
- Methadone and heroin addiction on the part of mothers results in the birth of addicted infants who risk being born prematurely and for having low birth weight, respiratory illness, and sleep disturbances.

B. Infections and Other Conditions

Infections can be passed to an embryo or fetus across the placental barrier or during the birth process. Table 3.3 describes some of these diseases.

- Rubella (German measles) can cause major developmental defects, including blindness, deafness, congenital heart disease, and mental retardation.
- Acquired Immunodeficiency Syndrome (AIDS) affects about 30% of babies whose mothers test positive for HIV. A baby can become infected prenatally or during exposure to the mother's blood at birth. However, the chances of infection are reduced by as much as 50% if the mother takes the drug AZT during pregnancy and delivery.
- Rh incompatibility can result in a mother forming antibodies that destroy the red blood cells of the fetus. Rh disease can be treated by blood transfusions; however, most cases are now prevented by an anti-Rh serum that prevents Rh-negative mothers from forming antibodies to their Rh-positive children's blood.
- Radiation exposure can lead to spontaneous abortion or prenatal death at high doses; it can cause mental retardation and may possibly cause malformations.
- Pollution by chemicals in air, food, and water can build up in the body and cause birth defects in unborn children. An example is "Minimata disease," which was caused when mercury from water contaminated by industrial waste became concentrated in fish, which were, in turn, eaten by pregnant women. In a city in Brazil, severe air pollution from industrial plants was associated with the death of many babies whose brains failed to develop. In the United States, there is concern about risks to pregnant women who live near chemical dumps.

IV. RECONSIDERING PRENATAL DEVELOPMENT

In examining prenatal development, some general principles become clear: sequence and timing of development are important, which implies the existence of sensitive periods; development consists of both differentiation and integration; development is uneven and is characterized by stagelike changes; and regressions in development occur during periods of reorganization. In many respects, prenatal development remains a mystery; however, these principles, according to many psychologists, can help us to gain some understanding of the processes involved.

V. BIRTH: THE FIRST BIO-SOCIAL-BEHAVIORAL SHIFT

At birth, important changes take place in the newborn's body and environment; the baby must obtain oxygen by breathing and nourishment by sucking. At this time, the social relationship between parents and child also begins.

A. The Stages of Labor

Labor, the process that forces the fetus out of the mother's body, occurs approximately 266 days after conception, and is customarily divided into three stages:

- During the first stage of labor, contractions of the uterus dilate, or open, the cervix—the opening of the uterus into the vagina. In a woman's first birth, this stage lasts about 14 hours.

- The second stage of labor begins when the baby's head enters the vagina and continues until the baby's head, then body, emerge from the mother's body.
- During the third stage of labor, the placenta and membranes are expelled.

B. Cultural Variations in Childbirth

The experience of giving birth depends, in part, on the traditions surrounding it in the culture in which the mother lives. These customs vary widely from culture to culture, but all give the mother and community a set of procedures to follow and a set of expectations about what will occur.

C. Childbirth in the United States

In the United States today, most women give birth in hospitals. The change to hospital-based birth has helped to lower infant mortality to 7.2 of every 1000 births and maternal mortality to 7.7 of every 100,000 women giving birth. However, medical intervention in childbirth is not without controversy.

- Drugs used to relieve the pain of childbirth may affect babies' breathing and sucking responses and other postnatal behavior. For women concerned about the adverse affects of drugs, alternative techniques—including breathing, relaxation, and the presence of a supportive companion during labor—can help to reduce use of medication during labor and delivery.
- Medical interventions—for example, induced labor or cesarean section—are thought to occur more frequently than is necessary. Alternative birthing arrangements, such as specialized birth centers, are associated with reductions in the use of spinal anesthesia and cesarean births. Despite reductions in fetal and maternal death rates, African American infants are still nearly twice as likely to die during the first year than all other infants, and their mothers are three times more likely to die during childbirth.
- The stresses of labor and delivery may actually help babies adapt to postnatal life; cesarean-born infants are more likely to have breathing difficulties than those born vaginally. A hormonal surge during birth puts the newborn into a state of quiet alertness that may last up to 40 minutes.

VI. THE NEWBORN'S CONDITION

Newborn babies weigh, on average, 7 to 7½ pounds (5½ to 10 pounds is the normal range) and are, on average, 20 inches in length.

A. Assessing the Baby's Viability

The neonate's physical and behavioral condition can be assessed using a variety of scales and tests:

- The *Apgar Scale* measures babies' heart rate, respiratory effort, muscle tone, reflex responsivity, and color at 1 and 5 minutes after birth. Total scores can range from 0 to 10;

a score of less than 4 indicates poor condition and the need for immediate medical attention.

- The *Brazelton Neonatal Assessment Scale* assesses more subtle behavioral aspects of the newborn's condition. It tests reflexes, muscle tone, motor capacities, responsiveness to objects and people, and infants' ability to control their own behavior and attention. Scales like Brazelton's do well in pointing out babies who need medical intervention and assessing development in the period following birth, but are less useful in predicting later characteristics—for example, intelligence or personality—from neonatal behavior.

B. Problems and Complications

Some babies are at risk for developmental problems, often because they are born prematurely and/or underweight.

- *Preterm,* or premature, infants are born at a *gestational age* of less than 37 weeks; the normal period of time between conception and birth is 37–43 weeks. Prematurity affects 10 percent of births in the United States. While expert medical care now allows more premature babies to survive, they may have immature respiratory, digestive, and immune systems. The causes of preterm birth are not well understood; however, mothers who are poor, very young, in poor health, who smoke, or who are carrying more than one fetus are more likely to give birth prematurely than those without these risk factors. However, more than half of all premature births are associated with no known risk factors.
- Infants falling into the lowest 10 percent of weight for gestational age are said to suffer from *fetal growth retardation.* This is associated with multiple births, maternal malnutrition, smoking or drug use, infections, chromosomal abnormalities, and abnormalities of the placenta or umbilical cord.

C. Developmental Consequences

The smaller a baby is at birth, whether preterm or not, the more likely that he or she will die or will suffer some permanent impairment. Low-birth-weight babies frequently have some decrease in coordination and in intellectual capacity. Premature babies of normal weight for their gestational ages are most likely to catch up with their full-term peers, although they may have problems with attention and visual-motor coordination during their school years. Those with low birth weights and medical complications are at risk for developmental difficulties. However, premature and low-birth-weight babies who grow up under supportive environmental conditions are less likely to suffer negative effects.

VII. BEGINNING THE PARENT-CHILD RELATIONSHIP

Human infants are helpless creatures; their relationships with their parents are crucial for their well-being. As discussed in the box "The Controversy over Mother–Newborn Bonding," instant mother–newborn contact is not necessary for developing a healthy long-term relationship.

However, extended mother–infant interaction has benefits, especially for at-risk babies. In any case, the events immediately after birth set the stage for future interactions.

A. The Baby's Appearance

In trying to understand the source of attachment between parents and infants, some psychologists have borrowed from ethology—the study of animal behavior and its evolutionary bases—the idea that the "babyness" of newborn infants' appearance leads adults to respond to them with caregiving behavior. There is evidence that adults find the large heads, protruding cheeks, and large, low-set eyes of infants to be appealing. Research shows that, beginning at about the age of puberty, children switch from preferring to look at pictures of adults to preferring pictures of babies. There is also evidence that adults interact more frequently with attractive babies than with those who are considered less attractive in appearance.

B. Social Expectations

When a baby is born, parents must begin to adapt to their actual child, not the child they may have imagined. From the time of birth, parents' reactions to their infants reflect their beliefs and expectations. Boys may be described as "big" and girls as "cute" regardless of their actual appearance. From the beginning, parents treat their infants in ways consistent with the community's ideas and knowledge about people and their future roles. The parent–infant relationship will serve as part of the foundation for children's future development.

Key Terms I

Following are important terms introduced in Chapter 3. Match each term with the letter of the example that best illustrates the term.

1. ______ amnion
2. ______ blastocyst
3. ______ chorion
4. ______ cleavage
5. ______ ectoderm
6. ______ endoderm
7. ______ epigenesis
8. ______ gestational age
9. ______ heterochrony
10. ______ heterogeneity
11. ______ inner cell mass
12. ______ mesoderm
13. ______ morula
14. ______ trophoblast
15. ______ zona pellucida

a. A membrane that develops into the fetal component of the placenta.
b. The layer of cells from which the lungs and digestive system develop.
c. The unevenness seen between the levels of development of different parts of an embryo is an example of this.
d. The layer of cells from which the bones and muscles are formed.
e. A thin but tough membrane that contains the fluid surrounding the embryo.
f. This extremely thin "envelope" forms the boundary that separates the zygote from the outside world.
g. The skin and the central nervous system develop from this layer of cells.
h. A cluster of identical cells that forms during the first few days after conception.
i. The name for the organism very early in development when, for the first time, two different types of cells can be distinguished.
j. A layer of cells within the blastocyst that develops into the protective membranes which will surround the developing organism.
k. The idea that new forms arise during development through interaction of existing forms with the environment.
l. A knot of cells within the blastocyst that develops into the organism itself.
m. About 24 hours after conception, the zygote divides into two daughter cells that, in turn, each divide into two daughter cells.
n. The amount of time that has passed since the fertilization of an ovum has occurred.
o. This refers to the fact that not all cells divide at the same rate during embryonic development.

Key Terms II

Following are important terms introduced in Chapter 3. Match each term with the letter of the example that best illustrates the term.

1. ______ Apgar Scale
2. ______ Brazelton Neonatal Assessment Scale
3. ______ cephalocaudal pattern
4. ______ embryonic period
5. ______ fetal alcohol syndrome
6. ______ fetal growth retardation
7. ______ fetal period
8. ______ germinal period
9. ______ implantation
10. ______ low birth weight
11. ______ placenta
12. ______ preterm
13. ______ proximodistal pattern
14. ______ stem cells
15. ______ teratogens
16. ______ umbilical cord

a. The period of prenatal development, lasting about 6 weeks, during which the body's basic organs take shape.
b. This structure links the embryo to the placenta.
c. The blastocyst attaches itself to the wall of the uterus.
d. The period of prenatal development that begins at conception and ends when implantation occurs.
e. This is illustrated by the fact that the embryo's arms begin to form earlier than its legs.
f. These come from the environment and harm the developing fetus by causing deviations in development.
g. This organ, made from tissues of both the mother and the embryo, helps the embryo obtain nourishment and dispose of wastes.
h. The period of prenatal development during which the organ systems develop sufficiently to allow the developing organism to be able to survive outside the mother's body.
i. Examples are that the upper arm develops before the forearm and the forearm before the hand.
j. Birth that occurs before the 37th week of gestation.
k. An assessment of the baby's physical condition at 1 and 5 minutes after birth.
l. An underdeveloped brain, heart disease, and malformations of the face are some of the indicators of this.
m. When this occurs, babies are particularly small for their gestational ages.
n. Babies have this if they weigh less than 5 pounds at birth.
o. This evaluates newborns' neurological condition by testing their behavior.
p. Each of these cells is capable of growing into a human baby.

Multiple-Choice Practice Questions

Circle the letter of the word or phrase that correctly completes each statement.

1. During the prenatal period, the one-celled ________ develops into a fully formed baby.
   a. ovum
   b. blastocyst
   c. zygote
   d. embryo

2. The germinal period of development begins at conception and ends when
   a. the organism divides into two cells.
   b. the organism is implanted in the uterine wall.
   c. the major organ systems are formed.
   d. the heart begins to beat.

3. The morula is made up of identical ________ .
   a. DNA strands
   b. germ cells
   c. stem cells
   d. chromosomes

4. The fluid-filled ________ protects and supports the developing embryo.
   a. amnion
   b. placenta
   c. blastocyst
   d. zona pellucida

5. The bones and muscles of the developing organism are formed from which layer of the inner cell mass?
   a. endoderm
   b. mesoderm
   c. ectoderm
   d. trophoblast

6. During prenatal development, the embryo's arms
   a. are formed earlier than the legs.
   b. are formed at the same time as the legs.
   c. are formed later than the legs.
   d. are formed later than the hands.

7. In the absence of testosterone during prenatal development, the sex organs will be ________ .
   a. male
   b. undifferentiated
   c. both male and female
   d. female

8. Studies of fetal hearing indicate that
   a. fetuses are capable of hearing, but the uterine environment is very quiet, so there is little to hear.
   b. fetuses "hear" only by feeling vibrations on their body surfaces, not with their ears.
   c. fetuses hear many sounds from outside their mothers' bodies, and can discriminate between them.
   d. fetuses do not hear sounds from the world outside, as the background noise level in the uterus is too high to allow other sounds to come through.

9. Research shows that women who are under stress during pregnancy
   a. secrete hormones that affect their fetuses' behavior.
   b. give birth to larger babies than women who experience peaceful pregnancies.
   c. give birth to babies who are placid and regular in their bodily functions.
   d. experience no special problems or advantages in their pregnancies.

10. Which of the following can cause birth defects?
    a. alcohol
    b. radiation
    c. environmental pollutants
    d. all of these

11. Abnormalities of the central nervous system, prematurity, and death of the baby are most strongly associated with severe malnutrition
    a. during the first trimester of pregnancy.
    b. during the second trimester of pregnancy.
    c. during the third trimester of pregnancy.
    d. only if it occurs during the entire course of the pregnancy.

12. Exposure to a teratogen during prenatal development
    a. always leads to fetal death.
    b. affects whatever system is developing at the time of exposure.
    c. affects all fetuses with comparable exposure in the same way.
    d. does not affect the fetus at exposure levels that are safe for the mother.

13. The baby emerges from the mother's body at the end of
    a. the first stage of labor.
    b. the second stage of labor.
    c. the third stage of labor.
    d. the fourth stage of labor.

14. The main disadvantage to the use of obstetric medications is that
    a. they are not effective in relieving the pain of labor.
    b. while they do not affect the fetus, they may adversely affect the mother.
    c. they enter the bloodstream of the fetus and may cause adverse effects.
    d. in order to use them, it is necessary to give birth in a hospital.

15. The "stress" hormones that babies produce during labor are thought to
    a. help their circulation and respiration adjust to life outside the womb.
    b. be the basis for psychological birth trauma.
    c. prevent them from making a smooth adjustment to postnatal life.
    d. have no real effect on them.

16. The _______ evaluates the baby's physical condition at 1 and 5 minutes after birth.
    a. Brazelton Neonatal Assessment Scale
    b. PKU test
    c. Bayley Mental and Motor Scale
    d. Apgar Scale

17. Women who _______ are more likely than others to give birth prematurely.
    a. are of middle-class socioeconomic status
    b. are carrying more than one fetus
    c. are in their twenties
    d. have no known risk factors

18. Which is *not* a sign of "babyness," as Konrad Lorenz described it?
    a. small head in proportion to body
    b. round cheeks
    c. large eyes
    d. high forehead

19. Parents tend to describe their newborns as
    a. "easy" if they are girls, and "difficult" if boys.
    b. "big" if they are boys, and "cute" if girls.
    c. "big" and "beautiful" regardless of sex.
    d. "resembling their mothers" regardless of sex.

20. Which of the following is *not* one of the general principles of prenatal development?
    a. Development proceeds in cephalocaudal and proximodistal patterns.
    b. The effect on development of environmental influences depends on their timing.
    c. Development includes repeated instances of differentiation and integration.
    d. Development is continuous rather than stagelike.

Short-Answer Practice Questions

Write a brief answer in the space below each question.

1. What are the major features of the germinal, embryonic, and fetal periods of prenatal development?

2. Explain how the timing of exposure to a teratogen determines its effect on development. What other factors influence the effects of teratogens?

3. Based on information about the sensory capacities of the fetus, how do you imagine its environment inside the uterus?

4. How does prenatal sexual differentiation occur in male? In females?

5. How does malnutrition affect prenatal development? Why is it difficult to determine the effect on development of nutritional deprivation alone?

6. What are the developmental consequences of preterm delivery and low birth weight? What factors affect the long-term outlook for babies with these conditions?

7. What happens during the process of birth? How do these events affect the baby?

8. How does the appearance of the newborn baby affect the behavior of parents and other adults?

9. What are some positive and negative aspects of parents' tendencies to have expectations about their newborns on the basis of the infants' sex?

Putting It All Together

As discussed in Chapter 1, developmentalists interpret the facts they collect in terms of several major questions about development:

- Is development continuous or do stagelike changes take place?
- What are the roles of genetic factors and environmental forces in development?
- What are the sources of individual differences?

Using what you know about prenatal development, find an example of each of the following as it occurs during the prenatal period:

- stages of development
- continuous change
- critical (or sensitive) periods
- genetic influence
- effects of the environment
- cultural influences

Sources of More Information

Azar, B. (1997, December). Behaviors of a newborn can be traced to the fetus. *APA Monitor,* 16.
Research on rats helps developmental researchers decipher the role of fetal behavior in preparing for postnatal life.

Azar, B. (1997, December). Learning begins even before babies are born, scientists show. *APA Monitor,* 15.
This article describes some of the clever methods researchers have developed to study fetal learning.

Kitzinger, S. (2003). T*he complete book of pregnancy and childbirth.* New York: Knopf.
This is a comprehensive discussion of pregnancy and the process of childbirth, aimed at helping the pregnant woman to understand what is happening and what to expect.

Lamaze, F. (1987). *Painless childbirth: The Lamaze method.* Lincolnwood, IL: NTC Contemporary Publishing.
A popular method of prepared childbirth is explained by the physician who brought it from the Soviet Union to France.

Nilsson, L. (1990). *A child is born: The completely new edition.* New York: Dell.
A photographic record of prenatal development.

Pasquariello, P. S. (Ed.). (1999). *The Children's Hospital of Philadelphia book of pregancy and child care.* New York: Wiley.
This book covers topics relating to pregnancy, birth, the newborn baby, and health and development in children up to 5 years of age.

Profet, M. (1995). *Protecting your baby-to-be.* Reading, MA: Addison-Wesley.
This book takes the view that pregnancy sickness serves the purpose of protecting the embryo during its most vulnerable period. Suggestions are included for managing pregnancy sickness and avoiding teratogens.

Vaughn, C. (1998). *How life begins.* New York: Bantam, Dell.
This is a readable discussion of prenatal development in a scientific context, written by a science journalist.

Answer Key

Answers to Key Terms I: 1.e, 2.i, 3.a, 4.m, 5.g, 6.b, 7.k, 8.n, 9.o, 10.c, 11.l, 12.d, 13.h, 14.j, 15.f.

Answers to Key Terms II: 1.k, 2.o, 3.e, 4.a, 5.l, 6.m, 7.h, 8.d, 9.c, 10.n, 11.g, 12.j, 13.i, 14.p, 15.f, 16. b.

Answers to Multiple-Choice Questions: 1.c, 2.b, 3.c, 4.a, 5.b, 6.a, 7.d, 8.c, 9.a, 10.d, 11.a, 12.b, 13.b, 14.c, 15.a, 16.d, 17.b, 18.a, 19.b, 20.d.

Infant Capacities and the Process of Change

During the first few postnatal months, infants are mainly adjusting to life outside their mothers' bodies, and parents are adjusting their lives to accommodate their new offspring. Some changes in infants' capacities seem to be the result of maturation of their nervous systems. For example, several reflexes present at birth, such as stepping and involuntary grasping, disappear during the first weeks or months. But learning also plays a role, and other reflexes are modified by use, becoming part of more complex behaviors, as when rooting, sucking, swallowing, and breathing become integrated with one another (and with maternal behaviors as well) in nursing.

Cultural variations in the ways parents organize their infants' experiences exert some influence on development. For example, infants from cultures—such as that of the United States—in which they are expected to sleep all night without waking to feed will, in fact, learn to sleep through the night sooner than infants from cultures in which this is not an important expectation. The various broad approaches to the study of development—biological-maturation, environmental-learning, constructivist, and cultural-context—each emphasize different factors in explaining the changes of the first months of infancy. But at the end of about 2½ months, it is possible to see how changes at all levels—biological, behavioral, and social—move infants to a new level of development, in a bio-social-behavioral shift.

Learning Objectives

Keep these questions in mind while studying Chapter 4.

1. What sensory and response capabilities are present at birth, and how does development of the central nervous system allow infants to expand their behavioral capabilities?
2. In what ways does experience with the environment affect maturation of the nervous system?
3. How do changes in infants' feeding and sleeping patterns during the first months after birth help them become coordinated with the schedules of their families?
4. What emotions are expressed by young infants? Why is it often difficult for their parents to tell why they are crying?

5. How do cultural practices affect the way infants' environments are arranged?
6. How does each of the four theoretical perspectives account for the changes that occur during early infancy?
7. What learning processes are infants able to use in order to respond to occurrences in their environments?
8. In what ways do biological, behavioral, and social factors contribute to the reorganization of behavior that occurs at about 2½ months of age—the first postnatal bio-social-behavioral shift?

Chapter Summary

I. DEVELOPMENT OF THE BRAIN

Before babies are born, their brains and central nervous systems support basic sensory and motor functions. At birth, the brain contains most of the cells it will have; however, it will continue to grow, becoming four times larger than it is in the newborn infant. The basic unit of brain activity is the *neuron,* or nerve cell.

A. Neurons and Networks of Neurons

Each neuron has an *axon*—the main protruding branch that carries messages to other cells in the form of electrical impulses, and *dendrites* through which it receives information from other cells. Messages are carried from one neuron to another by a chemical *neurotransmitter* that bridges the gap (called a *synapse*) between the axon of the transmitting neuron and a dendrite of the receiving neuron. The combination of a sending and a receiving neuron is a neuronal circuit. The brain grows in size after birth partly because of increases in *synaptogenesis*—the formations of new connections among neurons—made possible by increases in the number of dendrites and axon terminals, as shown in Figure 4.1. It also becomes larger because of myelination, a process in which the axons of neurons become covered with *myelin,* a fatty coating that insulates them and increases greatly the speed at which they can transmit impulses.

B. Experience and Development of the Brain

Development of the brain, like development of behavior, comes about through interaction of the organism with the environment. During the prenatal period, *experience-expectant* processes of brain development (under genetic control) provide an oversupply of synapses. Those that are not needed will die off selectively in a process called *synaptic pruning* that continues until early adulthood. While experience-expectant synapses are created before they are needed, in *experience-dependent* brain development, synapses are generated in response to experience. This is demonstrated in Rosenzweig's work with rats, in which subjects were housed in either a standard laboratory environment or in an enriched environment. Those in the enriched environment had larger and heavier brains with more synaptic connections and larger amounts of neurotransmitter; they also performed better on tasks such as maze learning.

C. The Central Nervous System and the Brain

As shown in Figure 4.4, the central nervous system has three parts: the *spinal cord* extends down the back and contains the spinal nerves that carry messages between the brain and specific areas of the body; the *brain stem* at the top of the spinal cord, which controls breathing, sleeping, and elementary reactions such as blinking and sucking; and the *cerebral cortex,* which is divided into two hemispheres, each of which has four lobes, separated by deep grooves and specialized for different functions. The human cortex also has large "uncommitted" areas, allowing the brain to change in response to the experiences children encounter as they develop. At birth, the spinal cord and brain stem are the most highly developed areas of the central nervous system; the cerebral cortex is relatively immature and is not well connected to the lower brain areas. As the cortex matures and becomes more efficiently connected to the brain stem and spinal cord, the infant's abilities expand. The *primary motor area* is the first area of the cortex to undergo important development. Structural developments in this region (following a cephalocaudal pattern) allow infants first to raise their heads voluntarily, to control their arms, trunks, and legs. Important changes in the *primary sensory areas* (including those responsible for touch, vision, and hearing) take place during the first 3 months after birth. Different parts of the cortex continue to develop at different times in infancy, childhood, and adolescence. For example, the frontal cortex, involved in voluntary behaviors including those that require planning, gradually begins to function during infancy and continues to develop throughout childhood.

II. SENSING AND RESPONDING TO THE ENVIRONMENT

Psychologists have disagreed about the extent to which newborn infants are innately able to perceive and act upon the world. Fluctuations in neonates' state of arousal make it difficult to determine precisely what they are able to perceive and do.

A. Sensory Processes

Newborns' sensory systems are all functioning, but some capacities are more mature than others (heterochrony). Psychologists study infants' sensory capacities by observing their reactions to stimuli—for example, does a child turn his or her head in the direction of a sound? Another common method relies on infants' tendency to pay less and less attention to a repeatedly presented stimulus (*habituation*); if the stimulus is changed in a way that makes it seem new to the infant, he or she will once again pay attention (*dishabituation*).

- Newborns turn their heads toward the sources of sounds, startle when they hear loud noises, and can distinguish—and prefer—the human voice compared to other sounds. Young infants are also able to perceive distinctions between the basic speech sounds called *phonemes,* which are the smallest categories in speech that carry meanings. They can even distinguish phonemes that do not occur in the language spoken around them. For example, Japanese infants, in contrast to Japanese adults, perceive the phonemes /r/ and /l/ as different even though they do not differ in the Japanese language.

- Infants' vision is not fully developed at birth. They have difficulty discriminating between colors that are equally bright; however, by about 2 months of age their color vision is equal to that of adults.

  Newborns are quite nearsighted, with an acuity that has been estimated as about 20/300. However, they can see fairly clearly objects at a distance of one foot, about as far away as their mothers' faces are during nursing. At 2 to 3 months, infants can coordinate the vision of both eyes. By the time they are crawling, at about 7 or 8 months of age, their acuity is close to that of adults.

  Newborns actively scan their environments. They engage in endogenous looking, which originates in the neural activity of the brain and occurs even in the dark. They also demonstrate exogenous looking, which is stimulated by the external environment, for example, by changes in illumination.

  As demonstrated by Robert Fantz, newborn babies prefer to look at patterned figures rather than unpatterned ones. Movement appears to play an important role in helping infants learn the boundaries between objects; for example, when two objects are separate, they do not move as one unit. Infants' abilities to distinguish objects improves over the first months. Their vision is best under conditions of high contrast, and at first they scan only the high-contrast portions of simple figures. By 3 months of age, their scanning has become much more sophisticated and better-controlled.

  Studies by Robert Fantz in the early 1960s demonstrated that newborns could distinguish a schematic face from a facelike figure in which the features had been scrambled. These studies used stationary stimuli. More recently, other investigators, using moving, naturalistic stimuli, have shown that infants only 9 minutes old will turn toward a schematic face and infants 2 to 7 hours old can distinguish their mothers' faces from the face of a stranger.
- Newborns have well-developed senses of taste and smell and can discriminate among a variety of odors. When tested a few minutes after birth, they show a preference for the smell of their mother's milk over that of another woman. They prefer sweet tastes and make characteristic facial expressions in response to different flavors.
- Newborns are sensitive to touch, to changes in temperature, and to changes in position; these senses have been active for some time, beginning early in the prenatal period.

B. Response Processes

Infants are born with a number of ways to respond to or act on the world.

- They are equipped with an array of *reflexes*—well-integrated, involuntary responses to specific types of stimulation. Table 4.2 describes some of the reflexes present at birth. Some reflexes disappear in the first months after birth, as higher brain centers mature;

others disappear and reappear as parts of more mature behavior, and some appear to be transformed more directly into more mature behavior.

1. In some studies—notably those of Andrew Meltzoff and Keith Moore, newborn infants have demonstrated the ability to imitate the facial expressions of adults. Older babies are able to imitate sounds and a wide variety of movements; there is disagreement about whether the two kinds of imitation represent the same process.
2. Except for getting their fingers to their mouths, newborn infants' contact with objects appears purely accidental. However, research by Claus von Hofsten has shown that they engage in "pre-reaching," a form of visually initiated reaching in which infants reach in the direction of an object but are unable to coordinate reaching and grasping movements. At about 3 months of age, with development of the visual and motor areas of the cortex, pre-reaching is transformed into visually guided reaching, in which reaching and grasping movements work together.

- Integration of Sensory and Response Processes

  From birth, infants appear to perceive that stimuli from different sensory modalities go together. An example of intermodal perception is infants' ability to turn their heads in the direction of a sound that they hear. They also expect the sight and sound of a novel object to be coordinated. There is also evidence that newborns are able to discriminate between information coming from their own actions and information coming from the environment.

III. THE QUALITIES OF INFANT EXPERIENCE AND BEHAVIOR

What characteristic qualities do infants display when responding to new events?

A. Emotion

In everyday usage, the word *emotion* refers to the feelings aroused by experiences.

- In addition to feelings, developmentalists recognize emotions to have physiological, communicative, cognitive, and action aspects. Technically, *emotion* is a feeling state produced by the distinctive physiological responses and cognitive evaluations that motivate action. They communicate to others and regulate interactions with others.
- Which emotions are present at birth? According to one view, emotions develop from two primitive states, contentment and distress, through a process of differentiation. For example, joy is thought to differentiate from contentment at about 3 months, and anger and fear from distress at 4 months and 6 months. Another view is that a set of core, primary emotions is present at birth. In support of this view are observations that infants display facial expressions that, to adults, look like indications of surprise, interest, joy, fear, and sadness. While there is evidence for a universal set of emotions and corresponding facial expressions, both from cross-cultural research and from observations of infants' expressions in response to events, it is difficult to know whether infants' facial

expressions have the same meanings as those of adults. But whatever emotions are present at birth, these emotions will become entwined with the physical, social, and intellectual aspects of children's development.

B. Temperament

Many psychologists believe that *temperament*—reflecting activity level, sociability, and the tendency to react to the world in characteristic ways—is already present at birth. Alexander Thomas, Stella Chess, and their colleagues found that babies could be classified as *easy* (playful, adaptable, and regular in biological functions), *difficult* (irritable, negative toward new experiences), and *slow to warm up* (low in activity level and needing some time to adapt to new situations). Other categories of temperament have been developed by Denise Newman and her colleagues in New Zealand and by Mary Rothbart and her colleagues in the United States. Statistical analyses suggest that the different scales have a great deal of overlap.

Cross-cultural comparisons have found some differences between groups; for example, Chinese children were found to be less active than American children; this may be a cultural difference, as high levels of activity and impulsiveness are discouraged by Chinese parents. Genetic influences are also agreed to be important. Stephen Suomi's research with monkeys uncovered a gene in which one allele is associated with a highly reactive temperament while a different allele is associated with a calmer temperament.

Longitudinal studies have found stability in temperamental traits such as irritability, persistence, and flexibility in children who were followed periodically through childhood and adolescence.

IV. BECOMING COORDINATED WITH THE SOCIAL WORLD

Coordination of babies' inborn abilities with their parents' caregiving skills allows babies' basic needs to be met. In addition, when babies and parents coordinate their schedules—for example, for eating and sleeping—babies fit smoothly into the lives of their families and the life patterns of their communities. The box "Sleeping Arrangements" tells some of the ways in which parents of various cultures accomplish this goal.

A. Sleeping

Peter Wolff, studying newborns' activity patterns, found that they display seven different states of alertness, in four of which they are asleep or nearly asleep. Electroencephalographic research indicates that different brainwave patterns accompany these levels of arousal.

For the first 2 to 3 months of life, babies begin their sleep periods with active or REM (rapid eye movement) sleep, and later enter quiet or NREM sleep. After a few months, this pattern is reversed.

Newborns sleep about two-thirds of the time, but their sleep comes in many short periods. As they grow older, sleep periods become longer and begin to coincide with adult day/night schedules.

Both cultural expectations and brain maturation affect how quickly babies adopt adult-like sleep cycles. American expectations for babies to sleep through the night early in infancy may be at the outside limit of what young infants can adjust to. The box "Sudden Infant Death Syndrome" discusses the possibility that nervous system immaturity is associated with the occurrence of SIDS.

B. Feeding

Adults and babies must also coordinate feeding schedules. If fed on demand, newborns prefer to feed about every 3 hours; most babies are able to go 4 hours between feedings by the time they reach 2½ months of age. By 7 to 8 months of age, babies are feeding about four times per day, an approximation of the adult eating schedule.

C. Crying

Crying tells parents that something is wrong. In infants all over the world, crying increases from birth to about 6 weeks of age, then begins to decrease in frequency. At first, crying is coordinated by structures in the brain stem; it is several months before the cortex becomes involved, at which point "voluntary" crying becomes possible. Adult listeners can distinguish among different kinds of cries and can distinguish between normal cries and the cries of "at risk" babies. Adults react to infants' cries with increased heart rate and blood pressure, and even, among nursing mothers, with milk flow.

Hunger is a major cause of crying, but often it is difficult to tell exactly why an infant cries. Some infants who cry excessively are said to have "colic."

V. MECHANISMS OF DEVELOPMENTAL CHANGE

During early infancy, existing behaviors become more efficient and new behaviors develop. A goal of developmental science is to explain how new forms of behavior arise.

A. From Sucking to Nursing

Nursing is a good example of a behavior arising in early infancy. At birth, rooting, sucking, swallowing, and breathing are not yet smoothly coordinated. By 6 weeks, however, the components of nursing occur in an efficient, integrated sequence. Since each of the four broad developmental frameworks introduced in Chapter 1 emphasizes different factors in explaining its development, nursing is a behavior that can be used to compare these approaches.

B. The Biological-Maturation Perspective

The biological-maturation perspective emphasizes that the maturational processes bring about development, and assigns only a small role to the environment. According to the biological-maturation approach, development of brain structures allows babies to interact with the environment in more complex ways. Supporting evidence comes from the observation that babies born with intact brain stems but without cerebral cortexes can suck, yawn, stretch, and cry; they also show habituation. However, they do not develop the well-coordinated behaviors, such as nursing, seen in normal babies the same age.

After birth, there is a dramatic increase in the number and efficiency of connections between the brain stem and the cortex in the central nervous systems of normally developing babies. This supports the biological-maturation view. However, it does not rule out the possibility that much of this development is brought about by infants' interaction with their environments.

C. The Environmental-Learning Perspective

The environmental-learning perspective emphasizes the role of *learning* in the coordination of innate reflexes with environmental events. Habituation and imitations are types of learning; habituation is described earlier in this chapter. Other types of learning are *classical conditioning* and *operant conditioning*.

- Through classical conditioning, previously existing behaviors come to be elicited by new stimuli. Babies are then able to anticipate events rather than simply react to them. Classical conditioning was first described by Russian physiologist Ivan Pavlov. In his studies, a tone served as a *conditional stimulus* (CS), which was paired with food in the dog's mouth—an *unconditional stimulus* (UCS). This UCS invariably caused salivation—an *unconditional response* (UCR). After many pairings, presentation of the CS alone caused the dog to salivate—a *conditional response* (CR) had been learned.

  It appears that newborn infants can learn expectancies through classical conditioning. For example, a co-worker of Pavlov showed that a baby could learn to open its mouth and make sucking motions in response to the sound of a bell that was previously paired with the sight of a glass of milk. Classical conditioning has been demonstrated in infants within hours of birth if the infants are alert and the stimuli used are biologically relevant. Lewis Lipsett and his colleagues found that 20- to 30-day-old infants, conditioned to blink in anticipation of a puff of air to the eye, were found by Lewis Lipsett and his colleagues to retain the behavior when tested 10 days later. However, babies who were only 10 days old at the time of training showed no sign of remembering what they had learned.
- While classical conditioning explains how behaviors come to be elicited by new circumstances, operant conditioning provides a means for addition of new forms of behavior to infants' repertoires. Actions that produce rewarding consequences are repeated; such a consequence is called *reinforcement.* Actions that are not followed by reinforcing consequences, or that are punished, will not be likely to be repeated. Einar Siqueland demonstrated that newborns could learn to either turn their heads (experimental group) or keep their heads still (control group) in order to obtain the opportunity to suck on a pacifier (reinforcing stimulus). Other investigators have demonstrated operant learning using such reinforcers as milk, sweet substances, an interesting visual display, and the sound of a heartbeat or the infant's mother's voice. There is evidence that during the

first several months of life, infants improve in their ability to remember newly learned behavior.

The environmental-learning perspective tends to view developmental change as a continuous process based on processes of learning that are in place at birth. Because it tends to discount the effects of genetic variation, this perspective has its greatest difficulty in accounting for individual differences in behavior.

D. The Constructivist Perspective: Piaget

The constructivist perspective originated in the work of Jean Piaget, who criticized as incomplete both the biological-maturation and the environmental-learning theories of his day. Piaget viewed infants as active organisms whose actions shape the ways in which the environment acts on them. He also believed that development occurs as a series of stagelike changes.

- In Piaget's view, development begins with the infant's inborn reflexes; these are early examples of *schemas*—mental structures that serve as models for action in similar situations. Schemas are strengthened and transformed through two processes of *adaptation: assimilation* (the process by which experiences are incorporated into existing schemas) and *accommodation* (the process by which schemas are modified so that they can be applied to both old and new experiences). For example, infants may assimilate breast, bottle, pacifier, and fingers to the inborn sucking schema. Since different techniques are necessary for sucking on these different objects, the infant must accommodate the sucking schema to each. *Equilibration* is a balancing of assimilation to existing schemas and accommodation to the requirements of environmental experiences, bringing children to a new level of development. Soon, however, biological changes or environmental demands will create new imbalances that will in turn push children's development even further. Piaget identified four major stages of development corresponding to infancy (sensorimotor), early childhood (preoperational), middle childhood (concrete operational), and adolescence (formal operational).
- During the *sensorimotor stage* adaptation mainly consists of coordinating sensory perceptions and simple motor responses. Piaget identified six substages within it, the first two of which are described in this chapter.

  In substage 1 (birth to 1 or 1½ months), infants mainly learn to coordinate and control their first schemas, the reflexes present at birth. The most important aspect of this practice is that the reflexes themselves produce further stimulation, which then stimulates even more reflex activity.

  Substage 2 (from about 1 or 1½ months to 4 months) is characterized by *primary circular reactions:* infants now repeat, for the pleasure of it, actions that are centered on their own bodies, such as sucking their fingers, waving their hands, or kicking their feet. These actions are called circular because they lead back to themselves, serving to prolong interesting events; Piaget considered this the first sign of cognitive development.

Piaget's view of the infant's reflexes was that they are schemas for action; he emphasized the role of infants' constructive activities in shaping the way the environment exerts its effects.

E. The Cultural-Context Perspective

The cultural-context perspective, like the constructivist perspective, believes that development occurs as individuals act on their environments and that biological factors and environment play equal roles in development. However, the cultural-context perspective emphasizes cultural variations in the way that adults arrange their interactions with their children.

- Nursing is a behavior that is universal, but that is also culturally organized. For example, children may be breastfed by their mothers, fed by a wet nurse, or given infant formula in a bottle. More important for development than these variations in feeding practices, though, are the larger cultural patterns of which they are a part. For example, some cultures routinely breast-feed babies for two years or more, a practice that helps to space births and protects babies from malnutrition.

VI. INTEGRATING THE SEPARATE THREADS OF DEVELOPMENT

Children's behaviors, such as nursing, do not develop in isolation, but as part of a complex system. The strategy of Robert Emde and his colleagues, described in Chapter 1, involves tracing developments in the biological, behavioral, and social domains as they relate to one another. Bio-social-behavioral shifts occur when developments in these areas create a reorganization of behavior, signaling the onset of a new stage of development. The first postnatal bio-social-behavioral shift occurs when infants are about 2½ months of age.

VII. THE FIRST POSTNATAL BIO-SOCIAL-BEHAVIORAL SHIFT

The first postnatal bio-social-behavioral shift occurs, in full-term babies, at about 2½ months after birth, and results from the convergence of developmental changes that had, before this time, proceeded separately. A good example of this process is the way changes in infants' smiling are related to other aspects of their development. The developmental changes contributing to this shift are listed in Table 4.6.

A. The Emergence of Social Smiling

Infants' early smiles do not appear to be related to any specific events in the environment. Then, between 1 and 2½ months of age, infants begin to smile in response to any external stimulus. Finally, at 2½ to 3 months of age, infants' smiles become truly social—they smile in response to others' smiles and, in turn, elicit others' smiles. At this point, parents report a new quality of emotional contact with their infants. This sharing, called primary intersubjectivity, involves only face-to-face communication.

B. Biological Contributions to Social Smiling

Robert Emde and his colleagues observed that infants' earliest smiles were controlled by events occurring in the brain stem. These have been called "REM smiles" because they are associated with drowsiness and REM sleep. These were replaced at about 2½ months of age by smiles that were not associated with REM sleep. At about 2½ months of age, maturation is also occurring in the visual system, allowing babies to focus their eyes on people and to process visual information more effectively. This helps to make social smiling possible.

C. The Social Smile and Social Feedback

Feedback from the social world—in the form of others smiling back—is important in the development of social smiling. Blind infants, unable to make these visual connections, may not shift to social smiling at 2½ months. According to Selma Fraiberg, parents of blind infants often use touch to stimulate their babies' smiles; in this way, they establish the kind of social interaction seen in sighted babies and their parents. These observations demonstrate that maturational processes alone do not lead to the development of social smiling; interaction with others is also necessary.

VIII. SUMMING UP THE FIRST 2½ MONTHS

During the first 2½ months of postnatal life, infants grow larger and stronger, their nervous systems develop, and they perform behaviors such as nursing more efficiently. These developments take place in close coordination with their caregivers' behavior. When changes in the biological, social, and behavioral realms converge, a qualitatively new level of development occurs. In the case of social smiling, at about 2½ months after birth, maturation occurring in the visual system leads to a transformation of smiling, previously an unrelated behavior; this, in turn, allows a greater social reciprocity between infants and their caregivers, which helps lead to a greater range of emotional expression on the part of infants.

Key Terms I

Following are important terms introduced in Chapter 4. Match each term with the letter of the example that best illustrates the term.

1. ______ accommodation
2. ______ adaptation
3. ______ assimilation
4. ______ axon
5. ______ dendrite
6. ______ emotion
7. ______ equilibration
8. ______ experience-dependent
9. ______ experience-expectant
10. ______ intermodal perception
11. ______ myelin
12. ______ neuron
13. ______ primary circular reaction
14. ______ primary motor area
15. ______ primary sensory area
16. ______ reflex
17. ______ schema
18. ______ sensorimotor stage
19. ______ temperament

a. The time of life during which developments in behavior primarily involve coordination between motor behaviors and sensory circumstances.
b. A baby learns to suck differently to get milk from a bottle than to nurse from his mother's breast.
c. A process through which schemas are strengthened and transformed.
d. A baby sees its hand pass across its field of vision, finds this interesting, then repeats the movement over and over again.
e. This balance between existing schemas and environmental experiences is a "back and forth" process that brings the child to new levels of development.
f. The area responsible for the sense of touch is the first to become active.
g. Development in this part of the cortex allows changes such as that from pre-reaching to voluntary reaching.
h. A baby uses her sucking schema to explore a pacifier.
i. This type of well-integrated but involuntary response comprises much of the newborn's behavior.
j. This substance coats nerve fibers, allowing nerve impulses to travel more efficiently.
k. According to Piaget, the infant's early reflexes (for example, sucking) are primitive examples of this unit of psychological functioning.

l. This involves formation of neural connections in advance of need.
m. Without this structure, neurons could not receive messages from neighboring cells.
n. Some examples of this—including anger, pleasure, and surprise—appear to be present at birth.
o. Knowing, for example, that a sound goes with a particular visual image.
p. This is another word for "nerve cell."
q. One example of this is "slow to warm up."
r. The main protruding branch of a neuron along which messages are transmitted.
s. This involves formation of neural connections in response to experience.

Key Terms II

Following are important terms introduced in Chapter 4. Match each term with the letter of the example that best illustrates the term.

1. ______ brainstem
2. ______ cerebral cortex
3. ______ classical conditioning
4. ______ conditional response
5. ______ conditional stimulus
6. ______ dishabituation
7. ______ habituation
8. ______ learning
9. ______ neurotransmitter
10. ______ operant conditioning
11. ______ phonemes
12. ______ primary intersubjectivity
13. ______ reinforcement
14. ______ spinal cord
15. ______ synapse
16. ______ synaptic pruning
17. ______ synaptogenesis
18. ______ unconditional response
19. ______ unconditional stimulus

a. An infant learns to suck a pacifier in order to activate a mobile above her crib.
b. A baby makes sucking movements with his mouth when he sees his nursing bottle approaching.
c. This part of the nervous system controls vital functions such as breathing and inborn reflexes.
d. This part of the nervous system carries messages between the brain and the spinal nerves.
e. Through this process, infants learn to anticipate events rather than simply reacting to them.

f. A stimulus that automatically elicits some response (as a puff of air in the eye elicits blinking).
g. This kind of change in behavior comes about because of the infant's experiences of events in the environment.
h. This is the name for the gap between neurons across which nerve impulses must travel.
i. In Pavlov's study, a tone, which signaled that food was about to be presented.
j. When an infant smiles at his father he receives a smile in return; this makes him more likely to direct smiles at his father in the future.
k. This part of the nervous system allows infants to integrate new sensory information with memories of previous experiences.
l. This is a coordination of mood between infant and caregiver.
m. A response that automatically occurs to a particular stimulus (as when a baby turns his head in the direction of a touch on the cheek).
n. These are responsible for the difference in sound between "pear" and "bear."
o. A newborn who stops paying attention to the washing machine is demonstrating this response pattern.
p. When neural connections are not needed, they are eliminated through this process.
q. A baby who has stopped paying attention to the radio and perks up when the station is changed is demonstrating this response pattern.
r. This substance aids in the transmission of impulses from one neuron to the next.
s. This process is prominent during prenatal development and infancy, and again in adolescence.

Multiple-Choice Practice Questions

Circle the letter of the word or phrase that correctly completes each statement.

1. ________ are protuberances on a neuron that can receive electrical impulses from other neurons.
   a. Axons
   b. Cell bodies
   c. Dendrites
   d. Neurotransmitters

2. On which would a newborn best be able to focus?
   a. his mother's face while he nurses
   b. a mobile hanging over the far end of his crib
   c. a person standing across the room
   d. all of the above equally well

3. When 2-week-old babies are shown simple geometric figures,
   a. they look away.
   b. they focus on areas of high contrast.
   c. they systematically scan the outline of the figure.
   d. they look first at the outline, then scan the interior.

4. Infants who are regular in biological functions, playful, and adaptable have been labeled "easy" with respect to
   a. motor development.
   b. personality.
   c. temperament.
   d. emotion.

5. Babies' cries usually cause adults to
   a. react with increased heart rate and blood pressure.
   b. avoid contact with the babies.
   c. react with decreases in heart rate.
   d. react with signs of depression.

6. Nursing
   a. is present at birth in the same form as seen in older infants.
   b. develops greater efficiency and coordination during the first weeks of life.
   c. is composed of several reflexes that are and remain separate from one another.
   d. takes longer in older infants than in newborns.

7. Theorists with the ________ perspective view development during infancy as the result of changes in the physical structures and physiological processes of the organism.
   a. environmental-learning
   b. cultural-context
   c. constructivist
   d. biological-maturation

8. "Myelination" refers to
   a. a process of brain growth through the formation of new neurons.
   b. the formation of a fatty sheath around nerve fibers.
   c. a structural part of brain development that is nearly complete at birth.
   d. the formation of reflex arcs in the spinal cord.

9. Studies of how young infants react to speech sounds have shown that 2-month-olds
   a. cannot distinguish between closely related phonemes such as /pa/ and /ba/.
   b. can distinguish only among phonemes that occur in the language they hear spoken around them.
   c. can distinguish among phonemes even if they do not occur in the language spoken around them.
   d. can distinguish only among phonemes that they can pronounce.

10. The facial expressions of infants
    a. are very similar to those of adults experiencing different emotional states.
    b. are definitely known to correspond to their emotions in the same way adults' expressions correspond to the adults' emotions.
    c. are usually about the same, no matter what emotions they are experiencing.
    d. are variable, but do not correspond in any reliable way to their emotional states.

11. The age at which infants begin to "sleep through the night"
    a. is entirely determined by the level of maturity of their nervous systems.
    b. varies among infants but is, on the average, the same for babies in all cultures.
    c. is influenced by cultural practices and also by maturation.
    d. is determined entirely by cultural practices.

12. The _______ reflex involves flinging out the arms, then hugging them back to the center of the body.
    a. grasping
    b. reaching
    c. swimming
    d. Moro

13. Through ______ , babies learn to anticipate events that often occur together.
    a. operant conditioning
    b. imitation
    c. classical conditioning
    d. habituation

14. When an infant turns her head, she is given a taste of sugar water. After a series of trials, she turns her head consistently. This is an example of
    a. habituation.
    b. classical conditioning.
    c. imitation.
    d. operant conditioning.

15. Piaget's theory of intellectual development views infants as
    a. active, problem-solving organisms.
    b. helpless and unable to initiate behavior.
    c. completely dependent on the environment for stimulation.
    d. having intellectual potential that unfolds automatically as they mature.

16. Which might be a primary circular reaction?
    a. An infant opens his mouth for milk when he sees his mother approach.
    b. An infant repeatedly brings her hand to her mouth and briefly sucks her fingers.
    c. A baby learns to ignore the sound of the highway outside his window.
    d. A newborn copies his mother when she opens her eyes wide in a surprised expression.

17. Which is associated with higher rates of Sudden Infant Death Syndrome?
    a. maternal smoking
    b. breast-feeding
    c. putting babies to sleep on their backs
    d. all of these

18. Which is associated with the first postnatal bio-social-behavioral shift?
    a. social smiling
    b. complete development of the cerebral cortex
    c. walking
    d. the first meaningful spoken words

19. The ______ controls vital functions such as breathing and sleeping.
    a. cerebral cortex
    b. cerebellum
    c. brain stem
    d. midbrain

20. In which order do infants gain the ability to control their movements?
    a. arms and trunk, legs, head
    b. head, arms and trunk, legs
    c. legs, arms and trunk, head
    d. all parts at about the same time

Short-Answer Practice Questions

Write a brief answer in the space below each question.

1. What sensory processes are the most mature at birth? Which undergo the most developmental change during infancy?

2. What types of visual stimuli do newborns prefer to look at? What changes take place in their looking behavior over the first few months of life?

3. In what ways do researchers determine that infants are experiencing emotions? Can we know for certain that infant and adult emotions are similar? Why or why not?

4. What do psychologists mean by "temperament"? What evidence is there that it has a heritable component?

5. How do both mother and infant contribute to the development of efficient nursing?

6. How do infants form expectancies through classical conditioning? Describe a situation in which this might actually occur.

7. Show how biological, behavioral, and social factors interact in infants' development of social smiling.

8. What evidence is there that newborn infants engage in imitation? How does this behavior differ from imitation seen in older infants?

Putting It All Together

People of different cultures vary in their opinions about how childbirth and the rearing of children should be accomplished. From Chapters 3 and 4, find several examples illustrating the way differences in parents' beliefs and expectations result in varying experiences for their infants.

Sources of More Information

Brazelton, T. B., & Sparrow, J. A. (1992). *Touchpoints.* Reading, MA: Perseus Books.
This book, which covers the period from birth to 6 years of age, includes material on feeding, crying, and temperament as well as general developmental issues and problems.

Ginsburg, H. P., & Opper, S. (1988). *Piaget's theory of intellectual development.* Upper Saddle River, NJ: Prentice Hall.
This is a readable presentation of Piaget's work and theory, aimed at undergraduate-level students.

Gopnik, A., Meltzoff, A. N., & Kuhl, P. K. (2001). *The scientist in the crib:What early learning tells us about the mind.* New York: William Morrow.
The authors tackle questions about how babies come to make sense of the world around them.

Montagu, A. (1986). *Touching: The human significance of the skin.* New York: HarperTrade.
The author describes the importance of tactile interaction for human development.

Sears, W., & Sears, M. (2003). *The breastfeeding book.* Boston: Little Brown.
This is a fairly comprehensive book about breastfeeding, written by a nurse and a physician. It covers most topics of interest to new mothers (and fathers).

Wolf, C. (1998). *On the safe side: Your complete reference to childproofing for infants and children.* Kansas City, KS: Whirlwind.
This book deals with one of the major adjustments that must be made by families with new babies—making the home safe for infants and young children.

Answer Key

Answers to Key Terms I: 1.b, 2.c, 3.h, 4.r, 5.m, 6.n, 7.e. 8.s, 9.l, 10.o, 11.j, 12.p, 13.d, 14.g, 15.f, 16.i, 17.k, 18.a, 19.q.

Answers to Key Terms II: 1.c, 2.k, 3.e, 4.b, 5.i, 6.q, 7.o, 8.g, 9.r, 10.a, 11.n, 12.l, 13.j, 14.d, 15.n, 16.p, 17.s, 18.m, 19.f.

Answers to Multiple-Choice Questions: 1.c, 2.a, 3.b, 4.c, 5.a, 6.b, 7.d, 8.b, 9.c, 10.a, 11.c, 12.d, 13.c, 14.d, 15.a, 16.b, 17.a, 18.a, 19.c, 20.b.

The Achievements of the First Year

chapter 5

At no time after birth does development occur so quickly as in the first year. During their first 12 months, infants move from relative helplessness to independent locomotion. Gradually, they gain control over their bodies. By 1 year of age, they can reach for and grasp objects smoothly and accurately and let them go voluntarily; they can even, using thumb and fingers, pick up objects the size of a bead or a raisin.

Infants' growing cognitive abilities parallel the development of their motor skills. Toward the end of the first year, they demonstrate newly developed powers of memory and are able to coordinate actions to reach a goal. Linguistically, they are also making progress; their strings of babbling begin to resemble adult speech.

Changes are occurring in infants' social lives as well. By 7 or 8 months of age, they begin to be wary of strangers and to resist being separated from their caregivers. In fact, they depend on their caregivers' reactions to show them how to react in unfamiliar situations.

These many changes in different domains result in a bio-social-behavioral shift between about 7 and 9 months of age. At this time, infants are prepared for more active exploration of their physical and social worlds.

Learning Objectives

Keep these questions in mind while studying Chapter 5.

1. How do biological changes that occur in the first year allow infants to develop locomotion, coordinated reaching and grasping, and other voluntary motor behavior?
2. Why is there disagreement among developmentalists as to how much knowledge about the world is innate and how much has to be learned through experience?
3. How do the biological-maturation, environmental-learning, and constructivist viewpoints regard the abilities that infants demonstrate during the first year?
4. How much can infants remember? How do improvements in memory relate to growth in other cognitive skills?
5. What verbal and nonverbal forms of communication are used by infants and their caregivers?

6. What interrelations occur among biological, behavioral, and social factors to cause a reorganization of behavior at 7 to 9 months of age?

Chapter Summary

I. BIOLOGICAL GROWTH

Changes in babies' motor and cognitive abilities between 2½ months and 1 year depend on changes in the physical structures of their bodies and brains.

A. Size and Shape

Most babies grow about 10 inches and triple their weight during the first year—their fastest growth spurt until adolescence. Their bodies grow differentially; by 12 months, their heads account for a smaller and their legs a greater proportion of overall length than they did at birth. This lowers their center of gravity and makes walking easier.

B. Muscle and Bone

Infants' bones start to ossify, or harden, beginning with those of the hands and wrists. Their muscles become longer and thicker, another development that prepares them for walking.

C. Sex Differences in Rates of Growth

Girls mature faster than boys. By the time of birth, their skeletons are 4 to 6 weeks more mature than those of male newborns. By puberty, girls will lead boys in physical maturity by 2 years.

D. The Brain

While the entire nervous system continues to grow and increase in complexity between the ages of 3 and 12 months, it is the tremendous increase in the number of synapses, called *exuberant synaptogenesis,* that is most noteworthy. This proliferation of synapses, resulting in twice the number that the brain will have in early adolescence, allows infants to be prepared to establish neural connections for whatever types of experiences they may have. Those connections that are used frequently are strengthened; those that prove unnecessary—that is, are not used—eventually disappear.

The brain develops at different rates in different regions. For example, the visual cortex undergoes its proliferation of synapses at 2½ to 4 months of age, around the time of the first postnatal bio-social-behavioral shift. The motor cortex has its surge in synapse formation at about 6 months of age followed by the prefrontal and frontal cortexes at 9 months. Between 7 and 9 months, the increase in activity in the prefrontal cortex allows infants to have greater ability to regulate and inhibit their actions.

II. PERCEPTION AND MOVEMENT

Like adults, infants need to coordinate perceptual information with motor actions in order to explore the environment.

A. Reaching and Grasping

Babies begin to gain voluntary control over their reaching toward at the time of the first postnatal bio-social-behavioral shift. During the next months, their movements become quicker and more accurate. By 9 months, their grasping motions are well-integrated and automatic, and parents need to be sure their homes are "baby-proofed." By 12 months, babies can pick up small objects using thumb and fingers and are well coordinated enough to eat with a spoon and drink from a cup.

Rachel Karniol has identified a regular sequence in the way babies' development of the ability to manipulate objects. And Eleanor Gibson has noted that, as they gain control over their hands, babies appear to perceive that different objects lend themselves to different ways of interaction—for example, rattles lend themselves to being shaken, soft toys to being stroked.

B. Locomotion

Locomotion, the ability to move around on their own, gives babies more opportunities to explore the environment. It also serves to separate babies from their caregivers. This, in turn, sets the occasion for further development. Control over the movement of infants' bodies proceeds in a cephalocaudal (head-to-toe) direction; for example, they can hold their heads up earlier than they can sit unaided. There is wide variation in the ages at which children reach various milestones in motor development, as shown in Table 5.1.

As shown in Figure 5.8, babies' crawling progresses through phases. Newborns engage in a pushing movement, controlled by subcortical reflexes, that can propel them forward. This reflexive pushing disappears at about 2 months of age, and is not replaced by coordinated crawling on hands and knees until 5 or 6 months later.

Once crawling allows them to explore the environment in a new way, infants begin to display wariness of heights, typically between 7 and 9 months of age. Research by Joseph Campos and his colleagues, using the "visual cliff," has demonstrated that it is infants' experience in moving around on their own that leads to this fear of heights.

C. The Role of Practice in Motor Development

Is practice necessary for the development of early motor skills? Wayne and Margaret Dennis discovered that Hopi infants raised traditionally (strapped to cradle boards) were no later, on average, to walk than those raised by less traditional parents. This suggested that practice is not necessary for the development of walking.

However, other observations from various cultures suggest that giving babies practice in specific motor skills—walking, for example—causes them to learn these skills at somewhat earlier ages. It is also sometimes true that restricting practice of a skill may delay its onset. For example, modern North American infants spend most of their time on their backs and little time in a prone (face down) position. This has resulted in a delay of the onset of crawling of as much as two months.

III. COGNITIVE CHANGES

Infants' *cognitive processes*—the psychological processes through which they acquire, store, and use knowledge about the world—develop rapidly between 3 and 12 months of age. Developmentalists disagree, to some extent, on when different milestones are reached; this disagreement is tied to the research methods used; it is difficult to determine what babies know and how they think given that it is not possible to ask them.

A. Constructing a Stable World

As discussed in Chapter 4, Piaget viewed development as arising from children's own actions on the world.

In referring to the earliest period of development as the sensorimotor stage, Piaget emphasized his belief that, during this period, children acquire knowledge through motor actions directed at the environment and guided by the sensory organs. The endpoint of sensorimotor development—the qualitatively different way of knowing about the world to which sensorimotor activity leads—is, Piaget believed, the ability to engage in *representation*—to be able to picture and think about the world without having to physically act upon it. According to Piaget, infants begin to represent object to themselves mentally at about 8 months of age; this ability is fully developed at 18–24 months of age. He believed that, during the period from 4 or 5 months to 12 months, infants begin to form the idea of objects as parts of external reality; before this time, he thought, infants are only aware of their own actions.

In substage 3 (4 to 8 months), babies perform secondary circular reactions, in which they repeat actions that cause interesting results in the outside environment; for example, kicking at a mobile in order to see the dangling objects move. Piaget saw this as an indication that babies are beginning to view objects as more than an extension of their own actions.

In substage 4 (8 to 12 months), babies become able to coordinate two different schemas in order to reach a goal (an example of *intentionality*). For example, a baby may sweep a cushion out of the way (one schema) in order to reach for and grasp a stuffed toy (a second schema). At this point, goal-oriented behavior is only directed at objects and people when they are present to the baby's senses.

- Piaget believed that newborns had no sense of *object permanence* but gradually developed it during the sensorimotor period. Until babies actively began to search for hidden objects at about 8 months of age, he thought, it was not possible to know that they believed in the objects' continued existence when out of sight. He believed that it was not until late in the second year of life that infants could keep an absent object in mind and also reason about the absent object. This notion has generated a great deal of research.

Studies have shown that the sequence and timing of Piaget's sensorimotor stages are quite reliable, even across diverse cultural environments. However, some researchers disagree with Piaget's reliance on overt action as both the necessary condition for and the measure of increases in babies' understanding. Perhaps, they argue, other factors are involved.

A series of studies by Adele Diamond suggests that babies' limited ability to remember and their tendency to repeat movements (*perseveration*) impair their performance on hidden object tests. So, for example, they may search for an object in a place where it was previously hidden (the "A-not-B error"), even when they have seen it hidden in a new location. Work by Esther Thelen and her colleagues supports the view that motor habits, rather than lack of belief in the permanence of objects, influence infant responses on object permanence tasks.

It is possible, by using experimental techniques that do not require action on the part of infants, to show that young infants seem to know more about hidden objects than they appeared to in Piaget's observations. For example, Renee Baillargeon and her colleagues used habituation and dishabituation to measure babies' expectations about the continued existence of a box obscured by a moving screen. They found that 3½-month-olds were surprised when a screen appeared to pass through the space where the object was supposed to be; thus, they reasoned, the babies must have continued to believe in the existence of the box even though it was not visible.

Research using methods that do not rely on overt action—for example, habituation/dishabituation and differential looking—has shifted the views of many developmentalists toward recognition that infants develop some form of many cognitive abilities earlier than was previously recognized. This view has also given rise to many products that are used by parents in the belief that they will enhance their babies' intellectual development (see the box "Bringing Up Brainy Babies"). However, not all researchers agree that the experimental results truly support the idea of infant precocity. Sometimes, they have conducted studies that point to alternative explanations of previous results. For example, Leslie Cohen and Cara Cashon found that infants' behavior in Baillargeon's experiment could be explained by factors related to the habituation/dishabituation procedure that was used. Research by other researchers has supported this view. It is clear that the processes used by researchers to measure development interact closely with the theories they will develop to explain development.

B. Additional Forms of Object Knowledge

The possibility that infants understand more about object permanence than was previously believed has given rise to investigations of other aspects of their knowledge concerning objects.

As was seen in Chapter 4, even newborns display intermodal perception—understanding that features of an object perceived in one sensory mode (vision, for example) go together with features perceived in another sensory mode (such as hearing). As infants' motor skills increase, intermodal perception expands beyond hearing and vision to include how objects feel. Arlette Streri and Elizabeth Spelke found that when 4-month-old infants have the ability to integrate sensory impressions from vision and touch; they were able to identify visually rings that they had previously explored only with their sense of touch. Apparently, infants do not need to go through an extended process of learning to understand that the basic perceptual properties of objects are related to each other.

Infants understand other things about the properties of objects. For example, Elizabeth Spelke and her colleagues found that 4-month-olds understand that objects cannot move through a solid physical obstruction; when a ball was dropped behind a screen, they stared less at the ball when it was seen lying on a shelf at the bottom of the display than when it was seen lying on the floor below the shelf, having seemingly passed through the shelf in violation of the laws of physics. Renee Baillargeon and her colleagues have demonstrated that 4½-month-olds also expect objects to obey the law of gravity; they stared longer at a block that appeared to be suspended in midair than at one that was supported by another block.

Alan Leslie and his colleagues have argued that their research demonstrates that 6-month-old infants have an appreciation of physical causality. They measured this by habituating infants to computer displays in which a square bumped a second square and the second square moved (showing causality); when shown a similar display in which the second square moved only after a delay, they stared longer at this apparently noncausal event.

Experiments by Karen Wynn, using a violation-of-expectations measure, appear to show that 4-month-old infants are able, in some way, to carry out simple arithmetic operations on small numbers of objects. However, there is disagreement among researchers as to whether infants really have some rudimentary ability to add and subtract, or whether they are responding to some other aspect of the experimental situation.

Researchers do not agree on how much knowledge about the world we can attribute to young infants. But Piaget's views on the importance of children's own activity in cognitive development have led to studies of the role of activity in the development of understanding. As discussed in the box "Action and Understanding," Richard Held and Alan Hein, working with kittens, discovered that experience with locomotion is necessary for developing an understanding of spatial relations. Joseph Campos and his colleagues demonstrated that babies who had experience with moving around in baby walkers not only developed fear of heights (as measured on a visual cliff) at an earlier age, but also were better at locating hidden objects than children of the same age without walker experience. Other research, by Martha Ann Bell and Nathan Fox, has shown that changes in activity of the frontal lobes—associated with success on object permanence tasks—accompany the onset of locomotion. Other work has demonstrated that babies whose locomotion was delayed by a neural tube defect became successful on an object permanence task after they became able to move around independently.

C. Categorizing: Knowledge About Kinds of Things

Categorizing is the process of responding to different objects as though they are equivalent because the objects are similar in some way. So, for example, all cats are similar in some ways and different from dogs. Peter Eimas and Paul Quinn found that 3-month-olds were able to learn quickly how to categorize different kinds of animals; for example, they formed a category corresponding to "cat" that excluded dogs. In another study, 3- and 4-month-olds appeared to respond to mammals as a category distinct from non-mammals and furniture. These studies used a differential looking procedure. Using a procedure in which 3-month-olds kicked their legs to make a mobile move, researchers found that the babies appeared to categorize the blocks dangling from the mobile on the basis of the form of the letters embossed upon them. The instances discussed above are examples of categorizing on the basis of perceptual features—how objects look, sound, taste, etc. Toward the end of the first year, infants become able to also form conceptual categories—that is, to categorize on the basis of such features as what things do and how they have come to be a certain way. Jean Mandler and Laraine McDonough found that, while 7-month-old babies responded to models of birds and airplanes as if they were the same, 9- to 11-month-olds treated them as members of separate categories.

There is controversy about whether infants are capable of conceptual categorization. Mandler believes that infants can, by 3 to 4 months of age, engage in perceptual analysis of stimuli, and that conceptual categorization requires another process that develops as infants gain more knowledge about the world. Some other researchers take the position that 9- to 11-month-old infants, who have not had direct experience with birds and airplanes, are simply making finer perceptual distinctions than younger infants.

- Can infants distinguish between animate and inanimate objects? Researchers agree that this distinction appears, with regard to objects, by 9 months of age; with regard to human beings, the idea of animacy may begin earlier.
- Developmentalists believe that the distinction between intentional and nonintentional actions is important in learning to distinguish between animate and inanimate objects. A block, for example, will not move unless someone pushes it; a cat, on the other hand, moves by itself. Some argue that actions must be "rational" in order to be considered intentional. At 9 months of age, infants act surprised when actions do not appear rational—that is, when they do not fit the limits of physical reality.
- It is clear that, from birth, infants respond to humans in a special way. For example, they may imitate a person opening his or her mouth, but will not imitate the action if modeled by a mechanical device.

  At 6 months of age, infants in a study by Maria Legerstee expressed no surprise when a person talked to someone behind a curtain and the curtain opened to reveal another person; they did express surprise if the curtain opened to reveal a broom.

D. The Growth of Memory

During the first year, infants improve in their ability to remember what they learn. Carolyn Rovee-Collier and her colleagues found that, when they were taught to move a mobile by kicking it, 2-month-olds remembered their training for 24 hours but had forgotten after three days; 3-month-olds remembered their training for about a week. Research with the mobile and with other tasks has shown a steady increase with age in the length of time that infants can remember what they learn.

E. Recall and Wariness

Infants' ability to categorize and their ability to remember are linked to one another in important ways.

- Because of the steady improvement they have observed in infants' memory over the first year, Rovee-Collier and her colleagues consider it to be a continuous process that does not involve new, qualitatively different, principles of learning or remembering. The development of categorization can be viewed in the same way. However, other researchers believe that, just as, between 6 and 9 months, categorization appears to shift from having a perceptual to having a conceptual basis, a qualitative shift in memory also occurs. This shift involves the ability to recall objects and events (*implicit memory*) rather than simply being able to recognize them as familiar (*explicit memory*). Andrew Meltzoff demonstrated this in a study of deferred imitation—imitation of behavior witnessed at a previous time. Nine-month-olds were found to be capable of recognizing objects they had seen and also imitating behaviors performed with those objects—behaviors the infants had seen the experimenter perform but had never performed themselves. Harlene Hayne and her colleagues, using similar procedures, found that, while 6-month-olds imitated actions they had seen 24 hours earlier, their memories were disrupted if the objects on which the actions were performed (puppets) were changed; 12-month-olds performed the observed actions even when new objects were substituted.
- Once infants can recognize what is familiar, they also recognize other situations as unfamiliar. Rudolph Shaffer found that, while 4-month-olds immediately reached for an unfamiliar object, 6-month-olds hesitated for a short time, and 9-month-olds hesitated longer or turned away from the object. Some researchers have suggested that infants become wary when they search their memories for objects and events and find that they do not fit into a category of things they have encountered in the past.

There is disagreement about exactly when recall memory appears. Andrew Meltzoff and Keith Moore argue, on the basis of infants' imitation of facial expressions, that recall memory appears as early as 6 weeks of age. They suggest that, later in the first year, infants become capable of extending recall to objects as well as people. Other researchers feel that imitation of facial expressions is a specialized response, and recall ability can only be attributed to infants when they can bring prior information to mind. In any event, toward the end of the first year, developments in remembering, categorization, and infants' responses to strange events become intertwined.

IV. NEW SOCIAL RELATIONSHIPS

During the second half of the first year, babies begin to act fearful of unfamiliar adults and distressed when their primary caregivers disappear. This behavior seems to be connected to their improved abilities to remember, categorize, and to explore the environment actively.

A. The Role of Uncertainty in Wariness

Babies are fairly limited in the ways in which they can function in the world; therefore, they depend on adults to help them perform many actions that they will later be able to perform by themselves. Cultural-context theorist Lev Vygotsky called this a *zone of proximal development*. The adults perform only those parts of the action that the child cannot yet perform; thus, their actions are finely tuned to those of the child. By about 7 months of age, babies can classify adults as "those who can be trusted to help" or as "strangers." Because only familiar adults can be counted on to perform according to babies' expectations, babies may feel uncertain about how to interact with unfamiliar adults, and are therefore wary of them.

B. The Infant–Caregiver Emotional Relationship

The important developments taking place during the first year converge, toward the end of the year, with a change in the quality of the emotional relationship between parents and infants. According to Joseph Campos and his colleagues, the ability to get around on their own (locomotion) is an important factor in this process. They found that, once infants were able to crawl, their parents had more intense feelings about them, positive and negative, and that the infants themselves also exhibited stronger emotional expressions. For example, they seemed angrier when they had difficulty attaining a goal. Infants who crawled also became more upset when their parents left their sides.

At about the same time that infants begin to crawl and to react with wariness to unfamiliar people, their emotional relationships with their caregivers take on a new quality, which developmentalists call *attachment*. According to Eleanor Maccoby, the signs of attachment are:

1. Seeking to be near the caregiver.
2. Showing distress if separated.
3. Being happy when reunited.
4. Orienting toward (for example, watching, or listening for) the caregiver.

Attachment appears between 7 and 9 months of age and undergoes changes in later infancy.

C. The Changing Nature of Communication

As babies become more independent physically, they show different forms of communication with their caregivers. In early infancy, their face-to-face interactions display a kind of emotional sharing called *primary intersubjectivity*. But at around 7 months of age, a further development—*secondary intersubjectivity*—appears, allowing infants and caregivers to share feelings about events beyond themselves, for example, pleasure at seeing a familiar object or event.

- Another example of babies' new communication skills is *social referencing,* a form of communication in which babies' reactions to unusual situations are affected by their mothers' facial expressions—the mothers' reactions tell them "how to feel." Baby girls are more likely than baby boys to be wary of objects that make their mothers appear worried. Perhaps in consequence, mothers use more intense expressions when communicating with boys. Between 9 and 12 months of age, infants' social referencing becomes more selective. Tricia Striano and Phillipe Rochat found that 7-month-olds, confronted by a remote-control barking dog, "checked" repeatedly with the adult even when the adult did not look at them; in contrast, 10-month-olds stopped looking at the adult if the adult did not glance at them when the dog barked.
- While 5-month-olds do not follow their mothers' gazes when the mothers look to one side, 6- or 7-month-olds, if the situation is clear and simple, will follow the mother's gaze to see what she is looking at. The ability to look in the direction in which a caregiver points increases rapidly between 10 and 12 months.

Once babies move around on their own, new forms of vocal communication allow mothers and babies to remain coordinated even when out of sight of one another.

- As early as 4 months of age, babies can recognize their own names; by 6 months, they apparently recognize names for familiar objects, and by 9 months they begin to be able to identify phrases and to understand common expressions such as "Wave bye-bye." The ability to produce language has its roots in the cooing sounds that babies begin to make at 10 to 12 weeks of age. Babies coo and gurgle in response to the voices of others and will even take part in cooing "conversations" when their own sounds are imitated.

  Babbling (involving consonant-vowel combinations) begins at about 7 months of age, as a form of vocal play. By 9 months, they begin to drop sounds that do not belong to the language they hear around them. In *jargoning,* which begins toward the end of the first year, babies imitate the stress and intonations of the language they are learning, while putting together long strings of syllables. By 12 months of age, babies can understand about a dozen simple phrases and can say several words themselves.

  Deaf infants engage in vocal babbling only if they have residual hearing. If signed to, however, they babble with their hands.

V. A NEW BIO-SOCIAL-BEHAVIORAL SHIFT

Advances in motor skills—particularly in locomotion—are coordinated with new developments in cognitive domains and in social relationships, creating a new bio-social-behavioral shift between 7 and 9 months of age. Infants are now able to move independently, to recall more of what they observe, and to grasp and explore objects more skillfully. Their social interactions change as they become more aware of the differences between familiar and strange adults, and their caregivers adapt their own behavior accordingly. These new patterns of adaptation will serve them until the next reorganization occurs, a year or so later.

Key Terms

Following are important terms introduced in Chapter 5. Match each term with the letter of the example that best illustrates the term.

1. ______ attachment
2. ______ babbling
3. ______ categorizing
4. ______ cognitive processes
5. ______ deferred imitation
6. ______ explicit memory
7. ______ exuberant synaptogenesis
8. ______ implicit memory
9. ______ intentionality
10. ______ jargoning
11. ______ locomotion
12. ______ object permanence
13. ______ perseveration
14. ______ representation
15. ______ secondary circular reactions
16. ______ secondary intersubjectivity
17. ______ social referencing
18. ______ zone of proximal development

a. When a nurse enters the examination room and greets a 9-month-old girl, the infant glances at her mother's face, then smiles at the newcomer.
b. When Suzanne turns her gaze toward the front door, Brian, her 8-month-old also stares in that direction.
c. John's mother gets the applesauce on the spoon, then lets John guide it to his mouth.
d. An infant is doing this when she treats all dogs as being somehow the same.
e. A 7-month-old boy has learned to pull the ring his parents have dangled over his crib, causing a music box to play. He pulls it over and over again.
f. This growth spurt occurs in different areas of the brain at different times during the first year.
g. Allison watches her brother operate a new toy; later in the day, she performs the same actions on the toy.
h. Ben, a 10-month-old, immediately whisks his mother's handkerchief off a squeeze toy after his mother has covered it.

i. An 11-month-old sounds as if he is explaining something to his family; however, no one can understand a bit of what he says.
j. A baby plays with language sounds: "ba-ba-ba-ba-ba."
k. Through this process, Jessica can think about the family dog when he is out of the room.
l. Tim cries when his mother leaves the room, but gives her a big hug when she returns.
m. Jody's tendency to repeat the same movement over and over makes it difficult for her to search in a new place when looking for a hidden object.
n. Learning and memory are examples of these.
o. To achieve this, babies must be able to integrate the movements of many parts of their bodies.
p. This occurs when a 9-month-old is able to recall something without needing a clear reminder.
q. According to Piaget, this appears in infants' behavior during sensorimotor substage 4.
r. This occurs during the recognition of things that have been experienced before.

Multiple-Choice Practice Questions

Circle the letter of the word or phrase that correctly completes each statement.

1. What, if any, changes occur in infants' body proportions during the first year of life?
   a. The head becomes a larger proportion of total body length.
   b. The head becomes a smaller proportion of total body length.
   c. The head and body maintain the same relative proportions.
   d. The head and body each maintain the same overall size.

2. The _______—a part of the brain involved in voluntary behavior—undergoes a spurt in development between 7 and 9 months after birth.
   a. cerebellum
   b. brain stem
   c. frontal cortex
   d. hippocampus

3. Cross-cultural observations of the development of infants' motor skills show that
   a. infants of all cultures reach early motor milestones at the same ages, regardless of differences in childrearing practices.
   b. the amount of practice a child gets may cause motor milestones to be reached earlier or later than would otherwise occur.
   c. early motor milestones cannot be reached earlier through practice; however, they can be delayed by restricting movement.
   d. restriction of practice has a permanent negative effect on the acquisition of motor skills.

4. Piget referred to infancy as the _______ stage of development.
   a. concrete operational
   b. representational
   c. preoperational
   d. sensorimotor

5. According to Piaget, during the last few months of the first year infants are learning to
   a. modify their basic reflexes.
   b. make interesting experiences, centered on their own bodies, last.
   c. make interesting events in the outside world last.
   d. coordinate actions to reach a goal.

6. During the period between 3 and 12 months of age, the number of synapses in babies' brains
   a. reaches the number seen in early adolescence and then remains constant.
   b. increases rapidly in all brain areas at once.
   c. increase well beyond what will eventually be necessary.
   d. increases slowly but steadily in all brain areas simultaneously.

7. During their first 9 months, babies' fine motor skills
   a. do not increase appreciably.
   b. progress through a sequence that is the same in all babies.
   c. are controlled by subcortical reflexes.
   d. increase only for those skills that are trained by parents.

8. Studies of the effects of locomotion on perceptual-motor skills have demonstrated that
   a. experience with independent locomotion enhances performance on the visual cliff both in kittens and in human infants and leads to better performance by infants on hidden object tasks.
   b. locomotion is beneficial to performance on the visual cliff and on hidden object tasks, but it does not matter whether the kitten or infant moves independently or is carried around by someone else.
   c. experience with locomotion is beneficial to performance on the visual cliff by both kittens and human infants but has no effect on infants' performance on hidden object tasks.
   d. experience with locomotion aids kittens in their performance on the visual cliff but it has no effect on the performance of human infants.

9. Which is an example of primary intersubjectivity?
   a. A child turns her gaze toward the door when her mother looks that way.
   b. Seeing his mother's look of alarm, a child cries when approached by a large dog.
   c. A child takes turns smiling at his mother and being smiled at in return.
   d. A child is upset when he is left with a babysitter while his parents go out.

10. Between the ages of 7 and 9 months, infants begin to act ______ people and things that are unfamiliar.
    a. afraid of
    b. attracted to
    c. indifferent to
    d. attached to

11. With respect to parent-infant interaction, a "zone of proximal development" refers to
    a. the parent directly training the child to learn new skills.
    b. the parent allowing the child to learn new skills entirely on his or her own.
    c. the child following the parent around wherever the parent may go.
    d. the parent helping the child do things he or she cannot yet accomplish alone.

12. Which is *not* a sign of attachment to the mother during the first year of life?
    a. The child cries when his mother leaves the room.
    b. The child is perfectly happy to be left by his mother.
    c. The child follows his mother around the house.
    d. The child is happy when his mother returns after a separation.

13. Infants' earliest babbling sounds
    a. may contain the sounds of any language.
    b. contain only the sounds of the language they hear around them.
    c. are no different in deaf babies than in hearing babies.
    d. do not occur without reinforcement from parents.

14. Which is *not* part of the bio-social-behavioral shift that takes place between 7 and 9 months of age?
    a. the ability to crawl
    b. coordinating actions to reach a goal
    c. greater acceptance of strangers
    d. social referencing

15. Which is an example of conceptual categorization?
    a. A baby responds the same way to toy birds and toy airplanes.
    b. A baby responds differently to cats and dogs.
    c. A baby responds the same way to a flower mobile and a bird mobile.
    d. A baby responds differently to two rattles.

16. Which is true of babies' memory during the first year?
    a. Babies steadily improve in the length of time they can remember a behavior they have learned.
    b. Babies can remembered learned behaviors much longer if they are given a "reminder" before retesting.
    c. Both a and b are true.
    d. Babies' memory for learned behaviors is as good at 3 months as it is at 12 months of age, provided that the correct testing procedure is used.

17. Cross-modal perception
    a. has been demonstrated to occur in utero.
    b. is present by 4 months of age or earlier.
    c. is learned, through an extended process, over the course of the first year.
    d. is not learned until the second year of life.

18. The ability to bring to mind objects and events experienced in the past is called
    a. recognition.
    b. explicit memory.
    c. deferred memory.
    d. implicit memory.

19. Infants who are deaf
    a. babble in exactly the same way as hearing children.
    b. communicate vocally if raised in a spoken language environment.
    c. are both a and b.
    d. babble with their hands if raised in a signing environment.

20. Parents report that, once their babies have learned to crawl, the babies ______ than they did before.
    a. seem calmer
    b. exhibit more anger and frustration
    c. act more tolerant of their parents' absences
    d. appear more joyful

Short-Answer Practice Questions

1. How are improvements in memory and in locomotion related to infants' ability to search for hidden objects?

2. In what ways do changes in infants' central nervous systems correspond to changes in their motor and cognitive abilities?

3. What do cross-cultural studies tell us about the roles of nature and nurture in the development of motor skills?

4. What types of evidence have led researchers to believe that infants may believe in the continued existence of hidden objects even though they fail to search for them?

5. How does growth in infants' ability to understand and produce speech relate to changes in the types of nonverbal communication they exchange with their caregivers?

6. What behaviors indicate attachment between infants and their parents? What adjustments might parents make in their own behavior in response?

7. Describe two different methods you could use to test whether a 9-month-old infant could engage in conceptual categorization.

8. Describe the difference between recognition and recall. How do researchers measure each in infants?

Putting It All Together

Look back to Chapter 4 and find information about social smiling. Then give examples of other forms of parent-infant sharing from Chapter 5 and discuss the importance of this behavior during the first year of life.

Sources of More Information

Brazelton, T. B. (1983). *Infants and mothers: Differences in development* (Rev. ed.). New York: Dell.
The author follows the progress of an active baby, a quiet baby, and an average baby through the first 12 months of life.

Caplan, F. (Ed.). (1995). *The first twelve months of life: Your baby's growth month by month.* New York: Bantam Books.
This is a month-by-month look at the physical, cognitive, and social changes taking place during an infant's first year.

Carpenter, M., Nagell, K., & Tomasello, M. (1998). Social cognition, joint attention, and communicative competence from 9 to 15 months of age. *Monographs of the Society for Research in Child Development, 63*(4), Serial No. 255.
This is a monograph describing research on the development of infants' social-cognitive skills, beginning around the time of the first postnatal bio-social-behavioral shift.

Uzgiris, I., & Hunt, J. M. (1989). *Assessment in infancy: Ordinal scales of psychological development.* Champaign, IL: University of Illinois Press.
This book describes the standardized instrument, based on Piaget's research on sensorimotor development, that is used for assessing development in infancy.

Walden, T. A., & Ogan, T. A. (1988). The development of social referencing. *Child Development, 59,* 1230–1240.
This study examines the course of development of social referencing in infants from 6 to 22 months of age.

Zucker, K. J. (1985). The infant's construction of his parents in the first six months of life." In T. Field & N. Fox (Eds.), *Social perception in infants*. Norwood, NJ: Ablex.

Answer Key

Answers to Key Terms: 1.l, 2.j, 3.d, 4.n, 5.q, 6.p, 7.f, 8.r, 9.q, 10.i, 11.o, 12.h, 13.m, 14.k, 15.e, 16.b, 17.a, 18.c.

Answers to Multiple-Choice Questions: 1.b, 2.c, 3.b, 4.d, 5.d, 6.c, 7.b, 8.a, 9.c, 10.a, 11.d, 12.b, 13.a, 14.c, 15.c, 16.c, 17.b, 18.b, 19.d, 20.b.

The End of Infancy

Between 12 and 30 months of age, children develop in important ways—physically, cognitively, and in their social relations. During this time, they develop increasing control over their bodies, as reflected in "gross motor" skills such as walking and running, "fine motor" skills such as scribbling with crayons, and in the ability to feed and dress themselves and to control elimination.

New developments in thought allow children to reflect on what has happened in the past and to set themselves goals for the immediate future. Being able to call objects and events to mind helps them avoid some of the trial and error on which younger infants depend when solving problems.

While older infants are still dependent on their caregivers for support when coping with unfamiliar situations, they are learning to predict and understand their caregivers' periodic absences and returns. Development in the ability to communicate with language helps infants make their needs better known.

The changes of late infancy—physical, cognitive, and social—allow children a greater degree of independence and self-direction. Their behavior begins to reveal a sense of "selfhood" at this time. These developmental changes complement one another—changes in one area helping development in another. At the end of infancy, developments in physical growth and coordination, thinking and language skills, and greater self-directedness will result in a new bio-social-behavioral shift.

Learning Objectives

Keep these questions in mind while studying Chapter 6.

1. In what ways do children's developing motor skills allow them to do more things without adult help?
2. Why do developmentalists believe that older babies are able to represent things to themselves, including the emotional states of others?
3. How do imitation and play provide infants and toddlers with new opportunities for learning?
4. How do psychologists measure attachment between infants and their caregivers? How do the various theoretical orientations explain attachment?

5. What factors influence the pattern of attachment behavior seen in different infants?
6. What new behaviors lead developmentalists to conclude that, about the time of their second birthdays, children develop a sense of "self"?

Chapter Summary

I. BIOLOGICAL MATURATION

During the second year of life, children continue to grow substantially. For children raised in the United States, height increases, on average, from 29 inches to 38 inches and weight from 20 pounds to 33 pounds. Nearly all their teeth appear, and their bodies become more streamlined in appearance.

Important changes are also taking place in children's brains. Fibers that connect the frontal and prefrontal areas of the cerebral cortex with the brain stem become myelinated, leading to new patterns of interaction between thinking and emotion. Different areas of the cortex begin to work in greater synchrony, allowing new psychological functions to develop, including self-awareness, systematic problem solving, voluntary control of behavior, and language acquisition. Length and branching of neurons in the cortex approaches adult levels.

II. GAINING COORDINATION AND CONTROL

The developments in their nervous systems give children much greater control over physical movement.

A. Locomotion

According to Esther Thelen and her colleagues, babies can make the leg movements needed for walking at 7 month of age, but cannot yet shift their weight and move their arms in a coordinated way. Walking involves not only the development of motor skills but also increased sensitivity to perceptual input from the environment. Karen Adolph and her colleagues found that beginning crawlers (in this study, 8½-month-olds) could apparently perceive the steepness of slopes, although they did not adjust their movements. Interestingly, crawlers experienced with slopes had to learn to judge steepness all over again from an upright position when they learned to walk. Babies only need a few months of practice to be coordinated walkers. Figure 6.2 shows the sequence of development followed by most babies.

B. Manual Dexterity

Between 12 and 30 months, infants develop greater coordination of fine hand movements, becoming able to string beads, use scissors, and feed and dress themselves. Michael Mc-

Carty and his colleagues, observing tool use in 9- to 19-month-old infants, found that at 14 months, they were more likely to grip a tool correctly when using it on themselves (brushing their own hair, for example); 19-month-olds could adjust the orientation of a tool so as to be able to grasp it efficiently with the dominant hand.

C. Control of Elimination

Voluntary control of elimination appears to be the result of maturation. Some children can remain dry during the day by the time they are 2 years old, although many do not achieve complete daytime dryness until later. Nighttime dryness is more difficult and is not achieved until children are 3½ to 4 years old.

III. NEW MODES OF THOUGHT

Children's increased ability to control their actions is accompanied by more sophisticated modes of thinking. The cognitive abilities they developed during the first year of life—goal-directed problem solving, categorization, the beginnings of language, and some understanding of object permanence, causal relations, and basic physical law—will be expanded upon during the remainder of the period of infancy.

A. Completing the Sensorimotor Substages

Piaget described two additional substages that occur during later infancy and that mark the end of the sensorimotor period:

- In substage 5 (tertiary circular reactions)—12 to 18 months—children explore the world in more complex ways by deliberately varying the actions they use to reach their goals. They are not yet able to imagine the consequences of actions, so these actions must still be performed physically.
- In substage 6 (representation), 18- to 24-month-old children literally "represent" the world to themselves mentally. This allows them to plan solutions to problems before carrying them out. They are now able to imagine objects not present, imitate past events, engage in pretend play, and solve problems more systematically. The substages of the sensorimotor period are reviewed in Table 6.1.

B. Object Permanence

Children master the remaining stages of what Piaget called object permanence during the second year of life.

- Beginning at about a year of age (substage 5) they begin to be able to search for a toy in a place it has not previously been, so long as they see it being hidden there. (In substage 4, they did not search for objects in unfamiliar places.)
- Between 18 and 24 months, they achieve substage 6; now they can find a toy in a new

place even if they have not seen it hidden there, apparently reasoning that it must be somewhere nearby. They can also anticipate the path of a moving object.

C. Problem Solving

Developments in sensorimotor intelligence and in the ability to reason about the location of hidden objects are accompanied by changes in children's problem-solving behavior. Children in substage 5 carry out deliberate problem solving but are still dependent on trial and error. In substage 6, they become less dependent on trial and error and are better able to imagine the results of their actions before carrying them out.

D. Play

Play during the sensorimotor period parallels children's current stage of cognitive development. From 12 to 20 months of age, increasingly complex forms of play reflect children's developing mental skills. Twelve-month-olds begin to use objects as adults would use them—for example, banging a hammer on a block. Between 12 and 24 months, children begin to engage in *symbolic play* (also called *pretend play* or *fantasy play*), making one object stand for another—for example, stirring a cup of "coffee" with a twig. As children develop, their pretend play becomes more elaborate, as is seen in Table 6.2.

It is the view of many developmentalists that play serves important functions for cognitive and social growth. Piaget viewed it as an opportunity to consolidate new sensorimotor schemas; Anthony Pellegrini suggests that rough-and-tumble play also provides experience in dominant and submissive social relations. As predicted by the cultural-context approach, the amount, kind, and sophistication of play varies across cultures. Some developmentalists theorize that play provides children with the chance to acquire skills that will be important later. Interestingly, research has shown that toddlers' play often is more advanced whey they play with their siblings than when they play with their mothers.

E. Imitation

Piaget felt that deferred imitation—imitation of actions observed in the past—was an indication that children could mentally represent their experiences. However, whereas Piaget classified this as a substage 6 behavior, more recent work (discussed in Chapter 5) has indicated that deferred imitation makes its appearance as part of the changes occurring toward the end of the first year. An experiment by Andrew Meltzoff showed that infants of 6 to 9 months could imitate actions, directed toward objects, that they had observed 24 hours previously. Meltzoff and Elizabeth Hanna found that, by 14 months, children can learn from one another by imitation; they imitated actions even after a 2-day delay. More in line with Piaget's age estimates, Meltzoff has also found that 18-month-olds imitated actions that they had seen adults attempt but not complete. He argues that this is an indication that infants can represent to themselves the mental state of another person. Only 1 in 10 babies performed this task if a machine rather than a person attempted the action.

F. New Categorizing Abilities

Even very young infants appear to be able to recognize categories, in that they respond differently to experiences depending on a variety of categorical features. Rochel Gelman has pointed out that these are "natural" categories which come from the environment in which we live; much of the categorizing people do is based on features of the cultural environment. In consequence, people from different cultures organize categories in different ways, which need to be learned. The ability to categorize objects according to multiple features develops during infancy. During the second year of life, children begin to create categories from an array of objects. A study by Susan Sugarman explored classification in 12- to 30-month-old toddlers. Although 1-year-olds noticed similarities between objects, they did not yet place similar objects together. Eighteen-month-olds, on the other hand, created a "work space" and put several objects of the same kind—for example, all the boats in a collection of toys—in it. Twenty-four-month-old toddlers divided the objects into two groups, for example, boats and dolls, and 30-month-olds divided their collections into subcategories—for example, red boats and blue boats. Infants moved from being able to recognize categories to being able to make use of the categories in a flexible and systematic way.

G. Understanding Visual Representations and Models

Part of the shift in children's thought processes at the end of infancy is development of the ability to understand that pictures are representations of objects, not the objects themselves, and to make use of this information. Judy De Loache and her colleagues found that when 9-month-olds were shown pictures of objects, they treated them as if they were the objects themselves, trying to grasp them with their fingers. Twenty-month-olds rarely did this. De Loache and Burns tested whether 2-year-olds could make use of information in pictures to find a toy hidden in a room. They found that, while this was beyond most of the 2-year-olds, 2½-year-olds could usually find the toy hidden in the location shown in a picture. De Loache also investigated children's ability to use information demonstrated using scale models. She found that when 3-year-old children saw an adult hide a toy within a scale model of a room, they could use the information to find the toy in the room itself. In contrast, 2½-year-olds were confused by the task. But when De Loache and her colleagues told the 2½-year-olds that the room could be shrunk by a machine to become the model—removing the difficulty of keeping in mind the model's dual nature as symbol and object—the children were able to make use of the information from the model to find the object in the room. De Loache emphasizes that the most important element in the ability to make use of pictures and models is *dual representation*—the ability to engage in the mental representation of both a symbol and its relationship to the thing it depicts.

H. Relating Words, Thoughts, and Actions

Children's ability to use and understand language increases greatly during the second year of life. For example, 14- to 16-month-old infants can understand about 150 words and simple phrases; by 21 months, they can follow fairly complex directions and create their own multiword sentences. The use of language is an indication of representative thought; language use is also linked to other expressions of mental representation such as deferred imitation, symbolic play, and the ability to categorize. For example, symbolic play and language both involve the representation of objects, people, and events not present. Generally, during the time that children speak in one-word utterances, their symbolic play involves only one object or action; they begin to combine two actions in play and two words in speech at about the same time. Other investigators have found correspondences between growth in children's vocabularies and improvements in their abilities to find hidden objects, categorize, and solve simple problems.

IV. THE DEVELOPMENT OF CHILD–CAREGIVER RELATIONS

As babies begin to move around on their own, they need to be able to learn about the world while, at the same time, avoiding its hazards. The development of attachment, an emotional bond between children and their caregivers, helps provide a balance between security and opportunities to explore.

A. Explanations of Attachment

Because children in all cultures begin to resist separation from their caretakers at about 7 to 9 months of age, it has been suggested that attachment is a universal feature of development. Theorists have suggested several different explanations for why attachment occurs.

- Sigmund Freud's theory emphasizes the importance of *biological drives*—states of arousal such as hunger and thirst, that urge the organism into action in order to obtain the prerequisites for survival. Freud proposed that infants become attached to those who help them satisfy these drives. In particular, children become attached to the mother, who satisfies their need for nourishment. A problem with this explanation for attachment is that it has not been demonstrated that attachment results from satisfaction of the hunger drive.
- Erik Erikson proposed that, at each of eight stages of development from birth through old age, people meet and resolve a particular conflict. Erikson's theory stresses that attachment is related to children's development of trust in their caretakers during the earliest stage (from birth to 1 year) and to the development of ability to do things for themselves during stage 2 (1 to 3 years).
- John Bowlby's work had its roots in his observations of children who had been separated from their families by war. He found that children separated from their mothers exhibited fear, then despair and depression, and finally *detachment,* a state of indifference. Bowlby's explanation, based on principles of ethology, emphasizes the function of attachment to provide a balance between infants' need for safety and their need for varied learning experiences. It progresses through four phases during the first 2 years of life. First is "preattachment" (birth to 6 weeks), then "attachment-in-the-making" (6

weeks to 6–8 months), during which infants show the first signs of wariness. At about 6–8 to 18–24 months is the phase of "clear-cut attachment," characterized by *separation anxiety* when the caregiver leaves. The caregiver becomes a *secure base* from which the infant can explore, returning occasionally for reassurance. During the phase of "reciprocal relationships" (18 to 24 months and later), caregiver and child share the responsibility for maintaining the equilibrium of the system. According to Bowlby's view, the attachment relationship serves as an *internal working model* for guiding children's interactions with caregivers and others.

- The studies of Harry Harlow and his colleagues using animal models suggest that bodily contact rather than nourishment is important in fostering attachment, in contradiction to the drive-reduction hypothesis. Infant monkeys became attached to terry-cloth-covered "surrogates" in preference to wire-bodied ones, even when only the wire "mothers" provided them with food. But, attachment—and the sense of security it brings—did not, by itself, ensure healthy social development; monkeys who became attached to nonliving surrogates did not learn how to behave with other monkeys. Under normal circumstances, two-way interaction with a responsive caregiver teaches the infant how to relate to others of its kind. For surrogate-raised infants, this two-sided regulatory system does not develop; instead, a one-sided processes occurs in which all the adjusting is left to the infant.

B. Patterns of Attachment

Mary Ainsworth and her colleagues studied attachment in the *strange situation,* in which children were left alone in an unfamiliar room, approached by a strange adult, then reunited with their mothers. The key indicator of attachment, they felt, is the way a child reacts to the mother upon her return. Several patterns of attachment behavior have been identified. In *secure attachment,* the pattern found in about 65 percent of middle-class, U.S. children, infants are upset when their mothers leave, but are quickly reassured when they return. In *anxious/avoidant attachment,* found in about 23 percent, infants appear indifferent to their mothers and ignore them when they return. The approximately 12 percent of middle-class, U.S. children who exhibit *anxious/resistant attachment* become upset when their mothers leave, but struggle to resist comfort from them when they return. Other researchers have noted that some children are difficult to classify in terms of these categories. Mary Main and her colleagues have called their attachment behavior "disorganized." As described in the box "Attachment to Fathers and Others," research on attachment has tended to focus on infants and their mothers. However, infants also become attached to their fathers and other caregivers, and to peers and siblings as well.

C. The Causes of Variations in Patterns of Attachment

What leads to the various patterns of attachment observed in the strange situation?

- Some, though not all, studies show that, as first reported by Mary Ainsworth and Silvia Bell, infants whose mothers are sensitive to their needs are more likely to behave in a securely attached manner. Infants whose caregivers are abusive or insensitive are more likely to be insecurely attached or disorganized.

- Children's own characteristics can also affect attachment. For example, Michael Lewis and Candice Feiring found that infants who, at 3 months of age, spent more time playing with objects than interacting with their mothers were more likely to show signs of insecure attachment at 12 months of age.
- Family problems such as maternal depression, low socioeconomic status, and marital discord are associated with a greater incidence of insecure attachment.
- Cultural variations in child-rearing practices result in differences in babies' behavior in the strange situation. For example, communally raised Israeli infants are more often rated anxious/resistant than are U.S. infants or Israeli children who sleep in their parents' home at night. Figure 6.12 shows cultural variations in the proportions of children assigned to each of the main attachment categories. Marinus van Ijzendoorn and Abraham Sagi have pointed out that, overall, the pattern of results across many cultures is consistent with Bowlby's theory and Ainsworth's results. They argue for the possibility that cultural factors affect the precise way in which children's attachment behaviors develop.
- There is conflicting opinion about the significance of the different attachment patterns for children's later development. What is clear, however, is that—in all parts of the world—infants follow a similar pattern: beginning at about 7 months, more and more infants become distressed when they are separated from their mothers; this trend begins to reverse at about 15 months of age.

V. A NEW SENSE OF SELF

Two-year-olds' capabilities in thinking, motor skills, language, and the ability to do things on their own combine to give them a greater awareness of themselves as people.

A. Self-Recognition

Beginning at about 4 months of age, infants will touch a mirror image if something interesting is reflected there. Ten-month-olds can use a mirror image to find a toy being lowered behind their backs. However, it is not until about 18 months that children begin to identify their own images in the mirror. At that age, if a red spot is applied to a child's nose, he or she will try to rub the spot off after seeing it on the mirror image.

B. The Self as Actor

Between 18 and 24 months, about the time that children begin to use two-word utterances, they begin to describe their own actions in their speech.

C. A Sense of Standards

Children become more sensitive to adult standards of "rightness"; they notice when toys are broken or clothing is soiled. They may even feel responsible for living up to adult standards—for example, by being able to imitate adults' behavior. They seem to set themselves goals—perhaps, making a tower of all the blocks—and to check their progress in achieving those goals. Success is accompanied by a new kind of smile—a "mastery smile" indicating self-satisfaction.

D. The Emergence of Secondary Emotions

In addition to the six primary emotions displayed in early infancy (joy, fear, anger, surprise, sadness, and disgust), by 24 months of age, infants experience certain *secondary emotions* such as embarrassment, pride, shame, guilt, and envy. These emotions are linked to children's emerging ability to evaluate their behavior in terms of social standards. So, toddlers may display pride in a new ability or shame at having done something "bad."

VI. THE END OF INFANCY: A NEW BIO-SOCIAL-BEHAVIORAL SHIFT

Children's growing abilities to do more things for themselves, to engage in more complex categorization and problem solving, to express themselves in words and play, and to begin to follow adult standards combine to produce the stagelike transition characteristic of a bio-social-behavioral shift. The changes occurring at the end of the second and the beginning of the third year—listed in Table 6.3—mark the end of the period we call infancy.

Key Terms

Following are important terms introduced in Chapter 6. Match each with the letter of the example that best illustrates the term.

1. ______ anxious/avoidant attachment
2. ______ anxious/resistant attachment
3. ______ biological drives
4. ______ detachment
5. ______ dual representation
6. ______ internal working model
7. ______ secondary emotions
8. ______ secure attachment
9. ______ secure base
10. ______ separation anxiety
11. ______ strange situation
12. ______ symbolic play (pretend, fantasy play)
13. ______ tertiary circular reactions

a. When children are proficient at this, they can use information from a picture to locate an object.
b. A boy places pebbles in a bowl, stirs them around, and serves "soup" to his teddy bear.

c. Hunger and thirst are examples of these.
d. A child, sitting in a high chair, repeatedly drops peas onto the floor. Sometimes holding his arm straight out, sometimes to the side, he varies the position from which each pea is dropped.
e. Pride and embarrassment are examples of these.
f. A 1-year-old plays by himself in the living room, but comes into the kitchen periodically to make contact with his mother.
g. An infant takes part in an experimental study in which her mother leaves her alone in an unfamiliar room, and a strange adult tries to comfort her until her mother returns.
h. A 1-year-old screams when he notices that his mother has left the room.
i. A 2-year-old is able to predict her mother's coming and going on the basis of past experiences of being separated from and reunited with her.
j. This pattern of attachment is more common among German infants than among U.S. infants.
k. This pattern of attachment is the most common among middle-class U.S. infants.
l. This pattern of attachment is often seen in Japanese infants from traditional families.
m. This may happen in children who have been separated from their parents for a long time.

Multiple-Choice Practice Questions

Circle the letter of the word or phrase that correctly completes each statement.

1. Brain development during the second year of life is characterized by
   a. an increase in myelination.
   b. growth in the length and complexity of neurons.
   c. increased interaction among different areas of the brain.
   d. all of the above.

2. Children younger than ________ do not usually have enough control over elimination to be able to remain consistently dry while asleep.
   a. 1 year of age
   b. 2 years of age
   c. 3 years of age
   d. 4 years of age

3. In substage 5, tertiary circular reactions, children begin to
   a. repeat interesting action sequences without variation.
   b. carry out actions in thought rather than physically.
   c. vary the action sequences they use to reach a goal.
   d. imitate objects and events that are not present.

4. At the end of infancy, children are able to ______ the world to themselves.
   a. assimilate
   b. accommodate
   c. represent
   d. explain

5. Which is an example of symbolic play?
   a. using a banana as a telephone
   b. making cookies out of Play Dough
   c. serving a doll a cup of sand coffee
   d. all of the above

6. During substage 5, infants will search for a hidden object
   a. in a location where they have found it previously, even if they watch it being moved to another location.
   b. in a location where they have not found it previously, but only if they see it being moved.
   c. in a location where they have not seen it previously, even if they do not see it being moved.
   d. only if they have hidden the object themselves.

7. In play, children perform
   a. only actions that they have seen adults perform.
   b. actions that they do not ordinarily enjoy.
   c. actions developmentally more advanced than those they typically perform independently.
   d. actions developmentally less advanced than those they typically perform independently.

8. _______ imitation was formerly thought to appear in the middle of the second year of life; now there is evidence that it is present toward the end of the first year.
   a. Deferred
   b. Immediate
   c. Reflexive
   d. Assimilative

9. Children learn to recognize categories based on ________ before they learn to recognize categories that involve ______ .
   a. inanimate objects; animate objects
   b. artifacts; core domains
   c. objects; people
   d. core domains; artifacts

10. John Bowlby's explanation of attachment emphasizes the role of attachment in
    a. satisfying biological drives.
    b. building trust between infant and caregiver.
    c. balancing safety and exploration.
    d. promoting object permanence.

11. Harry Harlow found that his surrogate-raised infant monkeys
    a. always became attached to the wire surrogate, whichever surrogate fed them.
    b. always became attached to the cloth surrogate, whichever surrogate fed them

c. always became attached to the surrogate, wire or cloth, that fed them.
d. did not become attached to either kind of surrogate.

12. When toddlers play with their older siblings, their play is often
    a. more advanced than it is when they play with their mothers.
    b. about as advanced as it is when they play with their mothers.
    c. less advanced than it is when they play with their mothers.
    d. less advanced than it is when they play by themselves.

13. In Mary Ainsworth's "strange situation," _______ children calm down quickly and resume playing when their mothers return after a brief separation.
    a. securely attached
    b. anxious/avoidant
    c. anxious/resistant
    d. all of the above

14. Cross-cultural studies on attachment patterns indicate that
    a. similar distributions of attachment patterns occur in all societies studied.
    b. different cultures produce varying distributions of attachment patterns as measured in the "strange situation."
    c. good parenting practices produce the same distribution of attachment patterns in any culture.
    d. attachment as we know it exists only in societies with "nuclear" families.

15. Which evidence caused Andrew Meltzoff to conclude that, at 18 months of age, children can represent to themselves the mental states of others?
    a. They can imitate actions they have observed in the past.
    b. They can imitate actions that others have attempted, unsuccessfully, to carry out.
    c. They do not imitate attempted actions performed by a mechanical device.
    d. both b and c

16. Which is an example of a secondary emotion?
    a. embarrassment
    b. anger
    c. sadness
    d. all of the above

17. Children show signs of recognizing their mirror images
    a. starting shortly after birth.
    b. at about the time they develop separation anxiety.
    c. at about the time they begin to describe their own actions.
    d. at about the time they begin preschool.

18. According to Erik Erikson, the time around 2 years of age, children are involved in dealing with which issue?
    a. trust
    b. autonomy
    c. separation anxiety
    d. bonding with parents

Short-Answer Practice Questions

1. What parallels occur between children's language development and their symbolic play?

2. Psychologists believe that, starting at about 18 months of age, children begin to set goals for themselves and to become more aware of adult standards. What are some indications of this change? What changes in children's and problem-solving capabilities occur about the same time?

3. What are some of the ways we can tell that children have begun to mentally represent things to themselves?

4. Why do psychologists say that there are different kinds of attachment relationships between parents and babies? Why might nature allow for a certain amount of variability in the characteristics of attachment?

5. According to work by Judy De Loache and her colleagues, how do infants of various ages reach to information presented in pictures? Why is making use of pictorial information a challenge, even for 2½-year-olds?

Putting It All Together

In this section, you will need to put together information from Chapters 4, 5, and 6 to get a more complete picture of development throughout infancy.

I. Reviewing Piaget's substages of sensorimotor development:

Here are some behaviors that Piaget observed his own children performing during the sensorimotor stage. Match each behavior with the substage in which you would expect it to occur.

Substages

1. Reflexes
2. Primary circular reactions
3. Secondary circular reactions
4. Coordination of secondary circular reactions
5. Tertiary circular reactions
6. Representation

______ Laurent strikes at a pillow to lower it, then reaches over it to grasp a box of matches.

______ Laurent repeatedly brings his hand to his mouth in order to suck his fingers.

______ Lucienne sees her father hide a chain inside a slightly open matchbox. She looks at the opening, opens and shuts her mouth several times, and finally reaches in a finger to slide open the box and grasp the chain.

______ Laurent becomes quicker at finding the nipple when it touches him anywhere on his face.

______ Laurent lifts toys and lets them fall, varying his arm position each time.

______ Lucienne, lying in her bassinet, sees a doll hanging above her and kicks it. The doll sways, and Lucienne attempts to kick it again and again.

Try to think of another example of infant behavior that would illustrate each substage.

II. Studying infant development:

As children's sensorimotor skills improve, it becomes easier for psychologists to determine what they know. Describe the different techniques used for studying the abilities of infants of different ages in one of the following areas: language, object permanence, or categorization.

Sources of More Information

Ames, L., Ilg, F., & Haber, C. (1980). *Your two-year-old.* New York: Dell.
The authors describe typical 2-year-old behavior in the tradition of Gesell's maturational approach.

Brazelton, T. B. (1989). *Toddlers and parents: A declaration of independence* (Rev. ed.). New York: Delacorte.
This book describes individual differences among toddlers and discusses the developmental tasks facing children during later infancy.

Caplan, F., & Caplan, T. (1998). *The second twelve months of life.* New York: Berkeley Publishing Group.
This book describes the development of mental, motor, and language skills, month by month, during the second year.

Erikson, E. (1998). *The life cycle completed: Extended version.* New York: Norton.
This is a discussion of Erikson's psychosocial theory of development.

Kaplan, L. J. (1980). *Oneness and separateness: From infant to individual.* New York: Simon & Schuster.
A discussion of psychoanalytically-oriented theorist Margaret Mahler's ideas, this book chronicles infants' "second birth," in which, during late infancy, they develop individual identities.

Shatz, M. (1995). *A toddler's life: Becoming a person.* New York: Oxford University Press.
A developmental psychologist describes a study in the tradition of Piaget's observations, in which her grandson, Ricky, is followed from 15 months to 3 years of age.

Singer, D., & Singer, J. (1992). *The house of make-believe: Children's play and the developing imagination.* Cambridge, MA: Harvard University Press.
This book traces play from birth through adulthood, beginning with its roots in the activities of infants and toddlers.

Answer Key

Answers to Key Terms: 1.j, 2.l, 3.c, 4.m, 5.a, 6.i, 7.e, 8.k, 9.f, 10.h, 11.g, 12.b, 13.d.

Answers to Multiple-Choice Questions: 1.d, 2.d, 3.c, 4.c, 5.d, 6.b, 7.c, 8.a, 9.d, 10.c, 11.b, 12.a, 13.a, 14.b, 15.d, 16.a, 17.c, 18.b.

Answers to Putting It All Together I: 4, 2, 6, 1, 5, 3.

Early Experience and Later Life

For many centuries, philosophers have expressed a belief that children's earliest experiences have the greatest effect on their development—that "As the twig is bent, so grows the tree." Modern psychologists have, for the most part, agreed. But do early experiences invariably set the course of development? Chapter 7 explores this issue and related questions about what kinds of early experiences help children's normal development or hinder it.

One thing children need is the stimulation of interaction with other people. Babies raised in poorly staffed orphanages with little human contact have been found to be both mentally and socially retarded. The longer they live under these conditions, the less complete their recovery when they are moved to more favorable environments. On the other hand, those raised in well-staffed orphanages have fared better, even when cared for by as many as 24 nurses during their first 2 years! Children who have been totally isolated become severely retarded; still, under certain conditions, recovery is possible even for them.

Research shows that children whose environments combine a number of stress-producing factors are at risk for later psychiatric problems. However, some are remarkably resilient in the face of difficult life circumstances. Supportive extended families, good schools, and even the child's own temperament may help to counteract stresses.

Developmentalists cannot predict a child's course of development with certainty. There are enough discontinuities in development to make it difficult to know for sure how the circumstances of babies' lives help to shape the adults they will someday be.

Learning Objectives

Keep these questions in mind while studying Chapter 7.

1. What are optimal conditions for infant development?
2. What are the effects of separation of infants from their parents?
3. How do risk factors and protective factors act on children's development?
4. To what extent can children recover from early deprivation?

5. How do transactional models of development help us to understand the effects of early experience on later development?
6. Is it true that early experience has a greater impact on development than do experiences that occur later in children's lives?

Chapter Summary

I. THE PRIMACY OF INFANCY

Some theorists believe that children's earliest experiences are the most significant for their later development. This idea is called the *primacy* of the experiences of infancy. Chapter 7 takes up the question of whether—or to what degree—this is true. In particular, how does deprivation during infancy affect children's later development? As we will see, early experiences do have important effects but the nature of these effects depends on whether later experiences reinforce or counteract those of infancy.

Research on the effects of early deprivation is, of necessity, correlational and subject to limitations on the conclusions we can draw. In evaluating this research, keep in mind the box "Correlation and Causation" in Chapter 1. Researchers have more control over factors that influence development when they conduct experiments with nonhuman animals; however, they must be careful about making comparisons across species.

A. Modifying the Impact of Early Experience

While it is expected that extremely undesirable life circumstances will have effects on later development, two factors appear able to modify the impact of early experiences: one is a change in the environment, positive or negative; another is the bio-social-behavioral shift at the end of infancy that reorganizes physical and psychological functions into new patterns.

As argued by developmentalist Jerome Kagan, each new stage of development makes new demands and presents new opportunities.

B. Transactional Models

Transactional models of development, which trace the ways in which the characteristics of the child and the characteristics of the child's environment interact over time, are considered by many modern developmentalists to account best for the effects of early experience on development.

Transactional models are important for understanding how children from similar environments can have different developmental outcomes; they also help to explain how the same experience can have different effects at different points in development. These models are especially useful for understanding the development of attachment.

II. DEVELOPING ATTACHMENT

Does a child's early attachment status—secure, anxious/avoidant, or anxious/resistant—correspond to later behavior?

A. Continuity and Discontinuity

Studies examining children's patterns of attachment show that the stability of a child's attachment pattern depends on the stability of the child's life circumstances. Studies of the long-term effect of different patterns of attachment have yielded mixed results. Alan Sroufe and his colleagues reported that, at age 3½, children who had been judged "securely attached" in infancy were more curious, played more effectively with other children, and had better relationships with their teachers than children who had been judged "insecurely attached" in infancy. At 10 years of age, the "securely attached" children were more socially skilled, more self-confident, and formed more friendships during a summer camp experience. At 15, they were judged more open in expressing feelings and in forming relationships with other teenagers. Inge Bretherton hypothesizes that this apparent continuity occurs because infants' interactions with their caregivers help them build up an "internal working model" of the way to behave toward other people. The model will guide behavior as long as it is effective; however, it may change or be replaced in response to modifications of the child's environment, resulting in an apparent lack of continuity.

Some researchers have found no obvious relationship between attachment status in infancy and later behavior. For example, Michael Lewis conducted a follow-up study of 18-year-olds whose attachment status had been measured in infancy. He found no relationship between their current attachment to their parents or their mental health as young adults and their attachment status as infants. At present, developmentalists disagree about the long-term implications of early attachment status.

B. Out-of-Home Care: A Threat to Attachment?

The majority of women with jobs outside the home return to work before their infants are 1 year old; by the time they are 4 years of age, most North American children spend some time in nonparental care.

The effects on development of out-of-home care during infants' first year are still hotly debated. On one side, Jay Belsky cites findings that show less secure attachment on the part of children with extensive nonmaternal care experience during the first year. Other studies have examined the issue, focussing on the quality of care children receive. Results show a slight negative effect of extensive time in child care on children's attachment relationships, as well as on their social behavior and intellectual development. Other risk factors, for example, economic hardship or insensitive mothering, have larger negative effects. While it is in society's best interest for infants to grow up to be emotionally healthy and socially competent, there is disagreement as to how child care can and should be arranged to help this come about.

III. EFFECTS OF DEPRIVATION

Some children are reared under conditions of extreme deprivation. What are the effects on their later development? Children living in orphanages experience a much more extreme form of separation.

A. Children Reared in Orphanages

A well-known study by Wayne Dennis and his colleagues showed that normal infants placed in the unstimulating environment of a Lebanese orphanage shortly after birth were, by the end of their first year, developing at only half the normal rate. Those of the children who were adopted before age 6 eventually reached normal or near normal levels of development, depending on how young they were when adopted. At age 6, the girls who remained institutionalized were sent to live in another impersonal, unstimulating situation; by the time they reached their teens, they were severely retarded. The boys, sent to a more stimulating environment, made substantial recovery.

Kim Chisholm, studying children from Romanian orphanages who were adopted into Canadian families, found that children adopted before 4 months of age were indistinguishable from native-born Canadian children. Children who had spent 8 months or more in an orphanage became attached to their adoptive parents; however, they showed more evidence of insecure attachment and appeared more hungry for attention from adults compared to children with less experience in institutions. More recent studies of Romanian adoptees support the conclusion that institutional care is the cause of children's later problems. When children from equally high-risk families were assigned either to foster care or to an orphanage, those placed with families did not show the high levels of hyperactivity and attention deficits seen in the orphanage-raised children. Brain scans of children adopted from Romanian orphanages have shown deficits in the functioning of areas of the limbic system that are particularly responsive to stress.

Barbara Tizard and her coworkers studied children raised in better-equipped, more stimulating nurseries in England. Because they were cared for by large numbers of nurses, these children had no opportunity to form close attachments to their adult caregivers. When children were adopted between 2 and 8 years of age, they were nearly always able to form attachments with their adoptive parents. Those returning to their biological families fared less well, perhaps because their parents gave them less attention; still, they did better than the children who remained institutionalized.

Studies of formerly institutionalized children do not support the idea that children can only form attachments during a critical period in early infancy. However, children's later environments affect whether the lack of early attachments will prove to be a lasting problem.

The problem of providing adequate care for orphaned children is ongoing. Currently more than 12 million children in sub-Saharan Africa alone are living as orphans because they have lost their parents to the HIV-AIDS epidemic.

B. Isolated Children

Occasionally, cases are discovered in which children have been separated, not only from their parents, but from all human company. Victor, the Wild Boy of Aveyron, is one example. In another case, described by Jarmila Kolachova, twin boys were isolated in a closet until 6 years of age with only one another's company; eventually they recovered normal intelligence. Genie, a girl who was severely isolated for 11 years, recovered somewhat but never developed normal enough language or social behavior to be able to live independently. (See the box "Genie and the Question of Ethics Revisited" for additional discussion of Genie.) We still do not know exactly how long or how severe deprivation must be in order to cause lasting damage.

IV. VULNERABILITY AND RESILIENCE

Prevention science, a new area of research, examines the biological and social processes that lead to healthy development or to maladjustment. Its practitioners are especially interested in *risk factors*—those personal or environmental characteristics that increase the probability of negative outcomes. Risk factors do not themselves cause developmental problems, but interact in complex ways with other factors. Some children subject to these risk factors display *resilience*—they manage to develop normally in spite of adverse circumstances. The sources of resilience are called *protective factors*; they include characteristics of the child, the family, and the community.

A. Characteristics of the Child

Personal characteristics associated with greater developmental risk vary somewhat for different age children. In infancy, an "easy" temperament in infants is associated with resilience, while infants classified as "difficult" are at greater risk for psychological problems. In middle childhood, children who are easily distracted and have short attention spans are at greater risk. In evaluating the effect of personal characteristics on resilience, it is important to consider culture. For example, work by Marten De Vries in East Africa and by Nancy Scheper-Hughes in Brazil has shown that, under some circumstances, a "difficult" demanding temperament may contribute to an infant's survival. Werner and Smith's Kauai study revealed that children who were well-adjusted while growing up had been described by their mothers as "very active" and "socially responsive" in infancy.

B. Characteristics of the Family

A study of a large group of low-income children on the island of Kauai by Emmy Werner and Ruth Smith followed the development of children at risk for developmental problems because of prematurity, birth stress, low levels of maternal education, or psychopathology of a parent (for example, see how maternal depression affects infants' behavior in the box "Maternal Depression as a Risk Factor"). This study highlights family factors as buffers contributing to children's resilience in the face of risks that might affect their development. In particular, children from cohesive families who received ample attention from their caregivers and had a network of relatives and friends to provide support were less likely to suffer developmental problems than those without these advantages.

A Finnish study of adopted children at genetic risk for schizophrenia found that at-risk children tended to develop a psychiatric disorder more frequently than children from a lower-risk background, but only when they were adopted into dysfunctional families. When adopted into well-functioning families, their rate of psychiatric problems was similar to that of low-risk children.

C. Characteristics of the Community

Studies of community factors show that children from poor, inner-city areas are more at risk than those from poor, rural communities; children from affluent communities are less at risk than those from poor communities. Social support networks provided by social service agencies and by friends and relatives can reduce the impact of negative community characteristics. Good experiences at school also seem to counteract stressful home circumstances.

D. Characteristics of the Culture

There are cultural differences in how risks to children's development are interpreted and managed. For example, in many African cultures, *cross-fostering*—a system of child exchange within families—is routine; about one-third of South African children live in households that include at least one fostered child. Compared to middle-class U.S. children, African babies experience substantial shared caregiving by multiple family members. Therefore, the verbal interaction and mutual gaze they experience is also spread over a larger number of caregivers and is less concentrated on the mother than is the case for U.S. children.

The box "Children and War" describes how armed conflict affects children's development. Under the stress of war, parents may become more authoritarian and less emotionally positive in their interactions with children; children may experience irritability, separation anxiety, and sleep problems. But intervention programs and community cultural traditions can play important roles in mitigating the trauma of war.

V. RECOVERY FROM DEPRIVATION

Exposure to risk factors does not necessarily condemn children to poor developmental outcomes.

A. The Impact of Later Circumstances

Influences on development work not in isolation, but in combination with one another, as illustrated in transactional models. For example, Michael Rutter and his colleagues found that, in their sample, poor parenting practices observed in women who had been raised in institutions as infants were not a straightforward result of their early experience, but resulted from a chain of events which could be—and sometimes was—broken by more favorable life circumstances.

How might children best be helped to recover from early deprivation? Removal from the damaging environment is often not enough, as seen in the case of Genie or the Lebanese orphanage children. However, research studies with monkeys, and a few with human subjects, make some useful suggestions.

B. Harlow's Monkeys Revisited

As discussed in Chapter 6, Harry Harlow demonstrated that, when infant monkeys were deprived of normal social contact and raised by inanimate mother surrogates, the duration and timing of deprivation affected the monkeys' long-term behavior. Monkeys isolated only for their first 3 months developed normal social behavior when placed with a group of other monkeys. Monkeys isolated for their second 6 months after 6 months of normal interaction became aggressive and fearful when returned to the group, but recovered and later were able to mate normally. In contrast, those monkeys isolated for all of their first 6 months only partially recovered and later were unable to mate. Isolation for the first year of life produced monkeys who showed no tendency to recover spontaneously.

C. Recovery from the Effects of Isolation

Was birth to 6 months of age a critical period for normal social development? Harlow and his colleagues tried several methods, all ineffective, for easing isolated monkeys' transition to group interaction. However, when previously isolated female monkeys had infants, they began to recover (if the infants survived their abusive behavior). The longer they interacted with their infants, the more normal their behavior became. The researchers found that, by giving them 2- to 3-month-old monkeys to interact with, they could reverse the abnormal social behavior of 12-month isolates to the point that researchers had difficulty telling them from non-isolated monkeys.

D. Implications for Human Recovery

Both Harlow's monkey studies and research with human children suggest that interaction with younger children may be more therapeutic than interaction with peers in reversing the effects of social isolation. Wyndol Furman, Donald Rahe, and Willard Hartup found that when 2½- to 5-year-olds who had been judged to be "socially isolated" played, over a 6-week period, with children who were 1 to 1½ years younger, they more than doubled their social interactions with peers, while those who played for the same amount of time with peers showed much less improvement. This suggests that socially isolated children can be helped substantially by the proper arrangement of the environment.

VI. SHAPING DEVELOPMENTAL PATHWAYS

It is not only deprivation or other unusual life experience that influences development. Recent studies with nonhuman primates and other animals have shown that the behavior of parents affects the course of development of their offspring. For example, infant monkeys with high levels of "emotional reactivity" developed differently (were less exploratory and more anxious) when raised by their own, highly-reactive, mothers than when fostered by calm mothers during the first 6 months of life.

A. Optimal Conditions for Infant Development

How can caregivers best foster infants' development? Brazelton and Greenspan's "irreducible needs of children" and the United Nations' document "The Rights of the Child" are both expressions of the recognition that infants and children the world over share fundamental developmental needs.

Optimal rearing conditions are generally thought to involve mothers' responsiveness to their babies' signals. There is some evidence that this is true. However, mothers of different cultures have different strategies for raising children with the characteristics that are valued in their societies. For example, Japanese mothers strive to instill more interdependence and cooperation in their children than do American mothers. In contrast, children of a poverty-stricken area of Brazil, studied by Nancy Scheper-Hughes, need an independent, active and demanding temperament in order to survive in their environment; mothers in this community favor children who have these characteristics.

B. The Unpredictability of Development

Research on the effects of early experience points to both continuities and discontinuities between infancy and later developmental periods. Freud noted that when we trace development backward—from outcome to origins—the steps seem to have led, one to another, in an inevitable sequence. He also pointed out, however, that when we trace development forward, the sequence no longer appears inevitable. We see alternatives that might have occurred. It is just as well that infants' future abilities and characteristics are not perfectly predictable; otherwise, parents would have no opportunities to influence and enhance the development of their children.

Key Terms

Following are important terms introduced in Chapter 7. Match each term with the letter of the example that best illustrates the term.

1. ______ cross-fostering
2. ______ prevention science
3. ______ primacy
4. ______ protective factor
5. ______ resilience
6. ______ risk factors
7. ______ transactional models

a. The characteristics of individual children interact with changes in the caregiving environment; sometimes this results in continuity of characteristics and sometimes it results in discontinuity.
b. Studies how biological and social processes lead to maladjustment or to healthy development.
c. The idea that, for example, children's earliest attachments have the greatest effect on their later relationships.
d. Economic hardship and insensitive mothering are examples.
e. A child of refugees from a war-torn country becomes a well-adjusted adult.
f. Having a supportive extended family helps to counteract a child's problems at home.
g. This practice results in a child having multiple caregivers.

Multiple-Choice Practice Questions

1. The primacy of infant experience refers to the notion that the experiences of infancy are
   a. the earliest experiences people remember.
   b. more important for development than later experiences.
   c. the only experiences with any importance for development.
   d. qualitatively different from later experiences.

2. Studies of the effects of day care on infants have shown that
   a. there are slight negative effects of extensive day care experience on children's intellectual and social development.
   b. the number of hours children spend in out-of-home care is a more important influence on development than factors such as socioeconomic status or insensitive mothering.
   c. most day care facilities provide excellent care.
   d. children with extensive day care experience are more securely attached to their parents than those cared for at home.

3. An important scientific problem with studying children who have suffered isolation or other deprivation is that
   a. it is not ethical to study such children.
   b. the children are subject to multiple risk factors.
   c. the children are not randomly assigned to rearing conditions.
   d. both b and c.

4. In order for their children to adapt successfully to Japanese culture, Japanese mothers raise them to be
   a. active and demanding.
   b. independent and individualistic.
   c. quiet and passive.
   d. interdependent and cooperative.

5. Children reared in unstimulating Lebanese orphanages
   a. became severely retarded unless removed before about 6 years of age.
   b. were not affected intellectually, but failed to develop secure attachments.
   c. developed slowly during infancy but recovered later, even if they remained in the same environment.
   d. were not distinguishable from children raised in families.

6. Children studied by Tizard and her colleagues who had been raised in well-staffed English orphanages
   a. were never able to form attachments to adults.
   b. fared better when returned to their biological parents than when adopted into other families.
   c. formed attachments to their adoptive parents.
   d. had no lasting effects of their early orphanage experiences.

7. Which of these is a protective factor that is associated with resilience in the face of threats to children's development?
   a. having an "easy" temperament
   b. having a good adaptation to school
   c. having a support network of extended family and friends
   d. all of these are protective factors

8. Romanian orphans who spent at least 8 months in orphanages have been found to be _______ compared to children adopted early in infancy.
   a. indifferent to adults
   b. overly friendly to strangers
   c. insecurely attached
   d. both b and c

9. In a(n) ___________ model, the interaction between children's characteristics and their environments is traced over time.
   a. transactional
   b. environmental-learning
   c. stage
   d. biological-maturation

10. Inge Bretherton hypothesized that children's early experiences influence later social behavior by way of
    a. conditioned emotional reactions to certain people and situations.
    b. their effects on children's physical development.
    c. an internal working model of how to behave with others.
    d. long-lasting memories of events that occurred in infancy.

11. Infants of depressed mothers
    a. are not distinguishable in behavior from those of mothers who are not depressed.
    b. have lower activity levels in infancy but no long-term effects of their mothers' condition.
    c. have lower activity levels in infancy and lower scores on various developmental measures at age 3.
    d. do not show signs of depression, but are more likely to develop other severe mental illnesses.

12. For Harry Harlow's formerly-isolated monkeys, the best therapy leading to normal social behavior was
    a. interacting with humans.
    b. interacting with younger monkeys.
    c. interacting with other formerly-isolated monkeys.
    d. interacting with a mate.

13. Research shows that infants' attachment classifications are
    a. inconsistent in predicting later behavior.
    b. good predictors of later behavior.
    c. useless in predicting later behavior.
    d. nearly perfect predictors of later behavior.

14. Cross-cultural studies have indicated that, in conditions such as famine or other extreme deprivation, infants with _______ are more likely to survive.
    a. "difficult" temperaments
    b. depressed mothers
    c. many closely-spaced siblings
    d. "easy" temperaments

15. Overall, the data on continuity between infancy and later developmental periods shows that
    a. there is little or no continuity between children's characteristics in infancy and their later characteristics.
    b. development of a particular psychological process is a sequence of causes and effects that follows a course that, once set in infancy, is very difficult to change.
    c. it is possible to recover from any early experience of trauma or deprivation, no matter how long-lasting.
    d. there are many points at which it is possible for development to change course, due to changes in children's environments or personal characteristics.

Short-Answer Practice Questions

1. Discuss how optimal parenting strategies may differ between cultures whose life circumstances are very different. Give examples of this.

2. Describe an environment in which a child whose temperament is "difficult" might fare better than one whose temperament is "easy."

3. Explain how maternal depression can act as a risk factor in infant development. How can the risk be reduced?

4. What do studies of orphanage-raised children tell us about the effects of early experience?

5. Imagine that you have just encountered a 6-year-old child who has lived her whole life under conditions of extreme social deprivation. On the basis of what you know of similar cases in children and in infant monkeys, how would you go about designing a treatment program for this child?

6. Some children are resilient and develop well despite exposure to difficult circumstances in infancy or childhood. Discuss several factors that contribute to this resilience.

7. Give an example of a study that shows continuity between development during infancy and later periods; give an example that shows discontinuity. Briefly, explain why it is possible to obtain such seemingly contradictory results.

Putting It All Together

I. Chapter 7 makes the point that, because human studies of social deprivation are correlational in nature, we need to be careful in interpreting their results. Taking into consideration what you learned about correlation in Chapter 1, discuss why this is true. Next, discuss whether studies of infant monkeys and other animals are subject to the same problems of interpretation. How does this work add to our knowledge of the topic?

II. Sometimes, experiences during infancy interact with experiences during the prenatal period. Chapter 3 includes information on the effects of risk factors present at birth, such as undernutrition and prematurity. Sometimes these factors have lasting effects; sometimes, the effects are counteracted by other factors. Discuss possible similarities between these risk factors and such postnatal risk factors as social isolation in their effects on development.

Sources of New Information

Alexander, D. (1999). *Children changed by trauma: A healing guide.* Oakland, CA: New Harbinger Publications.
A specialist in community psychology advises on how to help children recover from traumatic experiences.

Blum, D. (1998, May/June). Finding strength: How to overcome anything. *Psychology Today,* 32–38, 66–73.
This article mentions Werner's work in Kauai and other studies that demonstrate the resilience of many people who lead successful lives despite difficult childhood experiences.

Dennis, W. (1973). *Children of the creche.* New York: Appleton-Century-Crofts.
A description of the author's well-known study of children raised in a Lebanese orphanage.

Dynerman, S. B. (1995). *Are our kids all right? Answers to the tough questions about child care today.* Princeton, NJ: Petersons.
The author combines an analysis of research on child care and interviews with parents and day-care providers. She presents useful information to guide parents in their search for high-quality child care.

Harlow, H., Harlow, M., & Suomi, S. (1971). From thought to therapy: Lessons from a primate laboratory." *American Scientist, 59*(5), 538–549.
A discussion of the work of Harlow and his colleagues with infant monkeys, including their work on rehabilitation.

Thompson, A. M. (1986). Adam—A severely-deprived Columbian orphan: A case report. *Journal of Child Psychology and Psychiatry, 27,* 689–695.
A demonstration of a child's progress after intervention to counteract severe deprivation resulting from poverty.

Wachs, T. (2000). *Necessary but not sufficient: The respective roles of single and multiple influences on individual development.* Washington, DC: American Psychological Association.
The author attacks the problem of variability in individual outcomes by showing how individual behavior is best understood as a result of influences from multiple domains, including, among others, genetics, neurology, nutrition, and culture.

Werner, E. E. (1995). Resilience in development. *Current Directions in Psychological Science, 4*(3), 81–85.
Emmy Werner describes the protective factors—individual, family, and community—that help children overcome great odds.

Answer Key

Answers to Key Terms: 1.g, 2.b, 3.c, 4.f, 5.e, 6.d, 7.a.

Answers to Multiple-Choice Questions: 1.b, 2.a, 3.d, 4.d, 5.a, 6.c, 7.d, 8.d, 9.a, 10.c, 11.c, 12.b, 13.a, 14.a, 15.d.

Language Acquisition

One of the most amazing accomplishments of children's preschool years is the rapid acquisition of language. With language, children can make their needs known more clearly and can state their opinions; they also become able to learn more easily from the experiences of others, including those of people who lived generations earlier.

Despite its importance for human beings, language development has yet to be thoroughly explained by developmentalists. No single theory is able to account for all the known facts; however, nativist and interactionist theories can each explain certain aspects of language acquisition.

As Elizabeth Bates has expressed it, language acquisition can be thought of as learning "to do things with words." In order to be able to do things with words, children must learn to produce the sounds and master the grammatical rules of the language they are learning; they must also learn to select words and constructions that will best express what they want to say.

What experiences must children have in order to learn a language? Certainly they must be exposed to the language itself. Adults provide children with informal language instruction in the course of socializing them as members of the family and community. And while adults in some cultures engage in more deliberate teaching, this is apparently not necessary for children to communicate in this uniquely human way.

Learning Objectives

Keep these questions in mind while studying Chapter 8.

1. What are the subsystems of language and how do they each contribute to children's developing language abilities?
2. How do the major theoretical orientations contribute to our understanding of language acquisition?
3. What basic biological features are necessary in order for children to be able to acquire language?
4. How does the social environment contribute to children's language acquisition?
5. What is the relationship between children's language development and their growing cognitive abilities?

Chapter Summary

Children's language abilities undergo explosive growth during the period from 2 to 6 years of age.

I. PRELINGUISTIC COMMUNICATION

While newborns are predisposed to pay attention to language and quickly learn to distinguish the sounds of their native language, their only means of vocal communication is crying. Their repertoire is supplemented by social smiling at about 2½ months of age, and is eventually expanded to include cooing, followed by babbling and jargoning. As discussed in Chapter 5, primary intersubjectivity, the face-to-face interaction that appears at about 3 months of age; it is followed, at about 9 months, by secondary intersubjectivity, in which the attention of both participants is focused on a third person or on object or activity. Social referencing is an example of this. Social referencing may be accompanied by pointing; by the time children are 18 months of age, pointing has a clearly communicative function.

II. THE PUZZLE OF LANGUAGE DEVELOPMENT

While a great deal is known about language, much about its acquisition remains poorly understood.

A. The Problem of Reference

It is still not known how children learn which objects or relations particular words refer to.

B. The Problem of Grammar

There is evidence that children are sensitive to *grammar*—the rules for sequencing the elements of a language—by the time they are 7 months old. However, it is evident from the errors they make that they do not learn these rules solely by imitating adult speech. Nor does *recursion*—the process of embedding sentences within one another—appear to be consciously taught. How, then, do these properties of language appear in children's speech?

III. FOUR SUBSYSTEMS OF LANGUAGE

Language is composed of four distinct subsystems that work together as a unified system.

A. Sounds

It takes children several years to master the pronunciation of the sounds of their native language. In the meantime, they compensate for difficulties in pronunciation through substitution and simplification. Newborns can perceive the differences among the sounds, or phonemes, of their language. But in order for children to attend to and pronounce these sounds, the sound differences must be associated with meaning differences, as /l/ and /y/ are in "lard" and "yard." Children must also learn to cope with the fact that words often contain more than one *morpheme,* or meaning-bearing part. For example, the word "transplanted" is made up of three morphemes—"trans," "plant," and "ed."

B. Words

The first real words appear late in the first year and acquire meaning through a joint effort between children and their adult listeners.

- As shown in Figure 8.3, there is wide variation in the ages at which children achieve different levels of language production. On average, they can produce about 10 words by 13 to 14 months of age; however, at this time, they can understand about 100 words. Children's first words tend to name familiar objects ("ball," "juice") or persons ("Mommy," "Daddy"), and to be closely linked to actions that the child can accomplish. Words naming objects that change and move ("car") or that communicate change in state or relation ("gone") are frequently used. Another frequently used word is "No!" And, as noted by Andrew Meltzoff and Alison Gopnik, beginning at about age 2, children used words ("Hooray!" or "uh-oh") to comment on their successes or failures.
- The meanings of words are not fixed. Still, as children become familiar with the ways words are used in their cultural group, their own word usage comes more into conformity with that usage. *Overextension* occurs when children apply a word too broadly; for example, by calling all animals "doggie." *Underextension* refers to too-narrow application of a word; for example, using the word "animal" only for mammals. Children must also learn to use words at an appropriate level of abstraction. Their first words tend to refer to objects at an intermediate level of abstraction ("dog"), although they are able to recognize examples representing other levels ("poodle" or "animal").
- As children notice that adults react to the sounds they make—which they do at 11 or 12 months of age—their speech begins to be used to make things happen without the children having to do the things themselves. Now, children can operate on the world in a "mediated" manner.
- Children's first words and phrases are tied to specific experiences they have had. But as they accumulate experience with objects and events they have learned to label, the organization of their vocabularies changes. Now, the meanings of words are influenced by the logical categories of the language rather than depending on particular situations. Researchers study the structure of children's vocabularies by asking them, when they hear a word, to respond with the first word that comes to mind, or by asking "Tell me all you can about ________ ."

C. Sentences

At what point do children's multiword utterances become sentences?

- Some investigators believe that each of a child's first words expresses a whole idea—a *holophrase.* Others, like Patricia Greenfield and Joshua Smith, believe that children's one-word utterances are one element in a communicative complex that includes gestures and expressions as well.

- Toward the end of infancy, grammar appears in children's speech as they begin to form utterances of two words. These are simple to interpret in context; however, out of context it can be difficult to know what a child means by a particular combination of words.

  The length of 2-year-olds' sentences in terms of "mean length of utterance" (MLU), measured in morphemes, increases rapidly, as shown in Figure 8.6, along with their vocabularies and grammatical abilities. Children come to make greater use of *grammatical morphemes* (such as "a" and "ing"), which create meaning by showing the relations between sentence elements. Children are sensitive to grammatical morphemes by the time they begin to produce multiword utterances. The sequence in which they actually appear in children's speech is roughly constant. Table 8.4 shows the order in which English-speaking children acquire these elements of language. Between 2 and 6 years of age, children learn to use many standard grammatical constructions. Eventually, they learn to construct "tag questions" ("It's your birthday, isn't it?") and subtle constructions based on abstract rules that even adults have trouble explaining.

  Not long after they begin to name objects, children begin to use figurative speech such as metaphors. While 2- to 6-year-olds use many metaphors, they have trouble understanding adult figurative speech unless it refers to simple actions or perceptual characteristics.

D. The Uses of Language

While learning words and the rules for putting them together, children also master the *pragmatic uses of language*—how to use speech in ways appropriate to their actions in particular contexts.

- Utterances can be thought of as conversational acts, actions that achieve goals through language. Even children's earliest utterances can be thought of as "proto-imperatives," intended to engage another person to achieve a goal, or "proto-declaratives," which serve as ways of referring. Even 2-year-olds are able to understand and respond to indirect commands ("Is the door shut?") as requests for action rather than information.
- In order to use language to accomplish goals, children need to learn the rules of basic conversation, such as the cooperative principle, described by philosopher H. P. Grice—that is, they must make contributions to the conversation at the required time and for the accepted purpose of the exchange. Sometimes children and adults deliberately violate conversational rules, for example, when they use figurative language such as irony. Also, the social conventions regulating the use of language vary across cultures.

IV. EXPLANATIONS OF LANGUAGE ACQUISITION

Currently, theories of language acquisition fall into two broad categories: nativist and interactionist.

A. The Nativist Explanation

A nativist explanation has been proposed by linguist Noam Chomsky, who has suggested that the ability to acquire language is innate and that language is not learned in the same way as other kinds of behavior. Instead, he considers the capacity to comprehend and generate language to be a special property of the human brain. In order to discover the conditions for language acquisition, Chomsky has examined grammatical rules that remain the same no matter what topic people talk about. He calls the sentences people produce the *surface structure* of language; *deep structure* is his name for the set of rules, shared by all languages, from which the surface structure can be derived. Chomsky has hypothesized that children are born with a *language acquisition device (LAD),* programmed to recognize rules of whatever language they might hear. When young children are acquiring language, they often are very resistant to grammatical correction, lending some support to the nativist position that there must be a specialized structure that guides language learning.

B. Interactionist Explanations

Interactionist explanations consider language acquisition to be closely linked either to children's basic cognitive development or to support from a structured social environment.

- Alison Gopnik and Andrew Meltzoff note a link between children's ability to reason systematically about absent objects and to vary the actions they combine in order to achieve a goal and their ability to talk about these things (for example, "gone" to indicate absence or "uh-oh" when a goal is not achieved). Elizabeth Bates and her colleagues have found that the grammatical complexity of children's speech is strongly related to the size of their vocabularies. This supports the notion that mastery of grammatical structures is a by-product of increasing vocabulary and of children's attempts to express increasingly complex thoughts.
- Cultural-context theorists emphasize the role of the social environment in shaping children's language acquisition. Jerome Bruner highlights the importance of formats—socially patterned adult-child activities such as peek-a-boo and bedtime routines. The formatted activities within which children acquire language provide a language acquisition support system (LASS), the environmental complement to Chomsky's LAD.

  More than 50 percent of the world's people are bilingual—they speak two or more languages. The box "Bilingual Language Acquisition" discusses explanations of how children acquire two languages simultaneously.

V. ESSENTIAL INGREDIENTS OF LANGUAGE ACQUISITION

What biological properties must an organism have to be able to acquire human language? And what aspects of the environment are crucial to the development of language and how do they operate? While none of the theoretical approaches provides a complete explanation, each helps to explain certain elements of language acquisition.

A. Biological Prerequisites for Language

Researchers have tackled the question of biological prerequisites in two ways: by inquiring whether other species can comprehend and produce language; and by observing how biological deficits affect language acquisition in human children.

- To what extent is the ability to learn language unique to humans? Chimpanzees raised in families do not learn speech, though they learn to comprehend many spoken words. Chimps have been taught to use manual language and to communicate through symbols on a keyboard. In particular, Sue Savage-Rumbaugh and her colleagues have had a great deal of success with Kanzi, a Bonobo ape. Non-human primates have learned to use language to make requests and comments, and can construct two-word utterances. They achieve the ability to produce and comprehend language at roughly the level of 2-year-old human children.
- Adults who suffer damage to the left side of the brain develop aphasia, a deficit in the ability to produce or to comprehend language; this suggests a localization of language function in the left hemisphere. Young children who suffer similar damage do not lose language; the greater plasticity of their developing brains allows the right hemisphere to take over language functions.

  Evidence from children with severe biological handicaps such as Williams syndrome suggests that at least some aspects of language develop separately from general cognitive ability. However, normal linguistic functioning needs a minimum level of biological growth and ability; for example, children with Down syndrome do not develop the ability to produce and comprehend complex linguistic constructions.

B. The Environment of Language Development

Interaction with other people appears crucial for normal language acquisition. For example, deaf children in hearing homes, who have restricted language experience but who participate in culturally formatted activities, may learn to communicate in "home sign," a kind of communication through pantomime they develop themselves. Home sign develops the basic features of language, including multiple-part utterances and recursion; however, like the language of children raised in linguistically impoverished environments, it does not develop the more subtle features such as complex grammatical distinctions. The box "Children Creating Language" describes the way Nicaraguan sign language developed from what was originally the home signs of a group of deaf children.

- Children learn language as part of family or community activity. For example, Elsa Bartlett and Susan Carey found that preschool children learned the name of an unfamiliar color after one experience in which their teacher introduced the color name into classroom conversation. This process—in which children form a quick idea of a word's meaning—is called *fast mapping*. Fast mapping can be explained by several cognitive principles used by children: the "whole object principle" (a new word appearing in connection with an object refers to the whole object); the "mutual exclusivity principle" (an object can have only one name); and the "categorization principle" (object labels extend to classes of similar objects).

- Interactions with others also help children learn word meanings. For example, Michael Tomasello and his colleagues found that mothers talking to young children tended to label objects that were already the focus of the child's actions or attention, making it easier for the children to figure out the referents of new words. It also appears that explicit rewards for learning language are not necessary; children's built-in reward for using new words is their greater ability to communicate.
- What role does deliberate instruction by adults play in language acquisition? In some cultures, adults use special teaching strategies; even in societies in which this is not done, adults talking to children may use a high-pitched voice and simplified vocabulary, and may emphasize the boundaries between idea-bearing clauses. This type of speech has been called *motherese*. Adults simplify all aspects of their speech when talking to children; they also expand children's utterances into grammatically-correct adult versions. Table 8.5 shows the simplifications typically made by U.S. adults speaking to small children. There is no conclusive evidence that explicit tutoring affects children's language development; however, the amount of language children hear is related to the rate at which they acquire vocabulary, according to the observations of Betty Hart and Todd Risley. Nevertheless, normally-developing children in all cultures become competent language users, regardless of specific teaching practices.

VI. THE BASIC PUZZLES OF LANGUAGE ACQUISITION RECONSIDERED

The questions of how children learn the meanings of words and how they learn the sequences in which words must be placed to express meanings are still only partially answered. Perhaps, as Jerome Bruner has suggested, language results from the union of the LAD and the LASS. And while explicit instruction appears unnecessary for early language acquisition, it plays a more important role as children grow older and receive specialized instruction in specific skills that will prepare them for adult life in their culture.

Key Terms

Following are important terms introduced in Chapter 8. Match each term with the letter of the example that best illustrates the term.

1. ______ conversational acts
2. ______ cooperative principle
3. ______ deep structure
4. ______ fast mapping
5. ______ format
6. ______ grammar
7. ______ grammatical morphemes
8. ______ holophrase

9. ______ language acquisition device (LAD)

10. ______ language acquisition support system (LASS)

11. ______ morpheme

12. ______ motherese

13. ______ overextension

14. ______ pragmatic uses of language

15. ______ recursion

16. ______ surface structure

17. ______ underextension

a. The belief that a baby's one-word utterances each carry the meaning of a whole sentence.
b. The way children form a quick idea of a word's meaning when they hear it in a structured situation.
c. An 18-month-old does this when he applies the word "doggie" to all four-legged animals.
d. The sentence "The boy who petted the dog was bitten" illustrates this property of language.
e. "Proto-imperatives" and "proto-declaratives" are examples.
f. A hypothetical structure that underlies children's ability to acquire language, according to linguist Noam Chomsky.
g. A child is doing this when she uses the word "dog" only for pictures of dogs but not for life dogs.
h. Some examples are "ing," "the," and "ed."
i. The rules that determine the ordering of words in sentences and the ordering of parts within words.
j. We violate this if we interrupt others during a conversation or make irrelevant remarks.
k. An example is saying "Who left the window open?" when you mean "Please shut the window."
l. Jerome Bruner uses this term to refer to the totality of the events within which children are led to acquire language.
m. All the grammatically correct utterances formed by speakers of a language are derived from this.
n. The ritualized routines of bedtime are an example of this.
o. A person using this speaks in a high-pitched voice and simplifies his or her speech in many ways.
p. This is observed simply by listening to the things people actually say.
q. This is the unit used in calculating a child's "mean length of utterance" (MLU).

Multiple-Choice Practice Questions

Circle the letter of the word or phrase that correctly completes each statement.

1. The aspect of language that deals with the ordering of words in sentences and the ordering of parts within words is called
   a. pragmatics.
   b. phonetics.
   c. semantics.
   d. grammar.

2. Which theorist has hypothesized a language acquisition device (LAD) that is programmed to recognize universal linguistic rules?
   a. Jean Piaget
   b. Lev Vygotsky
   c. Elizabeth Bates
   d. Noam Chomsky

3. The sounds that are meaningful in a particular language are called
   a. morphemes.
   b. graphemes.
   c. phonemes.
   d. holophrase.

4. Which utterance contains five morphemes?
   a. "Kitty!"
   b. "John is eating an apple."
   c. "She jumps rope fast."
   d. "Bobby, have some gum."

5. An example of a "tag question" is
   a. "He wore his new jacket today, didn't he?"
   b. "Where is my pencil?"
   c. "When did you say you were going?"
   d. all of the above are examples.

6. Which is an example of "overextension"?
   a. Using the word "bird" for both a parakeet and a baby chick.
   b. Calling a cow "doggie."
   c. Using the word "meow" to refer to all cats.
   d. Saying "fis" instead of "fish."

7. The term "holophrase" refers to
   a. the idea that children's one-word utterances may carry the meaning of entire sentences.
   b. adults' expansions of children's one-word utterances.
   c. children's belief that all words refer to "things."
   d. one-word exclamations used by children and adults.

8. Grammatical morphemes
   a. are the same in all languages.
   b. are likely to appear in all children's speech in about the same order.
   c. are rules for ordering words in sentences.
   d. do not appear in children's speech until the end of the preschool period.

9. Children who suffer brain damage to the left hemisphere at birth
   a. never develop the ability to use or comprehend language.
   b. learn to comprehend language but not to produce it.
   c. have their language functions localized to the right hemisphere.
   d. learn to produce language at the level of normal 2-year-olds.

10. Susan Goldin-Meadow found that deaf children whose hearing parents did not sign to them
    a. became mentally retarded.
    b. learned to speak on their own.
    c. developed a simple form of signing on their own.
    d. never developed any form of language.

11. Chimpanzees raised in human environments
    a. communicate with sounds but not with gestures.
    b. have successfully learned the rudiments of human vocal language.
    c. have learned to communicate in simple ways using nonvocal languages.
    d. have demonstrated language development comparable to that of 4-year-old children.

12. Which of the following is sufficient for children to acquire full use of language?
    a. hearing language on the radio or on television
    b. seeing people talk with one another even if the child cannot hear them
    c. being in an environment where others are communicating with one another, even if not directly with the child
    d. exposure to language in the context of activities of which language is a part

13. The speech of American adults to young children
    a. is not significantly different from their speech to adults.
    b. is more repetitive, but otherwise similar to their speech to adults.
    c. is slower, but is otherwise similar to their speech to adults.
    d. is simpler, with higher pitch and clearer pronunciation, than their speech to adults.

14. A toddler is using a "protodeclarative" when she
    a. points to a dog and says "doggie."
    b. hands her cup to her mother and says "more."
    c. says "yes" when her mother asks "Is the door shut?"
    d. looks at her mother when a stranger says "Hello."

15. The experiment by Bartlett and Carey, in which preschool children learned a new color name, illustrates the role of ______ in language acquisition.
    a. holophrase
    b. grammatical morphemes
    c. explicit teaching
    d. fast mapping

16. Children's ability to understand and use metaphor begins at about the time they
    a. first begin to produce sounds.
    b. begin to name objects.
    c. begin elementary school.
    d. reach adolescence.

17. Children's early words are most likely to be at the level of abstraction represented by which of the following examples?
    a. "animal"
    b. "poodle"
    c. "dog"
    d. any of the above equally

18. Elizabeth Bates found which relationship between the complexity of children's grammar and the size of their vocabularies?
    a. The larger children's vocabularies, the less complex the grammar they use.
    b. The larger children's vocabularies, the more complex the grammar they use.
    c. Grammatical complexity and vocabulary are both related to age, but are not related to one another.
    d. There is no relationship between grammatical complexity and vocabulary until children are at least 4 years of age.

Short-Answer Practice Questions

1. Why is it difficult for developmentalists to explain how children acquire language?

2. Discuss the factors that influence how adults interpret the utterances of 1- and 2-year-old children.

3. In what ways does language appear to be a reflection of thinking? In what ways does it seem to be unique? In what ways might it influence thinking?

4. To what experiences must children be exposed in order to acquire language? What happens if these requirements are not met?

5. What similarities and differences are there between language as acquired by human children and language as acquired by non-human primates?

6. How is the language acquisition of bilingual children similar to and different from that of children learning a single language?

Putting It All Together I

Match each milestone in language development with the age at which it occurs. You may want to refer back to material in earlier chapters.

______ Children can perceive the categorical sound distinctions used in all the world's languages.

______ Children's language typically contains overextensions.

______ Children's speech contains many metaphors.

______ Children begin to practice consonant-vowel combinations.

______ Children's vocalizations take on the intonation and stress patterns that characterize the language they are learning.

a. At birth
b. At about the middle of the first year
c. Toward the end of the first year
d. At 2 years of age
e. By 4 years of age

Putting It All Together II

Match up the facts about language development with the approach that is strongest at explaining them. Refer back to previous chapters when necessary.

______ Babies can distinguish categorical differences between phonemes.

______ Children's earliest "words" usually do not have clear meanings and have to be interpreted by adults.

______ Children acquire much of their early vocabularies by repeating the names they hear others give to objects.

______ Deaf babies begin to "babble" manually at about the same time as hearing babies begin to babble.

______ Changes in some of children's early sensorimotor accomplishments—for example, self-recognition—appear to be related to changes in the ways they use words.

______ Children engage in less egocentric speech when playing with children who cannot hear.

______ Compared with nonhuman primates, children pick up human language quite easily.

______ Children who are able to put together two-word utterances usually are also able to combine two symbolic actions in play.

a. Nativist theories
b. Interactionist theories

Sources of More Information

Boysson-Bardies, B. (1999). *How language comes to children.* Cambridge, MA: MIT Press.
A French psycholinguist explains the course of language development during the first two years of life.

Hart, B., & Risley, T. (1995). *Meaningful differences in the everyday experience of young American children.* Baltimore, MD: Brookes Publishing.
The authors, who work in the environmental-learning tradition, report on a study that demonstrates how the amount of language interaction between parents and children translates into differences in children's later achievement.

Lenneberg, E. (1969). On explaining language. *Science, 164*(3880), 635–643.
A discussion of the biological underpinnings of language development which demonstrates that varying approaches to the study of language acquisition need not be antagonistic.

Pepperberg, I. (2000). *The Alex studies: Cognitive and communicative abilities in grey parrots.* Cambridge, MA: Harvard University Press.
The subject of much of this research is an African Grey parrot named Alex; one of the most interesting aspects of the work is how language is acquired by interacting with others and by watching others interact with one another.

Pinker, S. (1994). *The language instinct.* New York: HarperCollins.
The author argues, in the nativist tradition, that language is an evolutionary adaptation used by humans for communication.

Savage-Rumbaugh, S., Shanker, S., & Taylor, T. (1998). *Apes, language and the human mind.* New York: Oxford University Press.
This volume presents information on language-learning by Kanzi, a bonobo, and its implications for the evolution of human language.

Answer Key

Answers to Key Terms: 1.e, 2.j, 3.m, 4.b, 5.n, 6.i, 7.h, 8.a, 9.f, 10.l, 11.q, 12.o, 13.c, 14.k, 15.d, 16.p, 17.g.

Answers to Multiple-Choice Questions: 1.d, 2.d, 3.c, 4.c, 5.a, 6.b, 7.a, 8.b, 9.c, 10.c, 11.c, 12.d, 13.d, 14.a, 15.d, 16.b, 17.c, 18.b.

Answers to Putting It All Together I: a, d, e, b, c.

Answers to Putting It All Together II: a, b, a, a, b, b, a, b.

Early Childhood Thought: Islands of Competence

Because of their lack of knowledge about the world, young children expend great effort to understand some of the situations they experience each day. Their lack of experience also results in uneven thinking abilities that may appear remarkably sophisticated when applied in familiar contexts, startlingly illogical in less familiar domains.

Piaget's account of thinking during early childhood is the starting point for several explanations of preschoolers' development, and the phenomena he observed, including egocentrism, precausal reasoning, and appearance/reality confusions, continue to be of interest to contemporary developmental psychologists. Today, some developmentalists believe that Piaget's theory is basically correct despite demonstrations of the unevenness of preschoolers' thought; information-processing theorists use computer-like models to understand these phenomena, and theorists who explain cognition in terms of mental modules search for the roots of development in the maturation of brain structures. Cultural context helps to explain the variability of young children's performances by examining the ways adults arrange the occurrence of basic contexts in which cognitive development takes place. There is still disagreement about whether the period from 2½ to 6 should be considered a separate stage or whether the development that occurs during this time is simply the accumulation of gradual changes.

Learning Objectives

Keep these questions in mind while studying Chapter 9.

1. What characteristics of young children's thinking seem illogical to adults?
2. Why does the unevenness of 2½- to 6-year-old children's abilities pose a problem for researchers attempting to explain development?
3. What evidence is there for theoretical perspectives that explain development in terms of general processes or in terms of innately-organized modules or domains?
4. How does culture influence the areas in which children will develop competence earlier than they develop it in other areas?
5. Can this period be considered to be a separate stage of development?

Chapter Summary

The performance of preschool children on tasks measuring memory and thinking skills moves between logic and illogic, competence and incompetence. Given the unevenness of young children's intellectual performance, should the years between 2½ and 6 be considered a distinct stage of development? And, whether or not this period is considered to be truly a stage, what factors account for the unevenness researchers observe?

I. BIO-BEHAVIORAL FOUNDATIONS OF EARLY CHILDHOOD THINKING

Beginning at about 2½ years of age, children undergo physical changes that affect how they experience and act upon the world.

A. Physiological Growth and Behavior

During early childhood, children's rate of growth slows to an even 2½ to 3 inches per year and their physical coordination improves. This allows them to explore new environments and have many new experiences, thus providing occasions for the development of new ways to think and act.

B. Maturation of the Brain

During early childhood, the brain grows from being 50 percent of its adult weight to being 90 percent of its adult weight; much of the enlargement is due to myelination, especially in the areas of the frontal cortex that are involved in planning new actions. Unevenness in both the levels of maturity of brain areas and the myelination of connections between areas can account for some of the unevenness seen in young children's performance on cognitive tasks. Culture plays a role in this process as well; culturally important activities promote experience-dependent proliferation in children's brains, thus influencing which areas are likely to undergo development.

II. FOCUSING ON GENERAL PROCESSES OF COGNITIVE CHANGE

Some developmentalists focus on general processes of change to account for development in early childhood. Piaget is the best-known advocate of this approach.

A. Piaget's Account of Early Childhood Thinking

According to Piaget's theoretical framework, once children have completed the sensorimotor substages, they are able to engage in representational thinking. By 7 to 8 years of age, they will be capable of *mental operations* such as logically combining, separating, and transforming information. During the *preoperational stage,* cognitive development can be viewed as a process of overcoming the limitations that stand in the way of logical thinking. A key to preoperational thinking, Piaget hypothesized, is the tendency to "center," or focus the attention on one aspect of a problem while ignoring others. As a result of this, a child might say that when a glass of milk is poured into a taller, thinner glass the amount of milk has increased. The inability to keep two aspects of a problem in mind has a role in three important characteristics of thinking during early childhood: egocentrism, confusion of appearance and reality, and precausal reasoning.

- Piaget believed that preschool-aged children consider the world entirely from their own points of view, and that this *egocentrism* is the cause of some of their difficulties in problem solving.

  One example of egocentrism is lack of spatial perspective taking. For example, in the "three mountain problem," when asked to select the view that would be seen by a doll placed at the opposite side of the diorama, preschoolers tend to choose a picture showing the scene from their own viewpoint instead.

  Young children's speech also has an egocentric quality. Piaget used the term "collective monologues" for conversations in which children engage in verbal turn-taking but in which no actual communication takes place; Piaget considered them to be examples of egocentric speech.

  It may also be difficult for young children to reason about what goes on in other people's minds. As children begin to overcome egocentrism, they also become more skilled in reasoning about what others are thinking. The ability to think about other people's thoughts and to form theories about how they think is referred to as a *theory of mind.* Apparently, children do not develop this ability until 4 or 5 years of age.
- Their tendency to focus attention on the surface attributes of a stimulus may make it difficult for preschoolers to separate appearance from reality. Rheta De Vries showed children a cat wearing a dog mask. Most of the 3-year-olds believed that the cat had become a dog, while the 6-year-olds were confident that such a transformation was impossible. Interestingly, while 4- to 5-year-olds realized that a cat could not become a dog, they had difficulty in correctly answering questions such as "Can it bark?" John Flavell and his colleagues found that appearance/reality confusion in children under 4 years of age appears in children from a variety of cultures.

  While, on the one hand, children appear to be able to distinguish real from pretend events in play (as when they ride on a broomstick instead of a pony), they display some confusion of real and pretend events (as when they have actual fear of a pretend monster) until well into middle childhood.
- When engaging in precausal thinking, preschoolers confuse cause and effect. This thinking is "transductive" (reasoning from particular to particular) rather than following the rules of inductive or deductive reasoning. For example, one child believed that, given their association with death, graveyards caused people to die and that, by avoiding graveyards, one could avoid death.

B. The Problem of Uneven Performance

Characteristics of preoperational thinking are summarized in Table 9.1; the examples show why Piaget considered young children to have difficulty in decentering their thinking. The box "Young Children as Witnesses" tells how young children's cognitive limitations prove challenging when it is important to get from them an accurate account of events, as in a court case. Piaget relied extensively on verbal interviews and specific tasks to evaluate young children's logical abilities. Studies using different methodology have suggested that, under some circumstances, children show evidence of abilities earlier than Piaget believed possible.

Helen Borke tested children's ability to overcome spatial egocentrism by modifying the "three mountain problem" to represent a more familiar scene. On this task, even 3-year-olds demonstrated that they could imagine perspectives other than their own.

There is evidence that young children's speech is not necessarily egocentric. For example, when instructing another person which toy to select from an array, they provide more information to a person who is blindfolded than to one who is not blindfolded. They also simplify their speech when talking to children younger than themselves.

Kate Sullivan and Ellen Winner demonstrated that 3-year-olds have some appreciation of other people's thought processes. In their version of a "false belief" task, the children were the deceivers rather than the deceived. Under these circumstances, 75% of children answered correctly compared with 25% in the standard task.

Catherine Rice, using a deception task, found that 3- to 4-year-old children showed understanding of the appearance/reality distinction when the knowledge was used as part of an ongoing activity that the child could understand. Carl Huelsksen and his colleagues demonstrated that 3- to 4-year-olds understood that a person who put on a costume was still the same person even though he or she appeared different; interestingly, the children had difficulty in verbalizing this knowledge.

Merry Bullock and Rochel Gelman showed that even 3-year-olds grasped the working of an apparatus which caused a Snoopy doll to pop up when a marble was dropped into one of two slots. Five-year-olds had more adequate verbal explanations of the task, suggesting why researchers find discrepancies between children's performance on Piaget's heavily verbal tasks and those using less verbally dependent measures.

- Piaget himself was aware of the ways that subtle variations in the structure of tasks resulted in differences in children's performance. While some developmentalists believe that Piaget's views are basically correct (that is, that knowledge must be constructed through action), others argue that new approaches are called for. Their theories fall into two broad categories: information-processing approaches, in which cognitive change and unevenness of performance are accounted for by increases in short-term memory capacity and in knowledge; and approaches that de-emphasize general mechanisms and focus on domain-specific psychological processes.

C. Information-Processing Approaches to Cognitive Change

Information-processing theorists, like Piaget, emphasize the importance of general principles in accounting for mental development; they also believe that nature and nurture play equal roles as sources of development. The *information-processing approach* views people's thought processes as analogous to the workings of a computer. Developmental changes can involve improvement in children's "hardware" (myelination, for example) or "software" (new cognitive skills). In one kind of information-processing model, information from the environment is seen as first entering a *sensory register,* from which it is read into *short-term (working) memory,* where it is stored for several seconds and combined with information about past experiences from *long-term memory.* As shown in Figure 9.5, the flow of information is coordinated by "control processes." According to this perspective, young children's cognitive difficulties are caused by limitations on their ability to process information. These include limits on children's ability to control their attention and on the speed at which they can process information; there are also limits on their knowledge, memory, and their strategies for acquiring and using information. Children's information-processing abilities improve with maturation of their brains, the development of more efficient strategies, and the increase of their knowledge.

As predicted by this approach, children display greater cognitive competence in domains in which they have extensive experience. For example, Micheline Chi and Randy Koeske found that a child who knew a great deal about dinosaurs was able to remember more items from a list of dinosaurs with which he was most familiar than he could from a list of those with which he was somewhat less familiar. Chi and her colleagues also showed that children knowledgeable about dinosaurs organize their knowledge in more sophisticated ways than novices do, for example, by classifying them according to attributes such as "meat eaters" and "plant eaters" rather than by less informative attributes such as size.

Robert Siegler has concluded, on the basis of these and other similar results, that all human cognition, whether in adults or children, is characterized by its variability. His view of cognitive development involves, not stages, but overlapping waves, each representing a different cognitive strategy. The strategies are in competition with one another and the ones that work best tend to be those that survive. Averaging performance over all the strategies yields a gradual increase in effective problem solving with age, rather than stagelike changes.

III. FOCUSING ON DOMAIN-SPECIFIC APPROACHES TO COGNITIVE CHANGE

While Piaget's approach and that of information-processing theorists emphasize the importance of general processes in cognitive development, some developmentalists have concluded that the content of children's reasoning—whether, for example, they are reasoning about rocks or about people—matters and that development is domain-specific.

A. Privileged Domains

Anne Hickman and Henry Wellman, on the basis of recordings of the conversations of 2- to 5-year-old children, concluded that four frequently-referenced cognitive domains are physical, psychological, biological, and social explanations for the behavior of people and objects. Children successfully matched modes of explanation to appropriate entities (for example, psychological explanations to people). Zhe Chen and Robert Siegler use the term *privileged domains* to describe the domains identified by Hickman and Wellman.

- "Naïve physics" refers to children's early understanding of physical phenomena—for example, objects bumping into each other or water freezing into ice.

  As is seen in Chapter 5, infants have some understanding of physical laws (for example, an object cannot pass through a physical barrier) and reason differently about the behavior of objects and the behavior of human beings. Kyong Kim and Elizabeth Spelke, studying children from 7 months to 6 years of age, found that, while 7-month-olds showed no understanding of the principles of gravity or inertia, 2-year-olds had the beginning of understanding; 6-year-olds had an appreciation of both concepts, though one that was not fully mastered. Terry Au conducted an experiment in which children as young as 3 months demonstrated their understanding that physical substances still existed even when they underwent radical transformations in form such as pulverizing and freezing.
- The tendency to understand people's actions in terms of their mental states can be thought of as "naïve psychology." By the end of the first year, infants have some understanding that other people's actions are caused by their goals and intentions. Two-year-olds can make the distinction between their own and others' desires and can use the words "want" and "like" correctly. Three-year-olds can reason about others' desires but still have difficulty reasoning about others' beliefs, as demonstrated by their performance on false-belief tasks. However, just as children show more advanced reasoning on Piagetian tasks when the problem is posed differently, they perform better on false-belief tasks when they are allowed to act as "coconspirators" with the experimenters.

  Theory of mind—the ability to think about other people's mental states—seems to be in transition at 3 years of age and to become more solidified when children are 4 to 5 years old. However, this is a gradual change; even 5-year-olds may misunderstand the mental states of others when there is a conflict of desires, as in a competitive game.
- Young children's knowledge of biology develops later than their understanding of physical and psychological phenomena. The starting point for "naïve biology" is making the distinction between living and nonliving things. Christine Massey and Rochel Gelman showed that 3- to 4-year-olds made correct generalizations about living creatures based on the distinction between self-initiated movement versus externally initiated movement. Young children also know that living things grow and change appearance and that, if neglected (for example, not given water) they may die.
- The social domain is concerned with knowledge about the rules of interpersonal interaction and social conventions. An important characteristic of this domain is that the behavior of one person depends on the behavior of others. Another important characteristic is the importance of temporal sequence—the order in which actions follow each other. Knowledge of appropriate social behavior is acquired through participation.

B. Explaining Domain-Specific Cognitive Development

There are three major approaches to explaining knowledge acquisition in privileged domains: these emphasize either modularity theory, skeletal principles, or the culturally organized environment.

- Some theorists explain cognitive development in terms of *mental modules*—innate mental faculties that receive information from particular classes of objects in the environment and produce corresponding domain-specific information about the world. Modularity theory extends into cognitive development Noam Chomsky's idea of language as a separate psychological system. Modules are thought to be domain-specific, to have innately specified organizing principles, and to be only loosely connected to one another. Music perception, face recognition, and perception of causality have been suggested as examples of mental modules. In a modularity view, there is no development, in the sense of qualitative change over time; the essential elements are there from the beginning and only become more complex through maturation of their parts.

  A line of evidence used to support modularity theory comes from studies of children with *autism*—a condition that interferes with a person's ability to relate normally to others. Simon Baron-Cohen and his colleagues conducted a study in which they asked children to arrange picture cards to make a story; the children were either mentally retarded, autistic, or normal. When the stories involved mechanical sequences, the autistic children outperformed the normal children; they were equally proficient on behavioral sequences involving obvious emotions. But when the stories involved mental events, the autistic could not create meaningful sequences and performed worse than children in the other groups. In contrast, the mentally retarded children performed at much the same level on each type of sequence. These results can be interpreted as supporting the existence of a "theory of mind" module.
- Modularity theories, like all theories that propose innate mechanisms, have trouble explaining change by any mechanism other than maturation—for example, the improvement in autistic children's behavior when they are engaged in intensive therapeutic programs. An alternative approach called "theory theory" acknowledges the importance of biological factors, but also includes the child's active, constructive efforts in acquiring domain-specific knowledge. This approach views children as testing theories about how the world works in much the same way as scientists do. Instead of invoking modules, "theory theorists" assume that children are born with *skeletal principles*—innate, domain-specific principles that direct cognitive processes toward relevant features in the environment, so that they pay attention to the right cues. Active theory testing is then necessary in order for development to occur.

  Like scientific theory testing, children's thinking within privileged domains is accompanied by causal explanations and generates reasonable predictions. Parents, with the information they provide, as well as teachers, peers, and children's personal experience, all are important in the process of theory testing.
- Skeletal principles are fleshed out for children as they participate in ongoing culturally organized activities with parents and other family members. How do children represent these activities to themselves? According to privileged-domain theorists, children construct generalized representations—or *scripts*—for routine events such as birthday parties, taking a bath, or going to restaurants. Scripts specify who participates in an event, the social roles they play, the objects that are used, and the sequence of the actions that

occur. Initially, scripts (taking a bath, for example) are more external to the child than internal; a bath is something done to, rather than done by, an infant. As children become more capable and more familiar with the scripted activity, they take on more active roles. Katharine Nelson points out that children rarely experience the world "raw"; instead, they experience it in a way that has been prepared according to the scripts provided by their culture.

Scripts include general knowledge (for example, what happens when you go to a restaurant) rather than specific information about a single experience (a particular restaurant visit). They are guides to action that tell children what to expect. Scripted knowledge frees them to attend to more than the superficial details of an activity; it also helps them coordinate their activities with others who share the same scripts. In addition, scripts help children acquire abstract concepts—for example, "having a meal" in general—by providing a framework into which specific examples can be fitted.

The cultural-context view of cognitive development emphasizes the importance of language in children's participation in culturally organized activities. Some cultures have many words for emotions; others have relatively few. It is possible that this has an effect on whether children develop "theory of mind" in the sense that privileged-domain theorists assume to be universal. In countries where talk about mental processes is prevalent, children who hear a great deal of conversation about mental processes tend to demonstrate competence earlier on theory of mind tasks. Cultural influences may be associated with beliefs that deviate from the knowledge that is thought to be part of privileged domains. For example, people may believe in magic, or in angels or other supernatural beings. As discussed in the box "Believing the Unimaginable: Stone Soup Revisited," magical thinking may exist alongside rational thinking throughout life.

- Cultures influence the unevenness of development by arranging the occurrence and determining the frequency of activities, by shaping the relationships among activities, and by regulating the level of difficulty of children's roles in activities.

IV. RECONCILING ALTERNATIVE APPROACHES

No single approach provides a complete explanation for the unevenness of young children's performance on tasks measuring cognitive ability. There is strong evidence for some domain-specificity; however, if development were entirely domain-specific, children would not generalize what they learn from one domain to another. It appears that general and domain-specific aspects of behavior exist side by side within the same child. Sometimes, abilities change in a stagelike way; at other times, change seems to occur gradually. Robbie Case, Robert Siegler, and Kurt Fischer have each proposed explanations for the sometimes stagelike, sometimes gradual-looking nature of developmental change. Each has found that context and support from the environment affect how stagelike developmental change appears; in general, change appears more stagelike when there is support from the environment and more continuous when support is absent.

Considering the contradictory views of children's performance during early childhood, it is easy to understand why Piaget and Inhelder considered it a "time of organization and preparation" for operational thinking, rather than a distinctive stage of its own.

Key Terms

Following are important terms introduced in Chapter 9. Match the term with the letter of the example that best illustrates the term.

1. ______ autism
2. ______ egocentrism
3. ______ information-processing approach
4. ______ long-term memory
5. ______ mental module
6. ______ mental operations
7. ______ precausal thinking
8. ______ preoperational stage
9. ______ privileged domains
10. ______ scripts
11. ______ sensory register
12. ______ short-term (working) memory
13. ______ skeletal principles
14. ______ theory of mind

a. Generalized event representations that specify the people, objects, and behaviors involved in, for example, birthday parties or visits to the dentist.
b. Children with this disorder do not relate normally to others; they may, however, demonstrate great ability in specific areas such as music and drawing.
c. A preschooler points to a picture in a book and asks, "What's this?" not understanding that her mother can only see the outside cover of the book and not the picture she is indicating.
d. This involves mentally combining, separating, or transforming information within a logical system.
e. Examples are physics, psychology, and biology.
f. Psychologists using this approach view children's thinking processes as analogous to the workings of a computer.
g. Children make use of this when they recall experiences from the past.
h. John tells his nursery school teacher, "When the trees outside move, it makes the wind."
i. We make use of this when we hold a phone number in mind long enough to write it down.
j. According to Piaget, this is a period during which children's thought is representational but not yet logical.
k. These are important in directing children's attention to relevant features of the environment.
l. The ability to think about the mental states of others.
m. According to some theorists, language is best explained as an example of this.
n. The first stop for incoming information in an information-processing model.

Multiple-Choice Practice Questions

Circle the letter of the word or phrase that correctly completes each statement.

1. In Piaget's framework, early childhood is associated with the __________ period of development.
   a. sensorimotor
   b. preoperational
   c. concrete operational
   d. postsymbolic

2. Which of the following characterize(s) young children's thought, according to Piaget?
   a. egocentrism
   b. inability to perceive physical causality
   c. ability to think logically
   d. inability to use representation

3. Which is an example of egocentric thought by young children?
   a. collective monologues
   b. simplifying their speech when talking to younger children
   c. giving more information to a blindfolded person than to one who is not blindfolded
   d. all of these

4. ________, like Piaget, believe that development can be explained by general principles.
   a. Neo-Piagetians
   b. Neuropsychologists
   c. Information-processing theorists
   d. Modularity theorists

5. Research on young children's memory has shown that their recall may be inaccurate when
   a. they are interviewed repeatedly about an event over a period of weeks or months.
   b. they are allowed to give their accounts and then are probed for more information.
   c. both a and b
   d. None of the above; preschoolers' recall is just as accurate as that of older children and adults.

6. Which occurs in short-term memory?
   a. Information is stored for several seconds.
   b. Information is combined with information from long-term memory.
   c. Both a and b.
   d. Information is stored for several weeks; if not retrieved by then, it is forgotten.

7. By the time children are 6 years of age, the brain has attained _______ of its adult weight.
   a. 25 percent
   b. 50 percent
   c. 65 percent
   d. 90 percent

8. Children's mental representations of routine events such as eating in a restaurant are called
   a. long-term memories.
   b. scripts.
   c. domains.
   d. modules.

9. During the period from 2½ to 6 years of age, children's physical growth
   a. continues at the same rate as during infancy.
   b. undergoes a spurt.
   c. slows to 2½ to 3 inches per year.
   d. slows to about 1 inch per year.

10. According to Robert Siegler, unevenness of performance on cognitive tasks occurs
    a. only during infancy.
    b. in 2½- to 6-year-olds.
    c. both a and b.
    d. in children of any age and in adults.

11. The unusual artistic ability of Nadia, an autistic child studied by Lorna Selfe, supports the ________ explanation of the development of drawing.
    a. mental module
    b. cultural-context
    c. information-processing
    d. all of the above equally

12. Which is an example of a privileged domain?
    a. the rules of interpersonal interaction
    b. the movements of objects
    c. theory of mind
    d. all of these

13. When Rheta De Vries put a dog mask on a cat,
    a. 3-year-olds believed the cat had become a dog.
    b. 4- and 5-year-olds could not give correct answers to questions such as "Can it bark?"
    c. 6-year-olds knew that the cat only looked like a dog.
    d. all of the above

14. The term "egocentrism," as used by Piaget, encompasses which of these behaviors?
    a. disregarding the feelings of others
    b. inability to take another person's point of view
    c. inability to think about objects that are not physically present
    d. all of the above

15. Which of these is characteristic of "precausal" reasoning?
    a. reasoning from general premises to particular cases
    b. reasoning from specific cases to general conclusions
    c. reasoning from one particular case to another
    d. all of the above

16. Chi and her colleagues found that children reason better about domains (such as dinosaurs) in which they have a great deal of knowledge. This supports a(n) _______ explanation of development.
    a. Piagetian
    b. information-processing
    c. modularity
    d. all of the above equally

17. Mental modules, as conceived by Chomsky, are thought to
    a. be applicable to any domain of knowledge.
    b. be organized according to innately specified principles.
    c. interact closely with one another.
    d. require a great deal of environmental input to carry out their functions.

18. In pretend play, young children
    a. only imitate behavior they have observed others perform.
    b. base their pretending only on situations they have experienced.
    c. may become afraid of monsters or other situations that they have created themselves.
    d. demonstrate that they can tell the difference between real and pretend in all situations.

Short-Answer Practice Questions

1. In what ways can young children's thinking be characterized as uneven? Why is this a problem for Piaget's theory of development?

2. What are some of the ways that changes in children's brains account for unevenness in their performance on cognitive tasks?

3. Develop a script, from a preschooler's point of view, for "eating in a restaurant." Develop the same script for a college student. How do these scenarios differ? Note particularly how the supportive roles played by other people differ between the two.

4. Describe examples of egocentric behavior in young children and examples of behavior that looks nonegocentric.

5. How does an explanation of development in terms of "skeletal principles" differ from an explanation in terms of mental modules? Why do some theorists consider this approach to be an improvement over modularity theory?

6. Trace the development of "theory of mind" in young children. What evidence is there that autistic children have special difficulty in this area?

Sources of More Information

Caplan, T. (1984). *The early childhood years.* New York: Bantam.
This book gives an overview of development during the preschool years, covering motor and cognitive development, social development, early literacy experiences, sexuality, and family situations.

Flavell, J. H. (1986, January). Really and truly. *Psychology Today,* 38–39, 42–44.
The author discusses the problems of understanding appearance/reality distinctions among preschoolers of several cultures.

Loftus, E. F. (1997). Memory for a past that never was. *Current Directions in Psychological Science, 6,* 60–65.
In this article, Elizabeth Loftus discusses how false memories of traumatic childhood events can be implanted even in older children and adults.

Newcombe, N. S., Drummey, A. B., Fox, N. A., Lie, E., & Ottinger-Alberts, W. (2000). Remembering early childhood: How much, how, and why (or why not). *Current Directions in Psychological Science, 9,* 55–58.
This article addresses the question of why people generally remember so little of their lives before about 5 or 6 years of age.

Paley, V. (1988). *Mollie is three: Growing up in school.* Chicago: University of Chicago Press.
The subtle changes in children's behavior that occur between the end of infancy and the onset of middle childhood are poorly documented in standard research on early childhood. In these case studies of preschool children, the author vividly describes the unevenness of their thinking and the enormous amount of work that small children put forth daily in their efforts to understand the world around them.

Selfe, L. (1983). *Normal and anomalous representational drawing ability in children.* New York: Academic Press, 1983.
In this monograph, the psychologist who studied Nadia provides a wealth of examples of extraordinary drawing ability by children, illustrating the kind of phenomena emphasized by modularity theories of development.

Answer Key

Answers to Key Terms: 1.b, 2.c, 3.f, 4.g, 5.m, 6.d, 7.h, 8.j, 9.e, 10.a, 11.n, 12.i, 13.k, 14.l.

Answers to Multiple-Choice Questions: 1.b, 2.a, 3.a, 4.c, 5.c, 6.c, 7.d, 8.b, 9.c, 10.d, 11.a, 12.d. 13.d, 14.b, 15.c, 16.b, 17.b, 18.c.

Social Development in Early Childhood

Socialization begins at birth with infants' first interactions with their parents, and throughout infancy the values, standards, and knowledge of their society help to organize children's experiences. But it is not until early childhood that children are able to actually construct an understanding of the workings of their families and their communities. At first, children follow the rules of their societies under adult constraint; eventually, though, they internalize standards and follow them on their own. Psychologists believe that a process called identification, in which children mold themselves after important people in their lives, is helpful in socialization, but they differ in their ideas of how identification comes about.

Preschool children face many important developmental tasks in addition to making sense of the rules that govern their environment. They are expected to learn to regulate their own behavior, control their impulses to hurt others, and to be helpful and cooperative when it is appropriate. They may need to cope with the addition of younger siblings to their families, and they must come to terms with their identities as males or females and master the sex-role behaviors appropriate to their society.

The task of socialization is by no means completed at the end of early childhood, but by then children understand their society's rules and expectations well enough to be ready for the increased responsibilities that accompany middle childhood.

Learning Objectives

Keep these questions in mind while studying Chapter 10.

1. How do children develop a sense of themselves as individuals and as boys or girls, and members of a particular ethnic or cultural group?
2. How do children come to follow social rules, even when adults are not directly supervising their behavior?
3. What contributions do the various theoretical perspectives make in explaining children's displays of aggression?
4. What are some effective ways of decreasing children's aggressive behaviors and increasing their prosocial behaviors?
5. In what ways are children's developing cognitive abilities related to their ability to understand other people's emotions and to regulate their own behavior?

Chapter Summary

Social development is a two-sided process. *Socialization* is the process by which children acquire the standards, knowledge, and values of the society in which they live. Part of this process is learning about *social roles,* such as son, daughter, or student. The other side of social development is the development of *personality,* a unique pattern of temperament, interests, emotions, and abilities that develops in interaction with the social environment. Temperamental characteristics are present at birth, as discussed in Chapter 4. Children will develop another important aspect of personality—*self-concept,* which involves how they view themselves in relation to other people. These processes of socialization and personality formation are closely intertwined; but there is also tension between them, as children experience conflict between their desires and the rules of their society. As they get older, children learn more about how to please and also about how to upset others.

I. ACQUIRING A SOCIAL AND PERSONAL IDENTITY

According to psychologists, socialization requires *identification,* a process in which children seek to be like significant people in their social environment.

A. Sex-Role Identity

While male and female infants seem much alike, by the time children are 3 years of age, their behavior is much more gender-typed. Boys and girls prefer different types of play, and they tend to prefer to play with others of their gender; this phenomenon is known as *gender segregation.* Chapter 10 explores the formation of sexual identity from the perspectives of the psychodynamic, environmental-learning, and cognitive approaches.

- According to Sigmund Freud, boys come to identify with their fathers though a process of differentiation from their mother, the parent with whom they had the closest relationship in infancy. During the *phallic stage* (around 4 years of age), Freud believed, a boy wants to take his father's place with his mother (the *Oedipus complex*); he then relieves the guilt these feelings evoke by distancing himself emotionally from his mother and becoming closer to (affiliating with) his father. In contrast, girls' identification with their mothers is a process of affiliation, rather than the differentiation that characterizes the formation of boys' sex-role identities. Girls, Freud thought, blamed their mothers for their lack of a penis. In response to their guilt feelings over rejecting their mothers and competing for their fathers' affection, girls repressed their feelings for their father and identified with their mothers.

  Critics have attacked various aspects of Freud's explanation, notably its characterization of women as "underdeveloped" men. They point out that, as discussed in Chapter 3, all human embryos initially follow a female path; thus, female development should not be thought of as secondary to male development. Also, research indicates that there is more to children's sex-role formation than resolution of the Oedipus complex.

- In contrast to Freudian theories that view identification as a way of resolving conflicts between children's fears and their desires, environmental-learning assume that sex-role identity is the product of two processes: modeling, in which children observe and imitate individuals of the same sex; and differential reinforcement, in which boys and girls are each rewarded for engaging in behaviors appropriate to their respective genders. Children do not acquire gender-role identity only by imitating their same-sex parents. The importance of siblings, for example, is supported by research by John Rust and his colleagues; they found that children with older siblings of the same sex showed the most sex-typed behavior and children with opposite-sex older siblings showed the least sex-typed behavior.

  Young children are sensitive to gender-oriented language and activities and to gender stereotypes. But while both boys and girls are knowledgeable about the more rigidly defined male stereotype, girls are more knowledgeable than boys about the female stereotype.
- A cognitive-developmental approach to sex-role acquisition was proposed by Lawrence Kohlberg; he viewed sex-role identification as a result of children's structuring of their own experience. First, they are able to label themselves as boys or girls. Next, they become aware that boys grow up to be men and girls grow up to be women. Finally, they understand that sex remains the same in all situations. This theory describes the stages of children's understanding; however, contrary to Kohlberg's prediction, they display sex-typed behavior well before they have achieved sex-role constancy.
- An alternative view of sex-role acquisition, gender schema theory, hypothesizes children acquire a *gender schema* that guides the way they select and remember information from the environment. Children form gender schemas for people, objects, and familiar events that also provide models for action. In any situation, they will be more likely to select, remember, and act upon information relevant to their own sex.

  Gender schema theorists differ in their views from Kohlberg in that they believe that children's schematic knowledge guides their gender-linked interests and behavior; they also employ an information-processing approach to describe the interaction of the cognitive and learning aspects of the system.

The main approaches to explaining children's development of sex-role identity are listed in Table 10.1. No single theory succeeds in integrating all the data concerning children's acquisition of sex roles. And none of them truly succeeds in integrating knowledge of the underpinnings of sex-role identity formation with the emotional factors described by Freud.

B. Ethnic Identity

The development of children's sense of racial or ethnic identity and their attitudes toward their own and other groups are important social issues. Several decades ago, when Kenneth and Mamie Clark asked African American and European American children, 3 years of age and older, to indicate preferences for dolls representing the two ethnic groups, they found that African American children seemed to prefer the white dolls. This was interpreted as indicating that minority children define themselves in terms of majority culture and have a negative self-concept. While later research has supported the findings, it has not supported the interpretations. Children's choices change with circumstances; for example, one study found that Native American children who were tested in their own language preferred dolls representing their own group. African American children's preference for white dolls has decreased over the years, according to more recent studies.

Developmentalists are interested in *racial socialization*—the race-related messages communicated to children by their parents. Among the types of messages communicated are: cultural socialization, emphasizing racial heritage and pride; preparation for bias, stressing discrimination and prejudice; promotion of racial mistrust, encouraging mistrust of the majority group; and egalitarianism, emphasizing equality of members of all races. Margaret Caughy and her colleagues, studying African American preschoolers, found that most parents incorporated a variety of racial socialization messages when interacting with their children. More communicated messages emphasizing cultural heritage (88%) compared to messages promoting mistrust (65%). Children whose parents promoted racial pride and included African items in their homes tended to have stronger cognitive abilities and problem-solving skills and fewer behavioral problems compared with the other children. This study indicates that formation of ethnic identity is a process that begins early in life.

C. Personal Identity

Children's sense of self becomes increasingly complex during early childhood. It can be conceived of as double-sided, containing both the "I" who exists over time and experiences the world in a particular way and the "me" that others see. When asked by developmentalists to describe themselves, they typically provide a loosely connected list of behaviors, abilities, and preferences. Their self-evaluations also tend to be unrealistically positive. The process of developing the sense of self is influenced by children's increasing ability to use language and by their participation with caregivers in a variety of routine, scripted activities. Caregivers also help children create a personal narrative—*autobiographical memory*—that helps them acquire an enduring sense of themselves. By the time they are 4 years old, children have internalized the narrative structures of their culture and can relate their experiences by themselves.

II. A NEW MORAL WORLD

As children acquire a sense of identity, they also learn to evaluate their behavior according to the standards of their communities.

A. Learning About Right and Wrong

At first, children's ideas of bad and good are strongly influenced by adults' reactions to their behavior. Piaget called this "heteronomous morality" (morality subject to externally imposed controls). As they get older and have more experience interacting with peers, according to Piaget, children develop a more autonomous morality in which rules are seen as agreements among people, not as decrees handed down by adults.

According to *social domain theory,* children must learn to follow three different kinds of social rules; these vary according to how broadly they apply and the consequences of breaking them. Moral rules are at the most general level; they cannot be transgressed and are found in some form in all societies. Social conventions are at the next level of generality; these are aspects of cultural scripts that specify things such as what people should wear in public and appropriate behavior for males and females. Social conventions vary a great deal between, and also within, societies. Rules in the personal sphere involve situations in which children can make decisions based on personal preferences. Children as young as 3 or 4 years of age can distinguish among the three kinds of rules. Examples of each appear in Table 10.2.

B. The Role of Internalization

Internalization is the process by which external culturally organized experiences—for example, those highlighting social rules—are transformed into internal psychological processes that organize how people behave—for example, by following social rules. According to Freud, people have three mental structures that develop from early childhood. The *id* is present at birth; it is unconscious, impulsive, and concerned with the immediate satisfaction of bodily drives. The *ego* develops when the infant is forced by reality to cope with the social world; it represents the first phase of self-regulation. By about 5 years of age, children's internalization of parental rules and standards results in the formation of the *superego*. This part of the personality functions as the child's conscience, which becomes evident in children's displays of guilt when they violate rules. It contributes to children's ability to regulate their behavior according to their new sense of right and wrong.

III. DEVELOPING SELF-REGULATION

While learning basic social roles, children also learn to act in accordance with their caregivers' expectations, even when they are not being directly monitored. "Self-regulation" involves the ability to control one's emotions, behaviors, and mental states; it develops over a long time and involves many different domains. The ability to regulate oneself is important in order for children to be able to function independently.

A. Regulating Thought and Action

Remembering to do something and solving a problem each involve self-regulation. Sometimes a task requires *effortful control*—the inhibition of an action that is already underway. These skills become especially important once children enter preschool.

Some studies have explored children's ability to resist temptation and comply with adult norms. For example, Lisa Bridges and Wendy Grolnick placed 3- and 4-year-old children in a room with an attractive toy, but instructed them not to play with it. They found that the children used a strategy of "active engagement"—directing their attention to other toys—in order to control their interest in the forbidden toy.

In another study, Grazyna Kochanska and Nazan Aksan videotaped 2- to 5-year-old children as they interacted with their mothers. They found that, when the mothers asked the children to stop playing and put away toys, only 10 percent engaged in "active compliance"; most had to be continually prompted. In a second session, the mothers asked the children not to touch a particular set of toys; this instruction was easier for the children to comply than the instruction to put away playthings, which involved effortful control.

Children's ability to control themselves is an example of internalization as described by Freud. Internalization is also important in the theory of Lev Vygotsky. Vygotsky viewed internalization as the process through which social regulations, organized in the zone of proximal development, are transferred to the child's psychological system.

B. Self-Regulation and Play

According to Vygotsky, play also has an important role in self-regulation. When children can separate thought (containing the idea or meaning of an object) from the object that is being thought about, they are regulating their thoughts and actions. An example would be a child talking into a block, using it to represent a telephone. Vygotsky believed that in this kind of imaginary play children demonstrate their greatest self-control.

Sociodramatic play, in which two or more participants enact a variety of social roles (for example, mother, baby, and children) is an especially important type of imaginary play. A study by Cynthia Elias and Laura Berk assessed 3- and 4-year-olds' sociodramatic play and their level of self-regulation. There was no relation between the two when the first measures were taken; however, several months later, the children who engaged in a great deal of sociodramatic play also showed high levels of self-regulation. This was especially true for the more impulsive children, who showed the greatest gains.

As discussed in the box "Coping with Chronic Illness through Play," children with chronic illnesses that require painful medical treatments and have frightening symptoms often use play and games to help them get through these stressful situations.

C. Regulating Emotions

Young children, in order to become competent members of their social group, need to learn to interpret the emotional states of others, be able to modify their own emotions, and learn to mask their true emotions when necessary.

As young children are able to better control their emotions, they are able to deal more effectively with the disappointments, frustrations, and hurt feelings that are common at that age. There is also evidence that children who can moderate their own distress when a hurt occurs to another child are better able to show sympathy to the playmate in distress. In order to sustain play, children must balance emotional expression and regulation.

- Babies are not born with the ability to regulate expression of their emotions in socially acceptable ways. During early childhood, children learn to recognize when other people are masking their feelings. Girls are generally better than boys at recognizing and displaying masked emotions. There are cultural differences in the ages at which children learn to, or are expected to, be able to mask their emotions.

The ability to behave appropriately in social situations that evoke strong emotions is called *socioemotional competence*; it involves awareness of one's own and others' emotional states, capacity for sympathy and empathy, and ability to differentiate inner and outer emotions. Preschool children rated high in socioemotional competence are liked better by their peers and teachers.

- A culture's values and beliefs help to shape children's emotions and self-regulation. For example, for U.S. children, shame, one of the secondary emotions, emerges only at the transition to early childhood. But, as reported by Michael Mascolo and his colleagues, for Chinese children it is one of the first emotional labels used. Figure 10.4 shows how differences in socialization of U.S. and Chinese children result in very different emotional responses to their successes and failures.

IV. UNDERSTANDING AGGRESSION

Learning to control aggression is one of the most basic tasks of young children's social development.

A. The Development of Aggression

Aggression is generally defined as an action intended to hurt another. As children develop, they begin to exhibit *instrumental aggression,* in which aggressive behavior is aimed at getting something they want, and person-oriented or *hostile aggression* aimed at establishing dominance. Judy Dunn observed an increase in instrumental aggression between siblings during the second year. At this time, teasing also becomes a more important part of aggressive exchanges between siblings. Also, at about 2 years of age, children begin to worry about "ownership rights," engaging in struggles over toys. Up until about 18 months of age, physical aggression and teasing occur equally often; later, teasing becomes more prevalent. In general, boys are more aggressive than girls; as girls approach their second birthdays they become less aggressive while boys of the same age become more aggressive. Girls, however, engage in more "relational aggression"—which involves harming other children's friendships or excluding them from a group—than boys do.

B. What Causes and Controls Aggression?

Developmentalists have noted that the earlier children develop problem behaviors relating to aggression, the more likely they are to behave in those ways later on. Thus, it is important to understand what causes aggressive behavior and how it can be controlled. Several biological influences on aggression have been proposed.

- Charles Darwin pointed out that members of a species are essentially in competition with one another to survive. According to this view, aggression is natural and necessary, and automatically accompanies biological maturation. Aggression is widespread among animal species, but is kept in check by the formation of dominance hierarchies. F. F. Strayer and his colleagues observed that 3- and 4-year-olds in a nursery school also formed dominance hierarchies; this reduced the total amount of aggression occurring in the group.

Genes have an indirect effect on aggression through their effects on physiologically based characteristics that, in turn, affect behavior. For example, the different levels of aggression between boys and girls is associated with the differences between them in testosterone levels. However, this influence acts in both directions, as testosterone levels rise in response to dominance over others or success in conflicts. Other factors linked to aggressive behavior include: activity levels (influenced by testosterone); levels of neurotransmitters and nervous system activity; "difficult" temperaments; and certain types of brain damage.

- Another explanation of aggression stresses the importance of social and cultural influences. In this view, aggression is learned; children imitate the aggressive behavior of others or are rewarded for aggressive behavior. For example, Gerald Patterson and his colleagues found that aggression by preschool children was generally followed by positive consequences for the aggressor. They also have observed that the parents of aggressive children often reinforce their children's aggressive behavior, either because they signal approval when the child is aggressive, or because aggression is a successful way for the child to halt parental coercion. The box "The Spanking Controversy" discusses the use of physical punishment and its effect on aggression. If attention reinforces aggressive behavior, one way to reduce it is to withhold attention from the aggressor and pay attention only to the victim. This approach may be accompanied by teaching appropriate verbal responses (for example, "I'm playing with this right now.") to the child who was aggressed upon. This technique does in fact reduce aggression in preschool classrooms.

  There is cross-cultural evidence supporting the idea that children model the aggressive behavior of adults. When Douglas Fry compared the levels of aggression of two Zapotec Indian towns in central Mexico, he found notable differences in levels of aggression. When the children of each town were observed, it was found that the children from the town with more aggressive adults performed twice as many aggressive acts as the children from the more peaceful town.
- Children's emotional reactions to events depend on how they interpret social contexts and how well they understand others' intentions and emotions. Negative feelings result when children are involved in a frustrating situation (for example, when another child takes away something that they are playing with). Whether an aggressive response is made, however, depends on the children's temperaments and past social experiences.

  Some theorists emphasize the importance of children's knowledge about emotions, what causes them, and how they are expressed. Children with advanced understanding should be less likely to behave aggressively. This view was supported by results of a study by Susanne Denham and her colleagues. Jessica Giles and Gail Heyman examined another factor: children's beliefs about whether being aggressive is an enduring trait or a changeable behavior. Children who believed that a person who was aggressive in one situation was likely to be aggressive again in the future (an "essentialist" view) were more likely to endorse aggressive solutions to conflicts.

Reasoning with children about aggression—cognitive training—is sometimes effective even with preschoolers. Shoshana Zahavi and Steven Asher found that children were better able to control their aggression when their nursery school teachers made them aware of the feelings of the children they aggressed against and suggested alternate ways of resolving conflicts.

Many people believe that *catharsis*—the opportunity to vent aggressive tendencies in harmless behavior—will reduce the incidence of actual aggression; however, no research has actually demonstrated that this is the case. Still, this idea is widely applied in psychotherapy with young children.

IV. DEVELOPING PROSOCIAL BEHAVIORS

Prosocial behavior is voluntary action that benefits others—for example, sharing, helping, and showing compassion. The psychological state that corresponds to prosocial behavior (in the same sense that anger corresponds to aggression) is "empathy"—sharing another person's emotions and feelings.

A. Understanding Others' Emotions

Six- or 7-month-old infants can tell how to feel about a situation by reading their mothers' facial expressions. By 2 years of age, children know that some things make people feel good and other things make them feel bad. Richard Fabes and his colleagues studied 3- to 6-year-olds' interpretation of other children's emotions. Three-year-olds usually interpreted others' emotions correctly, and by 5 or 6 years of age, children studied were in agreement with adults 80 percent of the time in their assessment of other children's emotional states. Linda Michalson and Michael Lewis, studying 2- to 5-year-old children, found that children could assess the hypothetical emotions of a girl in a story. The children could interpret positive emotions earlier than negative emotions, and older children were better than younger ones at assessing negative emotions.

B. Empathy

Empathy, sharing another's emotional response, is an important stimulus for prosocial behavior. Martin Hoffman has traced the development of empathy through four stages. During the first year, babies cry at the sound of another infant's cry (global empathy); this empathy is reflexlike, occurring even before infants have any real awareness of other people's feelings. During the second year, babies actively attempt to comfort another person who is in distress, though not always in ways appropriate to the other person (egocentric empathy). Preschoolers can empathize with a wider range of feelings and, through the media, with people they have never met or with story characters. Hoffman's explanation emphasizes children's ability to think about the feelings of others. Children's actual emotions are not emphasized in this explanation; Hoffman makes the assumption that, the more children understand others' feelings, the more they will adopt them.

C. Evidence of the Development of Prosocial Behaviors

As in Hoffman's theory, Nancy Eisenberg and her colleagues propose that empathy results in an emotional reaction like that experienced by another; however, they emphasize that empathy may turn either into "sympathy" (feelings of sorrow or concern for the other person) or into "personal distress"—a self-directed response. When another person's distress generates too much emotion in a child, a self-directed response is more likely to occur.

Studies of 6- to 8-year-olds have indicated that children who tend to have extreme emotional reactions need to be able to regulate their emotions in order to feel sympathy for others. For less-emotional children, the ability to focus attention on other people (rather than on themselves) is associated with feeling greater sympathy.

D. Promoting Prosocial Behavior

According to Joan Grusec, explicitly rewarding children for prosocial behaviors is not effective in increasing these acts. Two less direct but effective methods are *explicit modeling,* in which adults behave in ways they want the child to imitate, and *induction,* in which explanations are used. Because of its emphasis on reasoning and explanations, induction has more generally been used with older children; for example, Julia Krevans and John Gibbs observed that parents used it successfully with 12- to 14-year-olds. In real life, parents and teachers use a variety of techniques to reduce aggression and increase prosocial behavior.

VI. TAKING ONE'S PLACE IN THE SOCIAL GROUP

By the end of early childhood, children have accepted that conformity to social rules is inevitable. While they are by no means completely socialized, they have developed their own distinct ways of thinking and feeling and are continuing the process of personality formation from within the social group.

Key Terms I

Following are important terms introduced in Chapter 10. Match each term with the letter of the example that best illustrates the term.

1. ______ aggression
2. ______ differential reinforcement
3. ______ effortful control
4. ______ ego
5. ______ explicit modeling
6. ______ hostile aggression
7. ______ id
8. ______ induction
9. ______ instrumental aggression
10. ______ personality formation
11. ______ prosocial behavior
12. ______ social development

13. ______ socialization

14. ______ sociodramatic play

15. ______ superego

a. The process by which children acquire their society's values, knowledge, and standards.
b. A mother appeals to her children's pride and their desire to be grown-up in explaining how they should behave toward others.
c. This occurs when someone hurts another person intentionally.
d. This is needed in order for children to, for example, stop playing with an attractive toy and put it away.
e. Janet hits another preschool child in order to gain possession of the doll she is playing with.
f. This occurs when adults reward boys for doing masculine things and girls for doing feminine things.
g. This is a process with two aspects: in one, children become differentiated as individuals; in the other, they become integrated into the society of which they are members.
h. John calls a fellow kindergartner "stupid" just to hurt his feelings.
i. A baby cries when she hears another child crying.
j. Altruism, cooperation, and sharing are examples of these.
k. Rules are seen as absolute laws laid down by adults.
l. Parents demonstrate for their children how to "take turns" with a toy.
m. This part of the personality serves as the child's conscience.
n. This part of the personality supplies the child's psychological energy.
o. The primary task of this part of the child's personality is self-preservation.

Key Terms II

Following are important terms introduced in Chapter 10. Match each term with the letter of the example that best illustrates the term.

1. ______ autobiographical memory
2. ______ catharsis
3. ______ gender schema
4. ______ gender segregation
5. ______ identification
6. ______ internalization
7. ______ modeling
8. ______ Oedipus complex
9. ______ personality
10. ______ phallic stage
11. ______ racial socialization
12. ______ self-concept
13. ______ social domain theory
14. ______ social roles
15. ______ socioemotional competence

a. The Freudian stage during which children develop sexual jealousy toward the parent of the same sex.
b. A father encourages his children to hit a punching bag to "blow off steam," hoping it will prevent them from punching one another.
c. Children's conceptions of sex roles that guide their behavior and affect the way they select and remember information.
d. In acquiring sex-role identity, this occurs when children observe and imitate other individuals of the same sex.
e. A term for modeling oneself after another person.
f. This has occurred when children have accepted social rules and make an effort to follow them on their own.
g. Children's distinctive sense of themselves, including distinctive ways of thinking, feeling, and behaving.
h. Boys prefer to play with other boys and girls with other girls.
i. Jason tells his mother that he wants to marry her someday, "after Daddy dies."
j. The way children conceive of themselves in relation to other people.
k. This involves messages related to ethnicity that are communicated to children by their parents.
l. Categorizes the rules of societies according to how broadly they apply and the consequences of violating them.
m Examples are "daughter," "student," and "wife."
n. Ability to discern other people's emotions is an important component of this.
o. A personal narrative that is initially created by children and adults together.

Multiple-Choice Practice Questions

Circle the letter of the word or phrase that correctly completes each statement.

1. ______ is the process by which children learn the standards, values, and knowledge of their society.
   a. Personality formation
   b. Prosocial behavior
   c. Affiliation
   d. Socialization

2. According to Freud, identification in males
   a. requires that they differentiate themselves from their mothers.
   b. requires that they differentiate themselves from their fathers.
   c. results in their remaining affiliated with their mothers.
   d. occurs because they are rewarded for imitating appropriate behavior.

3. In thinking about moral issues, preschool children
   a. have no sense of right or wrong.
   b. believe in obeying the spirit of the law rather than the letter of the law.
   c. judge the rightness or wrongness of actions by adults' reactions.
   d. are inclined to question the judgment of people in authority.

4. In Freud's theory, which part of the personality serves as a person's conscience?
   a. the id
   b. the ego
   c. the superego
   d. the unconscious

5. When children are able to obey social rules even when no one is monitoring their behavior, they are exhibiting
   a. repression.
   b. self-regulation.
   c. empathy.
   d. prosocial behavior.

6. Which, in a study by Margaret Caughy and her colleagues, was the most prevalent category of racial socialization messages used by parents?
   a. mistrust of the majority group
   b. preparation for bias
   c. cultural socialization
   d. all of these, equally

7. When children exclude another child from a group or harm the other child's friendship with someone else, they are engaging in
   a. a defense mechanism.
   b. explicit modeling.
   c. instrumental aggression.
   d. relational aggression.

8. According to Kohlberg's theory, which of the following needs to happen in order for children to develop a sex-role identity?
   a. Children need to be reinforced by adults for performing behaviors associated with their gender and punished for performing behaviors associated with the other gender.
   b. Children need to resolve the Oedipus complex.
   c. Children do not need to do anything; sex-role identities are genetically based and develop with maturation.
   d. Children need to come to understand that their sex is a permanent and unchanging characteristic.

9. Aggression among children results from
   a. imitation of aggressive models.
   b. adults inadvertently rewarding aggressive behavior.
   c. inborn tendencies to compete with others.
   d. all of the above.

10. Physically punishing children for aggressive behavior
    a. may make children even more aggressive.
    b. is the most successful way to inhibit aggressive behavior.
    c. has no effect on children's level of aggression.
    d. provides catharsis for parents and helps them cope better with their children's behavior.

11. When newborns cry in response to another baby's crying, they are displaying the first signs of
    a. self-control.
    b. empathy.
    c. frustration.
    d. learning.

12. Ability to perceive the emotional states of others and to control the expression of one's own emotions are aspects of
    a. gender schema formation.
    b. socioemotional competence.
    c. the Oedipus complex.
    d. the process of differentiation.

13. Which leads to a reduction in aggression among children?
    a. formation of dominance hierarchies
    b. rewarding nonaggressive behaviors
    c. cognition training
    d. all of these

14. Compared with girls, boys engage in more
    a. physical aggression.
    b. verbal aggression.
    c. relational aggression.
    d. of all of the above.

15. Which of the following is most difficult for young children to do?
    a. initiate an action
    b. inhibit an action
    c. imitate a simple motor action
    d. accept a reward for performing an action

16. Which is necessary for children to be able to feel sympathy for others?
    a. ability to focus attention on other people
    b. ability to regulate one's emotions
    c. both a and b
    d. the tendency to feel emotions very strongly

17. Research on development of ethnic identity shows that
    a. children are not aware of racial or ethnic groups until 6 or 7 years of age.
    b. minority group children usually wish they belonged to the majority group.
    c. children usually prefer to play with dolls representing their own ethnic group.
    d. the racial or ethnic preferences expressed by children vary according to the circumstances of the interview.

Short-Answer Practice Questions

1. Briefly describe the psychodynamic, social-learning, cognitive, and gender schema approaches to explaining children's sex-role identification. What are the strengths and weaknesses of each?

2. What factors are thought to be responsible for human aggression? Why might there be sex differences in aggressive behavior?

3. What is known about the ways racial socialization occurs? What kinds of messages about ethnicity are associated with the best outcomes for children?

4. What is prosocial behavior and what is its course of development in children? How can prosocial behavior be increased?

5. What is socioemotional competence? Give some examples of how children could be helped to develop this ability.

Putting It All Together

In this section, material from Chapter 10 can be put together with information presented in earlier chapters.

I. One of the major accomplishments of early childhood is the growth of children's ability to regulate their own behavior. Show how developments in language ability and the growth of scripted knowledge help children to exhibit self-regulation and to interact socially with others.

II. Among preschoolers, the ability to reason about social categories such as sex is thought to influence the process of identification. Use examples to demonstrate the relationship between cognitive development (for example, categorization and perspective taking) and social development during early childhood.

Sources of More Information

Ames, L. B., & Haber, C. C. (1989). *He hit me first: When brothers and sisters fight.* New York: Warner Books.
This book discusses sibling rivalry from the biological-maturational perspective of the Gesell Institute.

Dunn, J. (1988). *The beginnings of social understanding.* Cambridge, MA.: Harvard University Press.
The author has studied children as they interact with their siblings in everyday family settings. The book is helpful in illustrating the relationship between cognitive and social development.

Eisenberg, N. (Ed.). (1992). *The caring child.* Cambridge, MA: Harvard University Press.
A discussion of topics related to theory and research on the development of prosocial behavior.

Freud, A. (1979). *Psycho-analysis for teachers and parents.* New York: Norton.
This book contains four lectures in which Sigmund Freud's daughter, a noted children's analyst, discusses the early stages of psychosexual development.

Galinsky, E., & David, J. (1991). *The preschool years: Family strategies that work.* New York: Ballantine.
The authors present practical solutions to the problems faced by parents of preschool children.

Hall, C. S. (1999). *A primer of Freudian psychology.* New York: Dutton/Plume.
This brief paperback account of Freud's thinking is one of the most accessible and comprehensive available.

Honig, A. S. (1985, January). Compliance, control, and discipline, Part I. *Young Children,* 50–58.
Honig, A. S. (1985, March). Compliance, control, and discipline, Part II. *Young Children,* 47–52.
These two articles discuss children's development of self-regulation and suggest techniques that can be used by adults to increase cooperation and compliance.

Paul, A. M. (1998, January/February). Do parents really matter? *Psychology Today,* 46–49.
A brief discussion of the ways genetic predispositions interact with environmental factors in affecting children's behavior.

Answer Key

Answers to Key Terms I: 1.c, 2.f, 3.d, 4.o, 5.l, 6.h, 7.n, 8.b, 9.e, 10.k, 11.j, 12.g, 13.a, 14.i, 15.m.

Answers to Key Terms II: 1.o, 2.b, 3.c, 4.h, 5.e, 6.f, 7.d, 8.i, 9.g, 10.a, 11.k, 12.j, 13.l, 14.m, 15.n.

Answers to Multiple-Choice Questions: 1.d, 2.a, 3.c, 4.c, 5.b, 6.c, 7.d, 8.d, 9.d, 10.a, 11.b, 12.b, 13.d, 14.a, 15.b, 16.c, 17.d.

The Contexts of Early Childhood

chapter 11

Children's development is influenced by the many contexts of their lives; their families, for example, belong to communities that, in turn, are parts of larger societies. Child rearing varies from society to society: a family of nomadic herders in North Africa and a family living in a New York City high-rise apartment will not teach their children the same survival and social skills. There are also differences in child-rearing practices within societies and corresponding differences in children's behavior. Many factors influence a family's child rearing, including the personalities of parents and children, the parents' occupational status, and the life stresses that affect the family at any particular time.

During early childhood, many children are cared for by relatives besides their parents or by child-care providers, either in other families' homes or in child-care centers. High-quality child care does not harm children intellectually; it has both positive and negative social effects.

Children also have out-of-home experiences in preschools—sheltered environments oriented toward enhancing their development. Special preschool programs have been created for economically disadvantaged children in the hope of giving them an educational "head start," and there is some evidence that preschool experience has at least some long-lasting positive effects on such children's later school achievement.

Even within the family, children are influenced by the world outside. Media such as television, newspapers, books, and computers help to shape the behavior and beliefs of family members in the United States. Research on the influence of television on children indicates that it can have both positive and negative effects, depending on how it is used. Print media, particularly books, provide children with an introduction to literacy.

By the end of the period of early childhood, children, while not completely socialized, will have a great deal of information about how their culture works and will be able to behave competently in a wide variety of situations with which they are familiar.

Learning Objectives

Keep these questions in mind while studying Chapter 11.

1. In what ways do different cultures' child-rearing practices serve to socialize children to behave in ways that are valued in those cultures?
2. What patterns of child-rearing practices are most common in U.S. families? What are the consequences of each?
3. How do stresses such as divorce, single parenthood, and low income act to trigger developmental or behavior problems?
4. What are the effects of the media on children—for example, television watching and exposure to literacy experiences and computer media?
5. What sorts of child-care arrangements are used by U.S. families? How does out-of-home care benefit children? What problems does it cause? What is the purpose of children's participation in preschool programs? How does preschool experience benefit children from disadvantaged circumstances?

Chapter Summary

Chapter 11 highlights the way the contexts in which young children develop influence the course of their development. These contexts—ranging from specific events within the family or preschool to global influences of mass media—may shape children's development directly or indirectly, through their effect on parents and other family members. Parent–child influence goes two ways, of course, and children's own characteristics also affect their development by influencing how their parents interact with them.

I. THE FAMILY AS A CONTEXT FOR DEVELOPMENT

When Beatrice and John Whiting organized observations of child rearing in six diverse locales around the world, they found differences, not only in the circumstances of children's lives, but in the overall patterns of their behavior. For example, children of the Gusii, an agricultural people in Western Kenya, were more likely both to offer help and responsible suggestions to others and to reprimand other children. The children of Orchard Town, U.S.A., were more likely to seek help and attention from others and to engage in horseplay with other children. This difference in behavior was partly a function of how the children spent their days. While the children of Orchard Town spent their time in school, the Gusii children were expected to contribute economically to their families by working and by taking on the care of younger children. An Orchard Town child usually lived in a *nuclear family,* consisting of a husband, a wife, and their children. A Gusii child lived in an *extended family,* which included many other relations as well. Each cultural group socialized children in ways that would help them to fit in as adult members of that particular society.

Families differ in many ways that affect children's lives; families also change in response to social and economic changes in their society. For example, today children are more likely to live in a *single-parent family*—a family headed by one parent, usually the mother—than they were in the 1950s when the Whitings carried out their research.

A. Family Structures and Dynamics

While the term *family* is traditionally defined as a group of people with shared ancestry, shared residence, and/or marital ties, in practice the concept "family" has fluid boundaries. Developmentalists use the term *family structures* to refer to how the family unit is organized (for example, nuclear, extended, or single-parent) and the term *family dynamics* to refer to the patterns of interaction among family members.

- According to historian Phillippe Ariès, the nuclear family is a product of modern society; however, there is evidence that it dates back as far as medieval times, and is therefore not simply a response to the migrations of individuals from rural areas to cities. There is evidence that nuclear families are, and have been, embedded in kinship lines that extend between urban and rural areas.

  The proportion of nuclear families has been declining in the United States in recent decades, with a corresponding rise in importance of extended families.
- According to the most recent U.S. Census, extended families are about 4% of the total; however, they are a much larger percentages in certain areas. Extended families are born of cultural tradition and economic hardship; thus, they are especially prevalent among people of African and Hispanic ancestry and among recent immigrants.

  Extended families are an important source of support for the children of young, single mothers.
- About half of all U.S. children will spend some part of their childhood in a single-parent home. Studies of children from single-parent families report a variety of social, behavioral, and academic problems. One difficulty is that the formation of a single-parent family may be associated with socioeconomic hardship and/or divorce.

  When Gunilla Weitoff and her colleagues conducted a study in Sweden comparing children from one- and two-parent families, they found that socioeconomic differences were the most important factor in differences between the two groups. However, even when this was taken into account, the children from single-parent families were at higher risk for a variety of problems.

  John Kesner and Patrick McKenry shed further light on the issue with a study of mainly African American families in the United States. In this sample, most of the single mothers had never been married and, thus, had not undergone divorce. In addition, most had supportive extended families. Under these circumstances, there were no differences between the children of one- and two-parent families in social skills or conflict management styles.

B. Parenting Styles and Family Dynamics

Anthropologist Robert Levine has proposed that families share three goals for their children: making sure that their children survive, acquire economic skills, and acquire the cultural values of their group. So, for example, where threats to infant survival are high, parents in diverse countries tend to adopt similar child-rearing strategies. Presumably, these are transmitted both through biological means and by observational learning.

- While child-rearing behaviors differ in many ways among U.S. families, developmentalists conceive of parenting styles as varying along two dimensions: one corresponds to the amount of control parents exert; the other corresponds to the amount of affection parents display. The parenting patterns to which these give rise are shown in Table 11.1.

  Diana Baumrind and her colleagues found that, when they measured the parenting styles of U.S. families, 77 percent of the families they studied could be classified as falling into one of three patterns: an "authoritarian parenting pattern," in which parents shape their children's behavior according to a set standard and stress obedience to authority; an "authoritative parenting pattern," in which parents encourage individualism and independence, while setting high standards for behavior; or a "permissive parenting pattern," in which parents provide less discipline and demand less achievement and maturity than do parents in the other categories. Baumrind found that the children of authoritarian parents tended to lack social competence, spontaneity, and intellectual curiosity; that the children of authoritative parents were more self-reliant and self-controlled; and that the children of permissive parents were relatively immature and less responsible than those of the other groups. There are limits to the generality of these findings. For example, children's own characteristics probably influence the child-rearing strategies adopted by their parents.
- Parents have the greatest influence in children's socialization. The box "Fathers" describes the importance of fathers in promoting the life satisfaction of their children. Siblings, however, also play an important role. Margarita Azmitia and Joanne Hesser found that young children were more likely to imitate and consult with an older sibling than with an older friend during a block-building activity. And Gene Brody and Velma Murray, in a study of single-parent, African American families, found that "no-nonsense parenting" by mothers was linked to higher competence in older children; the older siblings' competence was, in turn, linked to the competence of the younger siblings, so long as the siblings enjoyed a positive relationship.

C. Family Diversity

Contemporary families represent diverse ethnic backgrounds, cultural heritages, and lifestyles.

- Currently, more than 50 percent of immigrants to the United States come from Latin America, about 25 percent from Asia, 15 percent from Europe, and 8 percent from other areas.

  Different types of families may find different parenting styles to be appropriate. For example, Diana Baumrind's original studies were of white, middle-class, two-parent families. There is evidence that keeping close control over children's behavior—characteristic of authoritarian parenting—does not have the same effect in African American families; African American children whose parents adopted an authoritarian style did better in school than those whose parents adopted an authoritative style, according to recent research. And Ruth Chao found that Baumrind's parenting categories do not apply well to families using Chinese child-rearing practices, in which the idea of training young children for later life is an important value.

- Somewhere between 2 and 8 million U.S. families raising between 3 and 14 million children are headed by gay and lesbian parents. According to a study by Jane Ariel and Dan McPherson, children raised by gay and lesbian parents are just as healthy as those raised by heterosexual parents with respect to a wide variety of psychological measures.

D. Distressed Families

A variety of family-related risk factors can impede children's development.

- Approximately one in four U.S. children is currently living in poverty. While family income typically fluctuates across a child's lifetime, poverty during early childhood is more highly associated with risk to later achievement and adjustment than poverty during later periods. Poverty has an influence on child-rearing patterns. In families living at a near-subsistence level and families under stress, parents are more likely to adopt an authoritarian parenting style. Stressful events occur more often in poor families; low-income parents are also more likely to use authoritarian or inconsistent styles of child rearing.
- Many single mothers raising children are teenagers. Research has shown that children of unmarried teenage mothers are developmentally disadvantaged compared to children of older, married mothers. According to Frank Furstenberg and his colleagues, one factor contributing to this is that young mothers vocalize less with their babies, leading to lower cognitive ability; also, young unmarried mothers have limited financial resources, with all the disadvantages that accompany low income.

  Tom Luster and his colleagues found that "more successful" preschool-aged children of teen mothers tended to be those who lived in more intellectually stimulating and less stressful environments and who had mothers who had completed more education, who were more likely to be employed, and who lived with a male partner.
- Divorce, which affects more than 1 million children annually, leads to changes in children's lives that are often accompanied by academic and social difficulties. Following a divorce, the family experiences a drop in income; the mother may have to enter the workforce, which requires her to juggle home, child care, and work responsibilities. Also, the custodial parent may feel lonely and isolated; there may be, at least temporarily, a deterioration in parenting.

  Developmentalists have used several different models to account for the effects of divorce on children. In the "crisis model," divorce was viewed as a specific disturbance to which children adapted with time. The "chronic stress model" recognized ongoing problems that followed a divorce. Paul Amato's "divorce-stress-adjustment model," shown in Figure 11.5, incorporates various stressors and protective factors that influence family members. The "selection perspective" incorporates factors that might predispose people both to divorce and to other problems that tend to accompany divorce.

Divorce has different effects on different people, benefiting some while having a lasting negative effect on others.

- According to statistics, about 13 of every 1000 children are abused; half of these cases involve neglect of physical well-being, one quarter involve physical abuse, 13% sexual abuse, and the rest are emotional maltreatment or medical neglect. It is sometimes difficult to define abuse, as what is acceptable in one community may not be acceptable in another (for example, see the discussion of spanking in Chapter 10). Abuse is more likely to occur when families are under stress, and when mothers are young, uneducated, abuse alcohol or drugs, and receive little support from the child's father. Boys are more likely to be victims of physical abuse, girls of sexual abuse; half of all cases involve children 7 years of age or less.

  Abuse negatively affects children intellectually, socially, and emotionally. Seth Pollack and his colleagues found that, on a task in which emotional expressions were matched to stories, neglected children had trouble identifying emotions and had a bias toward selecting sad expressions; physically abused children had trouble identifying sadness and disgust, but were accurate at recognizing anger and had a bias for selecting angry expressions. There were no selection biases for nonmaltreated children.

  Abuse is less prevalent in places where physical punishment is frowned upon, for example, in Japan and Sweden.
- Children living in affluent families can also be at risk for emotional problems. Suniya Luthar and Bronwyn Becker found that students in the wealthy community they studied had high rates of depression and substance abuse. These children felt themselves under great pressure to achieve, and felt isolated from adults, and emotionally distant from their mothers.

II. EARLY CONTEXTS OF CARE

By three years of age, more than 90% of U.S. children experience regular nonparental care; more than 30% will spend more than 30 hours per week in child-care settings.

A. Varieties of Child Care

- In *home care,* children are cared for in their homes by relatives or babysitters; with this arrangement, they experience the least change from their normal routine.
- In *family care,* children are cared for in the day-care provider's home, along with children from outside their families. The routine is usually similar to that at home, but children are exposed to a more diverse group of children and experiences than they would be at home.
- Licensed *child-care centers* have attracted the most public attention and study. They generally place more emphasis on formal learning experiences. The programs at child-care centers vary in style and philosophy; some are school-like, while others allow children to select their own activities. Many receive public funding and are therefore more accessible to researchers, who can study how their particular characteristics affect children's development.

B. Developmental Effects of Child Care

As discussed in Chapter 7, the quality of care is important in determining its effects on children.

- Children under 3 years of age who spend time in child-care arrangements with more than six other children become sick more often; however, there is no evidence that this affects their overall development. Infants and toddlers in child-care centers also experience more stress during the day, according to research by Sarah Watamura and her colleagues, who measured cortisol levels in children's saliva. The intellectual development of middle-class children in day care is at least as good as that of their stay-at-home peers; low-income children seem to actively benefit in cognitive and linguistic development. Table 11.2 shows standards useful in determining the quality of child-care centers.
- Research results indicate both positive and negative effects of experience in child-care centers on children's social and emotional well-being. For example, children who attend day-care centers in the United States are more self-sufficient and independent, more cooperative, and more comfortable in new situations, though also less polite, less compliant with adults, and more aggressive than children who do not attend day-care centers. The greater the number of years children spend in full-time nonparental care, the greater the likelihood that they will have behavior problems in kindergarten. Children's relationships with their parents and the amount of stress parents experience—along with other aspects of the ecology—appear to be important factors in determining how children react to out-of-home care.

C. An Ecological Approach to Child Care

Deborah Johnson and her colleagues point out that ethnic-minority and immigrant children are often not included in research on child care. Using Bronfenbrenner's approach, they have developed a model (shown in Figure 11.7) of how the interacting components of macrosystem, mesosystem, and microsystem affect the types of care available to and utilized by families subject to racism and segregation.

D. Preschool

Preschools serve a primarily educational purpose and provide a sheltered environment scaled to children; the children, who may range in age from 2½ to 6, typically spend 2½ to 3 hours per day engaged in a variety of activities designed to enhance various aspects of their development. The emphasis is usually on exploration rather than on performing correctly on preassigned tasks.

- Project Head Start was begun in 1964 in an attempt to narrow the educational gap between low-income and middle-class children by providing preschool-aged children with learning experiences they might miss at home. Soon, it was a year-round program serving 200,000 children; today, it provides services to more than 750,000.

  Data on the benefits of Head Start participation are not clear-cut; they do show evidence of some intellectual, nutritional, and health gains, along with greater involvement by parents in their children's schooling. Follow-up studies have shown that children who had attended a preschool program were less likely to be assigned to remedial classes than children with no preschool experience. It has also been found that Head Start and other similar programs have had broader effects, when looking at measures such as crime rates and unemployment. However, success is related to the quality of the classroom experience and, while Head Start classrooms are generally considered "adequate," few are rated "high quality." Nonetheless, a cost-benefit analysis of Head Start has estimated that, for every dollar spent on the program, the public has saved seven dollars in decreased costs for welfare and incarceration.

III. MEDIA LINKING HOME AND COMMUNITY

Children's behavior is shaped not only by the members of their families and their communities, but by modern communications media such as books, television, newspapers, radio, videotape, CDs, and the Internet. Chapter 11 examines the influence of media.

A. The Lessons of History

When literacy was first introduced to Greek society, Plato argued that it would lead to a weakening of memory. Today, it is newer media that elicit concern. Chapter 11 considers how both the physical form and the content of media affect children's development.

B. Books

U.S. children from all social classes are exposed to print frequently enough that they develop "emergent literacy"—the idea that the letters and symbols they see convey meaning.

- Being read to by their parents or other adults helps children to develop emergent literacy. Being read to often at home helps children once they begin school. Parents, in their interactions with children over books, often construct a zone of proximal development, providing support tailored to their children's level of knowledge.
- Some adults worry that certain literary forms such as fairy tales or nonsense verse are harmful to children's development; still others, like the psychologist Bruno Bettleheim, defend them as beneficial. There are also complaints that children's books ignore or misrepresent people from certain strata of society; there is some evidence that this is true.

C. Television

There is no question that children are influenced by what they learn from watching television. Even infants imitate language and actions they hear and see on TV. Moreover, they identify with characters they see on television, as can be seen in their fantasy play and in the toys and cereals they prefer.

- A special concern about television viewing is that children may have difficulty separating the actors from the characters they portray or understanding that the events depicted are not really happening. Even 4- and 5-year-olds, for example, may believe that Sesame Street is a real place, and even 7- and 8-year-olds may believe that people who play married couples on television must be friends in real life.
- Techniques of television production such as close-ups, flashbacks, and changes of camera angle have meaning for older viewers but are confusing to preschool children, who may be unable to keep track of much of what they see. The fast-paced nature of television also allows little time for reflection. It has been hypothesized that T.V. watching causes lower willingness to expend the mental work needed to learn from written texts. However, research has not supported the idea that television watching induces generalized mental laziness.
- How does the content of television programming affect children's development? Television content differs systematically from everyday reality. For example, prime-time programming tends to stereotype people by sex, age, ethnic group, and occupation.

  Television also contains many violent episodes, and psychologists have found that, in the laboratory, children who view violent programs exhibit more aggression in their play. It has also been found that more aggressive children watch more violent programming. And studies have shown that children's aggressiveness increases when television is introduced into an area that has been without it; still, it is methodologically difficult to conclusively demonstrate a causal relationship between television viewing and aggression.

  Does educational programming help children in school, in peer relationships, and in moral reasoning? As with studies linking TV violence with aggression, the data are correlational, making it difficult to draw conclusions about the effectiveness of such programming. Longitudinal studies suggest some positive influence of educational programs on school performance, especially for boys, and some negative effects of viewing programs for general audiences, especially for girls.
- North American parents place few restrictions on the amount of television their children watch, though they do place restrictions on content. Aletha Huston and John Wright found that children benefit when their parents watch television with them; parents can explain plot devices and character motivations, and parents and children can discuss the values and moral issues raised by programs. In fact, however, parents spend little time watching television with their children; some developmentalists have created interventions to help concerned parents maximize televisions' educational potential and minimize its harmful effects.

IV. INTERACTIVE MEDIA

In modern, industrialized societies, computers and the Internet rank close behind television in popularity with children.

A. Form

Computer games promote a number of cognitive and academic skills and help children learn to carry out computer operations. Concerns about computer use center around its solitary nature. However, there is no evidence that regular computer users spend less time with peers than less frequent users. A related concern is that frequent computer use affects family relationships. Today, children often are more knowledgeable about computers than their parents, so family interaction over games and other activities may be infrequent.

B. Content

Kaveri Subrahmanyam and her colleagues found that there were at least short-term effects of playing violent computer games on children's aggressive behavior. Whether game playing is the cause of the aggression is not known. In general, boys are more likely than girls to play interactive computer games.

IV. ON THE THRESHOLD

Each new context to which young children are exposed provides new experiences and new challenges. In situations in which they know the scripts, young children appear surprisingly competent. However, they enter many situations with which they are unfamiliar. Then, their thought processes and powers of self-expression and self-control may be inadequate. At these times, they must rely on adult supervision or on organizing activities such as play, in order to coordinate with others.

Key Terms

Following are important terms introduced in Chapter 11. Match each term with the letter of the example that best illustrates the term.

1. ______ child-care centers
2. ______ extended family
3. ______ family
4. ______ family care
5. ______ family dynamics
6. ______ family structures
7. ______ home care
8. ______ nuclear family
9. ______ single-parent family

a. In this type of care, children's daily routines are least disrupted.
b. This provides support that is especially important to the children of young, unmarried mothers.
c. Some of these are school-like in their philosophies.
d. This arrangement is considered the norm among North Americans, but it is not as typical in recent decades.
e. In this child-care arrangement, care is given in the provider's home.
f. A group of people related by shared ancestry, residence, and/or marital ties.
g. About 50 percent of U.S. children will spend some time growing up in one of these.
h. A term that refers to family arrangements such as nuclear, extended, and single-parent.
i. A term that refers to patterns of interaction among family members.

Multiple-Choice Practice Questions

Circle the letter of the word or phrase that correctly completes each statement.

1. Diana Baumrind and her colleagues found that the parenting styles of middle-class Americans vary along dimensions of
   a. aggression and love.
   b. control and affection.
   c. guilt and initiative.
   d. confidence and empathy.

2. Nuclear families
   a. are the most common form of family structure in all human societies.
   b. have only become common during the last hundred years or so.
   c. are less common in the United States than they were 50 years ago.
   d. are equally common among all ethnic groups in the United States.

3. According to which view of divorce are most of the negative effects of divorce on children due to longstanding dysfunctional family patterns that existed before the divorce?
   a. chronic strain model
   b. crisis model
   c. divorce-stress-adjustment perspective
   d. selection perspective

4. Which is a possible source of misunderstanding when preschoolers watch television?
   a. They may not know how to interpret special techniques such as scene changes or flashbacks.
   b. They may not understand that the events on the screen are not really happening.
   c. They may not be able to distinguish the actors from the characters they play.
   d. All of the above.

5. Which is true about the effects of TV violence on children's behavior?
   a. Unrestricted viewing of violent programs is associated with more aggressive behavior.
   b. Children who watch nonviolent children's programs like Mr. Rogers' Neighborhood are just as aggressive as those who watch violent programs.
   c. Only children who are predisposed to be violent are affected by violent programs.
   d. Children who "blow off steam" by watching violent programs are less aggressive in their play than children who watch nonviolent programs.

6. Which of the following serves as a "literacy experience" for young children?
   a. listening to their parents read a letter aloud
   b. looking at the messages on cereal boxes
   c. bringing home a note from their preschool teacher
   d. all of the above

7. Bruno Bettelheim has argued that fairy tales
   a. are inappropriate for children.
   b. stimulate violence and aggression.
   c. are useful as a means of teaching sex-roles.
   d. help provide solutions to children's inner conflicts.

8. Children who attend child-care centers are __________ than those cared for at home.
   a. better behaved
   b. more self-sufficient
   c. more attached to their parents
   d. less intelligent

9. The most widely utilized form of child care for preschool children is
   a. care in organized child-care centers.
   b. care in the child's own home.
   c. family care.
   d. All of the above are utilized equally.

10. The more full-time, nonparental care children have in infancy and early childhood,
    a. the more likely they are to have behavior problems in kindergarten.
    b. the less likely they are to have behavior problems in kindergarten.
    c. the more polite and obedient to adults they are.
    d. both b and c.

11. The main purpose of preschools is to
    a. take care of young children while their parents work.
    b. give children a head start in learning academic skills such as reading and writing.
    c. provide children with opportunities to practice developmental skills in a scaled-down environment.
    d. get children ready for school by teaching them to perform correctly on assigned tasks.

12. The most recent follow-up studies of Project Head Start showed that
    a. the program had no effect on children's development.
    b. the program had a positive effect on children's achievement.
    c. the program completely closed the gap between children from low income families and those from middle-class families.
    d. the program left disadvantaged children even worse off than before.

13. Children whose parents use a(n) ________ parenting style tend to be less mature than those whose parents use other strategies.
    a. permissive
    b. authoritative
    c. authoritarian
    d. None of the above is correct.

14. Young children who attend child-care centers
    a. tend to become sick more often than those cared for at home.
    b. are as able intellectually as those cared for at home.
    c. are both a and b.
    d. have experiences at the center that are the same as those they would have at home.

15. Which is true about child maltreatment?
    a. The majority of children who are abused grow up to abuse their own children.
    b. Children who are mistreated rarely show signs of it in their daily behavior.
    c. Most cases of maltreatment involve neglect of children's needs.
    d. Middle-class children are just as likely to be physically abused as are those living in poverty.

16. Some people worry that playing violent computer games will cause children
    a. to be more aggressive.
    b. to have shorter attention spans.
    c. to find it difficult to work quickly.
    d. to be all of the above.

17. Azmintia and Hesser found that, while trying to complete a block-building task, young children were most likely to consult
    a. an older sibling.
    b. an older friend.
    c. a strange adult.
    d. all of the above equally.

18. Teen mothers who ________ are more likely to have "successful" preschool children.
    a. are educated
    b. are employed
    c. live with a partner
    d. are all of the above

Short-Answer Practice Questions

1. What differences can be observed among children whose parents use authoritarian, authoritative, and permissive child-rearing strategies? Why is it hard to say whether the strategies actually cause the differences in children's behavior?

2. Show how factors such as divorce and socioeconomic problems make it difficult to evaluate the effect on children of living in single-parent families.

3. What problems may young children have in understanding what they see on TV? How does their understanding improve over time?

4. In what ways do child-care and preschool experiences affect children's intellectual and social development? What positive effects have been noted? Negative effects?

5. How would you design an ideal child-care environment for a 3-year-old child? Explain how each element would be beneficial for the child.

6. The chapter points out that parents reading to children create a zone of proximal development. Explain how parents might do this in reading a "counting book" to a child.

Putting It All Together

Using information from Chapter 11 and previous chapters, give several examples of how parents and teachers in different cultures organize children's environments to socialize the children in ways appropriate to their culture.

Sources of More Information

Clarke-Stewart, A. (1993). *Daycare* (2nd ed.). Cambridge, MA: Harvard University Press.
A discussion of scientific and practical issues surrounding day-care by a researcher with considerable experience in the area.

Fields, M. V. (1999). *Let's begin reading right: A developmental approach to emergent literacy* (4th ed.). Upper Saddle River, NJ: Prentice Hall.
The author discusses how children learn to read and write and how parents and teachers support the process.

Goelman, H., & Jacobs, E. V. (Eds.) (1994). *Children's play in child care settings.* Albany, NY: State University of New York Press.
The chapters in this book discuss how child-care environments influence children's play and provide ideas that early childhood educators can use to design programs for children, including those with special needs.

Greenfield, P. M. (1984). *Mind and media: The effects of television, video games, and computers.* Cambridge, MA: Harvard University Press.
The author shows how various media can be used to enhance children's learning and to promote social development.

Singer, J. (1981). *Television, imagination, and aggression: A study of preschoolers.* Mahwah, NJ: Lawrence Erlbaum.
This book reviews the results of research into the effects of television on young children.

Trelease, J. (1995). *The read-aloud handbook* (4th ed.). New York: Viking Penguin.
This book discusses how being read to affects children's development and includes a bibliography of suggested stories and books for reading aloud to children of various ages.

Trotter, R. J. (1987, December). Project day-care. *Psychology Today,* 32–38.
The author interviews Ed Zigler, a psychologist who helped begin Project Head Start, about possible solutions to the child-care crisis facing U.S. parents.

Wallerstein, J. S., & Kelly, J. B. (1996). *Surviving the breakup: How children and parents cope with divorce.* New York: HarperCollins.
A discussion based on findings from the Children of Divorce Project, written for general readers.

Answer Key

Answers to Key Terms: 1.c, 2.b, 3.f, 4.e, 5.i, 6.h, 7.a, 8.d, 9.g.

Answers to Multiple-Choice Questions: 1.b, 2.c, 3.d, 4.d, 5.a, 6.d, 7.d, 8.b, 9.b, 10.a, 11.c, 12.b, 13.a, 14.c, 15.c, 16.a, 17.a, 18.d.

Cognitive and Biological Attainments of Middle Childhood

chapter 12

Between 5 and 7 years of age, children change in a number of ways. Their bodies and facial features become more streamlined and their smiles show gaps and permanent teeth coming in. Less visible changes in their brains support more graceful movements and more efficient thinking. They are entering the developmental period called middle childhood.

During middle childhood, children's height, weight, and strength increase steadily. These changes are matched by new cognitive abilities and increasing competence in the many social contexts to which they have been exposed since the end of infancy. Already skilled speakers of their language, these older children can follow complex directions and, when assigned tasks, can perform them without constant adult supervision. They are better at remembering things and their thinking is more consistently logical than it was during their preschool years.

A reflection of children's new abilities is that adults now send them to be educated in schools or assign them economically important work to do. These new activities, in turn, stimulate further cognitive and social development. The behavioral changes of middle childhood can be understood more clearly when they are considered in terms of the many contexts in which development takes place.

Learning Objectives

Keep these questions in mind as you study Chapter 12.

1. What characteristics of children's behavior during middle childhood lead adults to assign them greater responsibilities?
2. How do children's bodies change during the years of middle childhood? What factors affect their growth?
3. In what ways are changes in the structure and function of children's brains associated with their increased abilities?
4. How, according to Piaget, is children's thinking different than it was during early childhood? Is this new way of thinking universal across cultures?
5. What roles do increases in individual cognitive abilities (such as memory, the use of strategies, and knowledge about one's own thought processes) play in helping children develop more powerful ways of thinking?

Chapter Summary

In many cultures the first loss of baby teeth marks the beginning of middle childhood. It seems to be universal among cultures that when children are between 5 and 7 years old, adults begin to expect them to take on new responsibilities. Now, they can work independently, formulate goals, and resist the temptation to abandon their goals.

During middle childhood, children's activities take them farther away from home. As discussed in the box "Out and About on Your Own," there is need for them to use "wayfinding skills" in order to safely make it to school or a friend's house and back home again.

I. BIOLOGICAL DEVELOPMENTS

During middle childhood, children can do more than before, partly because they are bigger, stronger, and have more endurance.

A. Patterns of Growth

Between 6 years of age and the beginning of adolescence, children grow significantly, though more slowly than they did earlier. They increase in height from about 45 inches to about 60 inches and in weight from about 45 pounds to 90 pounds. Genetic and environmental factors interact to influence how much growth they experience.

- Both genetic and environmental factors contribute to height differences among children. Monozygotic twins resemble one another in height more than dizygotic twins, showing the influence of heredity. The effect of environment is illustrated by examples in which children move from one environment to another. For example, when the height of Mayan American children was compared with that of Mayan children living in Guatemala, Barry Bogin and his colleagues found that the Mayan American children were 4½ inches taller, on average. In some countries (Guatemala, for example), nutrition and health care have important effects on growth; in such cases, there is a large gap in size between children from well-off families and those from poor families. In places where nutrition is uniformly adequate, the size gap is smaller. Illness also slows children's growth; however, the deficit is quickly made up as long as nutrition is adequate.
- Body weight is also influenced both by heredity and by environment. In the United States, childhood obesity, which can lead to health problems and social discrimination, is a growing problem, as discussed in the box "Obesity: A Childhood Epidemic." Currently, about 15% of 6- to 11-year-olds in the United States are considered to be obese.

B. Motor Development

Motor skills, coordination, and agility increase during middle childhood. Advanced motor skills such as kicking and throwing require practice, as well as physical maturation in order to develop. Boys are more advanced in activities that require power and force; girls are better at fine motor skills or activities that combine movement with balance. Sex differences in motor skills become more pronounced over the course of middle childhood; they are due partly to physical differences but also partly to products of cultural expectations.

C. Brain Development

Children's brains undergo changes between the ages of 6 and 8: myelination, particularly in the frontal cortex, continues; synaptic pruning continues, accompanied by more stable connections among remaining neurons; children's electroencephalograms (EEGs) reveal a shift from a predominance of theta activity (characteristic of sleep in adults) to a predominance of alpha activity (characteristic of engaged attention); and there is an increase in *EEG coherence,* the synchronization of electrical activity in different areas of the brain. Robert Thatcher has pointed out the importance of increases in coordination between the electrical activity of the brain's frontal lobes and that of other brain areas. There is some evidence that children's patterns of brain activity are related to their performance on problem-solving tasks. For example, it was found that children who succeeded on a standard Piagetian task had a different pattern of brain activity than those who failed the task. However, because the evidence is correlational, it is difficult to be certain whether changes in children's brains are causing the changes in their behavior; alternatively, it is possible that changes in children's experiences contribute to the changes in their brains.

II. COGNITIVE DEVELOPMENTS: BRIDGING THE ISLANDS OF COMPETENCE

Developmentalists are interested in how the "islands of competence" that characterize early childhood are bridged so as to allow children to participate in more complex tasks in a greater range of contexts. One mechanism that has been proposed is improvement in children's working memory, allowing them to hold more characteristics of a situation in mind while thinking about it.

A. Piaget's Bridge: A Change in Logical Thinking

According to Piaget, the new behaviors that accompany middle childhood represent a new form of thought. *Concrete operations* are coordinated mental actions that fit into a logical system in a way that creates greater unity of thinking. Children's thinking is now more flexible; when solving problems, they can consider alternatives and even reverse their steps. The characteristics of concrete operational thought are outlined in Table 12.1.

- *Conservation* of quantity refers to children's understanding that the amount of something remains constant even when physical appearance changes, for example, when the level of water rises as the water is poured into a taller, thinner glass. Most 3- and 4-year-olds are misled by changes in physical appearance because they focus their attention on only one aspect of a stimulus, such as the height of the water; this is an example of "centering," as discussed in Chapter 9. When children become able to conserve liquid quantity, they understand that, logically, the quantity of water must remain the same even though it appears different. They justify their insistence that "there is still the same amount of water" with one of the following arguments: *identity,* "nothing was added so they are still equal"; *compensation,* "the new glass is taller but it is also thinner"; and negation or *reversibility,* "if you pour the water back into the original glass, it will reach the same level as before."

- The conservation of number task tests children's understanding that, when a one-to-one correspondence has been set up between two rows of objects, rearrangement of one of the rows does not change the number—the rows are still equal. Applying concrete operations to the number conservation task requires the task to argue that the number remains the same because, logically, "it has to be that way"; this is Piaget's main criterion for a stage-like change in thinking. The box "What's So Funny? Humor as a Window on Cognitive Development" shows how changes in children's level of reasoning also changes what types of jokes they think are funny.

B. Information Processing Bridges Between Islands of Competence

Most developmentalists agree with Piaget's description of the two-sidedness of children's thinking during middle childhood. However, they take different approaches to explaining how children's thinking develops this two-sidedness.

- According to many developmentalists, it is an increase in memory abilities that allows children to consider two or more aspects of a problem at once. Four factors seem to account for increased memory performance during middle childhood: brain-related increases in speed of memory processing and memory capacity; increase in knowledge about the things one is trying to remember; acquisition of more effective strategies for remembering; and an improved ability to think about one's own memory processes.

  Children are able to hold more information in memory. *Memory span*—the number of randomly presented items children can repeat immediately—increases from early childhood into adolescence; older children are able to process information more rapidly and make more efficient use of their memory capacity. Cross-cultural work supports this view. For example, it takes young children more time to encode longer items in memory; therefore, the words for numbers being shorter in Chinese than in English, Chinese children can recall more digits than their American age-mates, as discovered by Chuansheng Chen and Harold Stevenson. However, when memory capacity is measured using lists of words that are equally long in Chinese and in English, the researchers found no differences in memory capacity.

  Robert Kail and his colleagues found that 11-year-old children could retrieve information from long-term memory about six times faster than 4- and 5-year-olds could. Therefore, they can execute more cognitive operations in the same amount of time, allowing greater intellectual effectiveness.

  Older children generally have a greater *knowledge base* and, therefore, better-elaborated concepts to draw on when they need to remember things relating to a particular topic. For example, Micheline Chi found that 10-year-old children who are expert chess players remembered positions on a chess board better than college students did, though they were not as good at remembering random numbers.

While 1½- to 2-year-old children have been observed using simple tactics to help them remember, during middle childhood children become better able to make use of memory *strategies,* deliberate actions that help them to remember. Studies by John Flavell and his colleagues have demonstrated that 10-year-old children are more likely than 5-year-olds to use *rehearsal* in order to remember information. Other research results indicate that even kindergarten children are capable of using rehearsal; this suggests that what occurs during middle childhood is an increase in the effectiveness of strategy use. *Memory organization* also changes during middle childhood. For example, older children are more likely to link words to be remembered according to category (animal, color, etc.), whereas younger children may use sound features, such as rhyme ("cat" and "sat" for example). Children who do not spontaneously use rehearsal or organizing strategies improve their performance when they are taught the techniques. *Elaboration*—making connections between items to be remembered—is another strategy that begins to occur spontaneously during middle childhood and that is used more frequently as children get older.

Seven- and 8-year-olds know more about their own memory processes (*metamemory*) than younger children and are therefore more likely to correctly estimate how much effort will be required to remember particular items. They do not always apply their knowledge, however. William Fabricus and John Hagen created a task in which 6- and 7-year-old children used an organizational strategy on some trials and not on others; when they used the strategy, they usually remembered better. The researchers found that children who recognized the usefulness of the strategy were more likely to use it in a future session (99 percent compared to only 32 percent of the children who did not attribute their improved remembering to using the strategy).

- How do changes in memory result in changes in logical reasoning? Robbie Case and his colleagues believe that it is the increase in working memory capacity that allows children to think more logically. Their work on children's understanding of the domain of number showed that there was little difference between the performance of 6-year-olds and that of older children when questions could be answered by referring to only one "mental number line"; however, if two mental number lines needed to be coordinated, the 6-year-olds' performance deteriorated to a greater degree than that of 8- or 10-year-olds.

  Andreas Demetriou and his colleagues found that speed of processing, working memory, and logical problem solving build upon each other; this provides evidence of a link between general capacities and stagelike changes in more specific cognitive domains.

C. Cognitive Development as the Evolution of Strategies

Both Piagetians and developmentalists who seek to account for changes in logical thinking in terms of changes in memory view development in terms of discontinuous, stagelike changes. However, as discussed in Chapter 9, some developmentalists working in the information-processing tradition, Robert Siegler for example, characterize development as a gradual shift in the kinds of reasoning strategies children use. Siegler and his colleague

Kenneth Crowley studied strategy use in the game of tic-tac-toe. The 6- to 9-year-olds they studied could all use multiple strategies, but the mix of strategies they used changed with age. In common with the findings of theorists favoring stagelike changes, Siegler found that the advanced strategies used by children involved the same two-sidedness that is thought to be characteristic of middle childhood.

D. Additional Cognitive Bridging Mechanisms

In order to carry out the everyday activities children's are expected to perform during middle childhood, they need to be able to pay attention to a task, make plans for handling the task, and have some knowledge of their own thinking processes. Coding their experiences in language provides them with a large store of organized, retrievable knowledge.

- Infants attend to events that capture their notice and then habituate to them. During early and middle childhood, the quality and length of children's attention increases steadily. Children's ability to direct their attention also increases. For example, Elaine Vurpillot, in a study of 3- to 10-year-olds, found that older children's visual search strategies were more systematic than those of younger children. Other research has shown that, during early and middle childhood, children also acquire the ability to ignore distractions and gain voluntary control over what to pay attention to.

  The ability to formulate a *plan*—that is, a cognitive representation of the actions needed to achieve a goal—is another aspect of thinking that improves during middle childhood. William Gardner and Barbara Rogoff, in a study using a maze-solving task, found that when children were instructed that accuracy was the most important consideration, 7- to 10-year-olds planned all their moves ahead of time, while 4- to 6-year-olds planned only a portion of the route. When children were told that speed and accuracy were both important, children in both age groups planned only a portion of the route. Research on the "Tower of Hanoi" problem shows that, as when solving mazes, older children show greater ability to plan their solutions ahead of time compared to younger children.
- *Metacognition*—the ability to think about one's own thought processes—allows people to assess the difficulty of a problem and choose solution strategies accordingly. By 4 or 5 years of age, children begin to be able to explain what they are doing when they solve a problem; however, under more ordinary circumstances—that is, when not engaged in solving problems—they may not be aware of what they have been thinking about. John Flavell and his colleagues found that 5-year-olds did not report that they had been thinking about an unusual occurrence that they had just witnessed; on the other hand, two out of three 7- to 8-year-olds reported thinking about the event.
- Children's language capacities increase markedly during middle childhood. Vocabulary increases from the 10,000 words understood by 6- to 7-year-olds to approximately 40,000 words by the time children reach 10 to 11 years of age. As children learn more about the categories to which things belong, this knowledge is incorporated into their vocabularies; as they grow older they become better able to understand the hierarchical structure of categories, including subordinate-superordinate relations ("Are there more

brown beads or more beads?"). Another change in children's categorizing is the ability to organize a collection of objects, such as baseball cards, according to multiple criteria (such as league, team, and position). There are other improvements in language-related skills; for example, children become better able to keep a coherent conversation going and to take into account the knowledge or perspective of their conversational partner.

E. The Role of Social and Cultural Contexts

The role of social and cultural contexts in the changes that occur between early and middle childhood are highlighted by cross-cultural research.

- Are the cognitive changes thought to accompany middle childhood universal? Piaget believed that conservation would occur in children from all cultures, although children in some cultures might, due to differences in experience, acquire it sooner than others. Research has found that children in nonindustrial societies achieve concrete operations a year or more later than reported by Piaget; however, in some cases, researchers have found that even adults in certain cultures never seemed to show an understanding of concepts like conservation. It has become evident that unfamiliarity with testing procedures is partly responsible for these results. For example, Pierre Dasen and his colleagues found that rural Australian aboriginal children and Canadian Inuit children showed greater understanding of conservation after being familiarized with a similar task in a brief training session. Children participating in cross-cultural studies also perform better on conservation tasks when tested in their native languages. In one study, Raphael Nyiti found that Micmac Indian children in Nova Scotia performed less well on a conservation task than children of European descent when tested in English, but equally well when tested in Micmac. Apparently, concrete operations are an achievement of middle childhood for children in all cultures. However, cultural differences may influence children's performance on the specific tasks used to assess these skills.
- Cross-cultural studies show that the development of memory skills during middle childhood is subject to cultural variations. For example, Michael Cole and his colleagues found that, unless they had attended schools, tribal children in rural Liberia did not demonstrate the steady increase in free recall performance characteristic of U.S. children during middle childhood. Educated Liberian children, like their U.S. counterparts, learned the stimulus list quickly and made use of categories within the list (clothing, food, etc.) in recalling the items. The non-schooled Liberians, however, learned the list easily when the items were presented, not randomly, but as part of a story. Items were clustered in recall according to their roles in the story. Similar results have been obtained with Guatemalan children from a Mayan village. Remembering, like concrete operational thought, is used by people in all societies. However, specific forms of remembering—those most often studied by psychologists—are not universal, but are associated with formal schooling.
- A study of Navajo and European American children by Shari Ellis and Bonnie Schneiders revealed that the Navajo children spent nearly 10 times as long planning their way through a maze and made far fewer errors. This was of interest to the researchers be-

cause the two cultures differ in the emphasis on doing things speedily; while Americans of European ancestry tend to consider speed of mental performance to be a sign of intelligence, the Navajo place greater emphasis on doing things thoughtfully.

III. RECONSIDERING THE COGNITIVE CHANGES IN MIDDLE CHILDHOOD

During middle childhood, specific physical abilities and cognitive processes become more systematic and can be applied in a larger range of settings; however, it is the totality of these changes that leads adults to begin treating children differently at this time. Cross-cultural findings demonstrate the importance of the culturally organized environment in the changes that occur during middle childhood. The next two chapters will examine children's behavior in two important social contexts: classrooms and peer groups.

Key Terms

Following are important terms introduced in Chapter 12. Match each term with the letter of the example that best illustrates the term.

1. ______ compensation
2. ______ concrete operations
3. ______ conservation
4. ______ EEG coherence
5. ______ elaboration
6. ______ identity
7. ______ memory organization
8. ______ memory span
9. ______ metacognition
10. ______ metamemory
11. ______ plan
12. ______ rehearsal
13. ______ reversibility
14. ______ strategy

a. In answering a question about conservation, a child points out that two lumps of clay were the same weight to begin with and that nothing has been added or removed; therefore, they must still be equal although they now look different.
b. When asked if two lists of words are equally difficult to learn, a boy says that it will take longer for him to learn the longer list.
c. Understanding that objects' basic physical properties, such as weight, volume, and quantity, remain the same despite changes in appearance.
d. When applied to memory, this is a deliberate procedure that helps people remember things more effectively; for example, tying strings on their fingers or writing themselves notes.

e. A child realizes that the transformation performed in a conservation task can be undone; for example, by pouring the water back into the original container.
f. Ways of transforming information (combining, separating, etc.) that fit into a logical system.
g. A 10-year-old gets a phone number from "directory assistance" but has no pencil to write it down; she keeps it in memory by repeating it to herself over and over.
h. A boy notices that, when liquid is poured into another container, the greater height of the second glass is balanced by a decrease in width.
i. Children take advantage of internal structure in remembering a list of words, grouping the mammals together, the flowers together, and the fish together.
j. In a memory task, this occurs when a child notices and makes connections between some of the items to be remembered.
k. Children do this when they form cognitive representations of what they need to do to achieve a goal.
l. This is evidence that activity of the frontal lobes is coordinated with activity of other brain areas.
m. This increases from early childhood into adolescence.
n. An example of this is being able to judge the difficulty of solving a particular problem.

Multiple-Choice Practice Questions

Circle the letter of the word or phrase that correctly completes each statement.

1. Which shows the effect of the environment on growth during middle childhood?
   a. Monozygotic twins resemble one another more than dizygotic twins.
   b. Children of Mayan descent who live in the United States are taller than those living in Guatemala.
   c. The weights of adopted children are correlated with the weights of their biological parents.
   d. All of the above.

2. When children are between the ages of 6 and 8, their brains
   a. become more myelinated, especially in the frontal lobes.
   b. achieve greater EEG coherence.
   c. shift their electrical activity toward a greater preponderance of alpha waves.
   d. all of the above.

3. A child who, in correctly answering a question about conservation of liquid quantity, says, "They're still the same because, even though the level now looks higher, the second container is skinnier" is justifying her answer in terms of
   a. negation.
   b. reversibility.
   c. identity.
   d. compensation.

4. With respect to the development of motor skills during middle childhood, boys are generally more advanced than girls in
   a. fine motor skills.
   b. skills requiring power and force.
   c. skills involving balance and foot movement.
   d. all of the above.

5. Studies suggest that children's ability to find their way independently from one place to another
   a. is fully developed by about 6 years of age.
   b. improves rapidly between the ages of 6 and 12.
   c. does not develop until 12 years of age.
   d. is not age-related.

6. One reason for preschoolers' problems on conservation tasks is that they focus their attention on
   a. only one aspect of the stimulus situation.
   b. two aspects of the stimulus at the same time.
   c. other stimuli besides the ones presented.
   d. their own actions with respect to the stimuli.

7. Some of the increase in memory performance during middle childhood can be attributed to
   a. more efficient use of memory capacity.
   b. increased use of strategies such as rehearsal.
   c. an increasing knowledge base.
   d. all of the above.

8. Metamemory refers to a person's
   a. knowledge about the process of remembering.
   b. knowledge relating to the information being recalled.
   c. memory capacity.
   d. use of strategies to aid in remembering.

9. When children are using concrete operations, their answers on the conservation of number task are based on
   a. what must logically be true.
   b. the physical appearance of the stimulus display.
   c. what they wish to be correct.
   d. what the experimenter tells them is correct.

10. Schooled people have an advantage over unschooled people on which aspect of memory performance?
    a. memory capacity
    b. tasks using randomly presented items
    c. remembering stories
    d. none of these

11. What is the relationship between children's memory and their knowledge base?
    a. The greater the knowledge base children have about a topic, the better their performance on a topic-related memory task.
    b. If children have a large knowledge base on one topic, their performance is improved on tasks related to other topics as well.
    c. Knowledge base affects the memory performance of adults but not that of children.
    d. Knowledge base has no effect on children's memory performance.

12. During middle childhood, children are most likely to organize a collection of stamps in which of the following ways?
    a. Placing them in one large, undivided pile.
    b. Separating U.S. stamps into one pile and putting all other stamps in a second pile.
    c. Separating all the stamps into different piles according to country.
    d. Separating stamps according to country and, within countries, separating them according to subjects depicted (birds, people, etc.).

13. Researchers have found that teaching 4- and 5-year-olds to rehearse material they are asked to remember
    a. has no effect on their memory performance.
    b. is generally not possible.
    c. makes their memory performance more similar to that of older children.
    d. improves the memory performance of only those children who spontaneously use rehearsal.

14. Gardner and Rogoff found that age-related differences in performance on a maze-navigation task could be attributed to
    a. changes in knowledge base
    b. strategies used by teachers
    c. planning
    d. sex differences

15. In a study comparing the performance of Navajo and Euro-American children on a maze-solving task, Shari Ellis and Bonnie Schneiders found that
    a. Euro-American children solved the maze more quickly and with fewer errors than Navajo children did.
    b. Navajo children took much longer than Euro-American children to plan their route through the maze.
    c. Euro-American children made more errors on the maze than Navajo children did.
    d. both b and c are true.

16. By the time they are ________ years of age, children begin to be able to explain what they are doing when solving a problem such as determining whether two pictures are the same or different.
    a. 2 or 3
    b. 4 or 5
    c. 7 or 8
    d. 10 or 12

17. Barker and Wright found that 7-year-olds such as Raymond Birch were able to carry out which of the following?
    a. playing outdoors unsupervised
    b. taking care when crossing streets
    c. getting ready for school on his own
    d. all of the above

18. During middle childhood, adults give children increased freedom and responsibility
    a. in cultures all over the world.
    b. only in the United States and Western Europe.
    c. only in nonindustrialized cultures.
    d. only in cultures that value formal schooling.

Short-Answer Practice Questions

1. Why is it difficult to determine the extent to which biological development during middle childhood causes the changes in behavior that characterize this period? Give examples.

2. What are the characteristics of concrete operational thought, according to Piaget? What changes in their social relations become possible as a result of this new way of thinking?

3. What important changes take place in children's memory performance during middle childhood? How are these changes affected by cultural context?

4. What cultural factors affect the age at which children attain concrete operational thought in a particular content area? What aspects of task presentation are important?

5. What improvements take place during middle childhood in children's ability to plan ahead? How might these be related to changes in their ability to find their way from one place to another, as discussed in the chapter?

Putting It All Together

As children grow older, they learn more and more about the world. One thing they learn is that certain properties of people and objects remain the same despite changes in the way they look. Using examples, show how this knowledge develops in various ways during infancy, the preschool period, and middle childhood.

Sources of More Information

Cole, M., & Scribner, S. (1974). *Culture and thought.* New York: Wiley.
This book describes studies of cognitive development carried out in Liberia.

Elkind, D. (1981). *Children and adolescents: Interpretive essays on Jean Piaget* (3rd ed.). New York: Oxford University Press.
This book of essays was inspired by Piaget's theory of cognitive development.

Inhelder, B., & Piaget, J. (1969). *The early growth of logic in the child: Classification and Seriation.* New York: Norton.
The authors discuss their work on the development of children's skills in logical classification.

Kail, R. (1990). *The development of memory in children* (3rd ed.). New York: Freeman.
The author takes up important topics such as use of strategies, metamemory, and the role of knowledge base in memory.

Rogoff, B., & Lave, J. (Eds.). (1999). *Everyday cognition: Its development in social context.* Cambridge, MA: Harvard University Press.
This is a collection of essays by psychologists and other social scientists on the effect of context on the process of cognitive development.

Rogoff, B., & Chavajay, P. (1995). What's become of research on the cultural basis of cognitive development? *American Psychologist, 50*(10), 859–877.
This article discusses the transition that has occurred in research on culture and cognition from comparative cross-cultural studies to research on thinking in sociocultural activities.

Scribner, S., Tobach, E. (Ed.), Falmagne, R. (Ed.), Parlee, M. (Ed.), et al. (1997). *Mind and social practice: Selected writings of Sylvia Scribner.* New York: Cambridge University Press.
This is a collection of writings by one of the psychologists who has been instrumental in shaping the emerging field of cultural psychology.

Serpell, R. (1982). Measures of perception, skills and intelligence: The growth of a new perspective on children in a third world country. In W. Hartup (Ed.), *Review of child development research.* Chicago: University of Chicago Press.
The author reviews research on cross-cultural variations in perceptual and cognitive tasks and discusses ways that imposing Western cultural interpretations on behavior can be avoided.

Siegler, R., & Ellis, S. (1996). Piaget on childhood. *Psychological Science, 7*(4), 211–215.
The authors describe what they consider to be the important features of Piaget's theory, highlighting the importance of variability in children's thinking as a motivator of cognitive change.

Tanner, J. M. (1990). *Fetus into man: Physical growth from conception to maturity* (Rev. ed.). Cambridge, MA: Harvard University Press.
This is a comprehensive review of normal growth and development.

Answer Key

Answers to Key Terms: 1.h, 2.f, 3.c, 4.l, 5.j, 6.a, 7.i, 8.m, 9.n, 10.b, 11.k, 12.g, 13.e, 14.d.

Answers to Multiple-Choice Questions: 1.b, 2.d, 3.d, 4.b, 5.b, 6.a, 7.d, 8.a, 9.a, 10.b, 11.a, 12.d, 13.c, 14.c, 15.d, 16.b, 17.d, 18.a.

Schooling and Development in Middle Childhood

chapter 13

Throughout the world, middle childhood is a time when children are expected to begin to learn the skills they will need in order to be productive adult members of their societies. In modern, industrialized countries, children of this age spend much of their time in school, learning literacy, mathematics, and other culturally valued knowledge.

When children begin school, they already know a great deal about language and may know the names of the letters of the alphabet, a system that represents each significant sound with a different symbol. They can usually count numbers and objects, using their fingers or other body parts to help keep track of quantity. They are also experienced at making inferences on the basis of partial signs; for example, they know that if the car is not in the driveway, their friend next door may not be at home. In school, children will build on these skills, working within a specialized environment with its own rules and even its own ways of using language.

Many of the cognitive changes associated with middle childhood are not direct results of schooling; however, children who have been to school perform better on tasks that resemble school activities. Schooling has its greatest effect on opportunity: children who are not educated have less chance for later economic success.

Because of the importance of schooling for later success, there has been great interest in tests that will predict school performance, and intelligence tests are now routinely used for that purpose. In fact, psychologists do not agree on what intelligence is, but since tests of intelligence seem primarily to measure aptitude for schooling, they are moderately successful in predicting who will do well and who is likely to have problems. In addition to aptitude, students need environments conducive to learning in order to succeed academically. For many students, a supportive atmosphere at home, in school, and in the neighborhood can make the difference between success and failure.

Learning Objectives

Keep these questions in mind while studying Chapter 13.

1. In what ways does formal schooling differ from other ways of educating children, such as apprenticeships?

2. How do ideas about "top-down" and "bottom-up" processing affect strategies for teaching reading and mathematics?
3. What makes the "language of schooling" different from everyday language?
4. How do these differences affect children's school performance?
5. Which cognitive skills are improved by participating in formal schooling?
6. Why are intelligence tests used for measuring aptitude for schooling? What can be learned from these tests?
7. In what ways do genetic and environmental factors influence children's intelligence?
8. What sorts of things hinder children's ability to learn in school? How may these problems be remedied?

Chapter Summary

Education is important in shaping children's later lives. As shown in Figure 13.1, number of years of schooling is related to the amount of income people earn. Because many children have difficulty in some particular area of learning, the study of learning and development in school contexts is an active area of research for developmentalists.

I. THE CONTEXTS OF LEARNING

Although all children are raised to learn the basic knowledge, beliefs, and skills important in their culture, *education*—the deliberate teaching of specialized knowledge and skills—is not an important activity in all cultures. In hunter-gatherer societies, skills are taught as a part of everyday activity. Once societies become more complex, *apprenticeship,* which combines instruction with productive work, provides training for specialized occupations. In contrast to children taught in schools, apprentices learn through observation and practice, and put their skills to work from the beginning.

The earliest forms of formal *schooling* go back to about 4000 B.C., when young people were brought together to learn systems of writing and arithmetic. Schooling differs from apprenticeship training in several ways: motivation (school knowledge typically cannot be applied immediately); social relations (schoolteachers fill a more specialized role in children's lives); social organization (in school, many children of the same age learn under the supervision of a teacher); and medium of instruction (in school, a specialized type of oral and written instruction is used).

II. LITERACY AND SCHOOLING IN MODERN TIMES

It is only in more recent times, since the industrial revolution, that mandatory schooling and mass literacy have become widespread. At first, only children of the elite received a high level of education; today, many societies expect all children to attain such a level. This can, however, be a challenge to modern educational systems; in fact, many children do not complete the required schooling or do not master the basic skills upon which further learning depends. Because school failure is a political and economic problem as well as a personal one, it is important to understand the processes through which children acquire academic skills in school settings.

A. Acquiring Academic Skills

Instruction in schools throughout the world focuses on learning two basic symbol systems: written language and mathematics. There is some disagreement as to whether it is better to teach these by introducing basic skills first, then moving on to higher-level skills once these are mastered, or whether more complex tasks should be introduced at the earliest stages of instruction in order to hold students' interest.

- Reading is a complex system of coordinated skills and knowledge; the process of learning to read is still not fully understood.

  In "prereading," children begin to realize that the marks they see on paper correspond to elements of spoken language. They must also learn to "see letters"; this important aspect of reading is called *decoding,* the process of learning letter-sound correspondences.

  A first step in learning decoding is *phonemic awareness*—recognizing, for example, that the word "ball" begins with the sound "b." This process does not seem to occur without deliberate instruction; Benita Blachman, among other researchers, has shown that activities designed to enhance phonemic awareness can improve children's reading skills substantially. A difficulty in learning to read English is that there is often not a one-to-one correspondence between letters and sounds. Written letters are pronounced differently in different contexts and it is difficult to isolate individual phonemes, which normally do not occur alone. It is not surprising, therefore, that many children (25%, according to research by Marilyn Adams) who are taught to read using a "decoding first" strategy are unsuccessful.

  Reading requires children to coordinate "top-down" processes (integrating materials with previous knowledge) and "bottom-up" processes (sounding out letters to make words, combining these, etc.). There is disagreement among teachers over how much emphasis should be given to each type of process in early reading instruction—whether to emphasize decoding or use a "whole-language" (comprehension-first) approach.

B. Learning Mathematics

In order to learn mathematics, children must acquire a distinctive set of concepts and also must master a special notation system.

- According to Rochel Gelman and her colleagues, learning arithmetic requires the coordination of *conceptual knowledge* (the ability to understand the principles that underpin a problem); *procedural knowledge* (the ability to carry out a sequence of actions to solve a problem); and *utilization knowledge* (the ability to know when to apply particular procedures). Children must learn to use mathematical knowledge in a variety of contexts. For example, Terezinha Nunes found that Brazilian children working as street vendors easily solved problems in a work-related context but made errors when the same types of problems were presented as strictly mathematical questions.

- In order to learn mathematics, children must first learn to read and write numbers. Once they learn the first 10 digits, they must learn to write larger quantities using the concept of place value; it may take years to master this. As in reading, children must use both bottom-up and top-down processes in order to carry out arithmetic operations correctly.
- Disagreement about the best way to teach mathematics centers on the importance of practicing basic skills versus emphasizing the importance of understanding, and solving real-world problems. Today, it is agreed that drill in computation and practice in generalizing computations to meaningful problems are both important and necessary parts of mathematics instruction; however, achieving a balance between the two is challenging for teachers.

B. The Social Organization of Classroom Instruction

As mentioned earlier in the chapter, the social organization of the classroom—typically one teacher to between 25 and 40 children—is different from forms of enculturation and apprenticeship that occur in other contexts.

- In schools, children usually sit in parallel rows, facing front, while the teacher sits at a desk in front of them. In school, language is used in ways that are different from its typical use in other contexts. *Instructional discourse*—a distinctive way of talking and thinking that is typical in school—provides students with information about the curriculum and with feedback about the correctness of their answers while providing the teacher with information about their progress. A feature of instructional discourse is the *initiation-reply-feedback sequence*; frequently, this takes the form of questions to which the teacher already knows the answer. In the specialized language of school, context does not always help children interpret the teacher's questions and they have to focus on language itself in order to master the information presented.
- Alternative forms of classroom instruction modify the more traditional "recitation script" in the direction of more activity-based, project-oriented approaches in which teachers spend little time working with the class as a whole and most of their time moving among small groups. Alternative forms of instruction have been developed for reading and mathematics. Computers provide another mode of classroom instruction, as discussed in the box "Computers in Schools."

  An example of alternative instruction in reading is *reciprocal teaching,* a method created by Ann Brown and Annmarie Palincsar; it was developed as a way to integrate decoding and comprehension skills. In this approach, a discussion leader initiates an exchange that includes questions about content, summarizing, clarifying, and predicting what will happen next. This approach is an application of Vygotsky's idea of a "zone of proximal development." It allows children to participate in "reading for meaning" even before they have acquired all the component abilities that are ordinarily necessary for reading independently. Studies have shown the procedure to be effective in improving children's reading skills.

  An alternative to teaching mathematics in a "bottom-up" way is "realistic mathematics education," widely used in the Netherlands. Paul Cobb and his colleagues have developed a similar program, which makes use of models and real-world problems. Children are expected to be able to justify the reasoning behind their solutions and understand the reasoning behind other children's solutions. A study by Jo Boaler examined differences between two classrooms in England, one which used a traditional "recitation script" approach to teaching mathematics and the other of which used a "problem-oriented" approach. Students who learned under the traditional format scored better on standardized tests testing knowledge of mathematical procedures; however, students who learned under the problem-oriented approach did better on questions that required them to apply their knowledge to a novel problem.

III. STUDYING THE COGNITIVE CONSEQUENCES OF SCHOOLING

Schooling provides children with large amounts of practice in deliberate remembering and systematic problem solving. In order to specify the contributions of schooling to changes in cognitive function that occur during middle childhood, psychologists compare the performance of children who have attended school with the performance of those who have not.

A. Using the School-Cutoff Strategy

In places where there is a minimum age for beginning school, it is possible to compare children whose birthdays are just before the cutoff date with those who have just missed the cutoff; this is called the *school-cutoff strategy.* Frederick Morrison and his colleagues found that attending first grade increased children's recall ability and their use of active rehearsal; other studies have shown that conservation of number, coherence of storytelling, and number of vocabulary words they understand improve as a consequence of age, rather than as a consequence of schooling.

B. Comparing Schooled and Nonschooled Children

Another method of assessing the cognitive consequences of schooling is to study societies in which schooling is available to only a portion of the population.

- The evidence suggests that schooling does not affect children's attainment of concrete operations. However, as discussed in Chapter 12, school experience may increase children's familiarity with testing procedures, making their performance appear more advanced than that of nonschooled children.
- Schooling appears to be the factor underlying cultural differences on standard memory tests. Children from other cultures who go to school demonstrate memory performance more similar to that of their North American peers than to that of other children in their villages who do not attend school. These differences are most pronounced in cases in which the materials to be remembered are not connected by an everyday script; they disappear when the materials are part of a meaningful setting. No evidence suggests that schooling increases actual memory capacity.
- Schooling seems to influence the degree to which children can reflect on and talk about

their own cognitive processes and explain how they reach solutions to problems. Schooling also affects metalinguistic awareness, children's ability to think about their own language-using skills. For example, Sylvia Scribner and Michael Cole found that, while both educated and uneducated Vai people in Liberia could judge the grammatical correctness of sentences spoken in the Vai language, only the educated people could explain what made some of the sentences ungrammatical.

C. The Second-Generation Impact of Schooling

Schooling also affects children indirectly, through the parenting practices of adults. Robert LeVine and his colleagues found that mothers who have been educated had children with lower rates of infant mortality, better health, and better academic achievement. This could be traced to habits and skills the mothers themselves had learned in school, for example, making use of information from health, education, and social welfare providers and interacting with their children in ways that prepare them for the school setting. In a study of Mayan mothers conducted by Pablo Chavajay and Barbara Rogoff, more educated mothers teaching their children to solve a puzzle gave them instructions, while less educated mothers simply participated with the child. Both methods are effective; however, the one adopted by the more educated mothers is more similar to the kind of learning children will encounter in school.

D. The Evidence in Overview

Schooling does not appear to change in a general way the basic cognitive processes associated with middle childhood. Schooling increases children's knowledge base, teaches them specific information-processing strategies that make them more effective in performing school-related tasks, and changes their attitudes and life situations in ways that are passed on to their own children through their child-rearing practices. One of the most important effect of schooling on children's lives is the opportunity it gives them to command more highly paid jobs which lead to greater economic power and increased social status.

IV. APTITUDE FOR SCHOOLING

For many years, the idea of "intelligence" has influenced discussion of the question of why some children learn more easily in school than others. While all languages have words that describe people's ability to solve problems, the exact meanings of the terms differ across cultures. More traditional societies tend to give equal importance to social and cognitive components of intelligence; in North America and Europe, the cognitive dimension is more important. In North America today, children's scores on intelligence tests influence the kind of education they receive and the kind of work they will do.

A. The Origins of Intelligence Testing

Once mass education became widespread, educators became interested in finding out why some children had difficulty learning in school. In 1904, Alfred Binet and Theodore Simon were commissioned by the French Minister of Public Instruction to develop a screening exam to identify children who needed special instruction. Binet and Simon based their test on the premise that a child who performed at the level of the average 7-year-old on their tasks had a mental age (MA) of 7, regardless of his chronological age. An intelligent child would have a mental age greater than his chronological age, while the MA of a dull child would be less than his chronological age. While Binet and Simon felt that performance on their test was determined by both "nature" and "nurture," they specified no way in which the effects of these factors could be separated.

B. The Legacy of Binet and Simon

Variations of Binet and Simon's test have come into wide use. In the United States, Lewis Terman of Stanford University modified it into the Stanford-Binet Intelligence Scale. David Wechsler developed intelligence tests for use with adults and children. Both the Stanford-Binet and Wechsler tests measure performance on a variety of subscales, which measure abilities such as general information, comprehension, and the ability to solve arithmetic problems. Other tests, such as the Peabody Picture Vocabulary Test and Raven's Progressive Matrices, focus on one type of ability.

The concept *intelligence quotient (IQ),* introduced by William Stern, refers to MA/CA 100 (where MA is a child's mental age and CA is the child's chronological age). So, for example, a 10-year-old with an MA of 11 would have an IQ of 110. A further refinement was the development of the "deviation IQ," based on the fact that the raw IQ scores of a large population form an approximately normal distribution. This makes it possible to compare the scores of children of different ages. The procedure underlying today's IQ tests, like those of the test developed by Binet and Simon, are as follows: create a set of test items on which the performance of children of the same age will vary; order the items in terms of difficulty; and make certain that performance on the test corresponds to school performance.

C. Enduring Questions about Intelligence

The essential properties of intelligence continue to be a matter of debate for developmentalists. There are questions to be answered about how intelligence should be defined, what causes variations in intelligence scores, and why variations in IQ scores predict variations in school performance.

- Intelligence is usually thought of as a general characteristic of people's behavior, and indeed, performances on separate subscales within IQ tests are correlated. However, some scholars feel that a single dimension is inadequate to characterize intelligence; L. L. Thurstone, for example, argued that there are seven "primary mental abilities" and developed the Primary Mental Abilities Test, which has subscales to measure each. Howard Gardner has proposed a theory of "multiple intelligences," including, among others, linguistic, musical, logical-mathematical, and social intelligence. And Robert Sternberg has proposed a "triarchic" theory of intelligence that includes analytic, creative, and practical abilities. IQ tests measure primarily those aptitudes that relate to success in school, and in fact school tasks do differ in systematic ways from those encountered in other settings. Among other differences, school problems are formulated for learners by other people, are clearly defined, have a single correct answer, and come with all the needed information to deal with them. In contrast, in everyday settings, learners have to recognize or formulate problems for themselves and seek new information in order to solve them.

- Along with disagreements about the nature of intelligence, psychologists disagree about the sources of differences in intelligence test scores. The debate is complicated by differences found between the average scores of members of different ethnic groups. According to the *innatist hypothesis of intelligence,* differences in scores are due to inborn variations and cannot be eliminated through training or other environmental manipulations. Beginning in the 1930s and 1940s, this view was balanced by the *environmentalist hypothesis of intelligence,* which views intelligence as greatly influenced by experience. Support for the environmental view comes from data showing that, worldwide, there has been a steady increase in intelligence test scores since the time that testing began.
- Currently, psychologists recognize that both genetic and environmental factors contribute to the intelligence test performance of individuals, just as they contribute to most other characteristics. It is difficult to specify the exact contribution of each for the same reasons detailed in Chapter 2—that it is difficult to specify the genetic and environmental contributions to any human behavior. What psychologists do know is that IQ scores predict, to a moderate degree, children's performance in school. But, because all intelligence tests draw on a background of learning that is culture-specific, comparisons of intelligence between cultural groups are extremely difficult to make. Studies indicate that within-group differences may have a substantial genetic component; however, because of noncomparability of environments, there is no evidence that average score differences between ethnic groups are due to genetic factors. In addition, because heritability is a population statistic—meaning that it applies to groups of people, rather than to individuals—measures of heritability do not tell the percentage of a person's IQ score that is attributable to heredity; instead, they estimate the percentage of variability within a group of people (raised under similar conditions) that is attributable to heredity. Differences in IQ between African American and European American children all but disappear when socioeconomic differences between the groups are taken into account.

V. PERSONAL AND SOCIAL BARRIERS TO SCHOOL SUCCESS

Personal, family, and community influences affect the likelihood of children's success in school.

A. Specific Learning Disabilities

Children with *specific learning disabilities* do poorly in school despite having normal intelligence test scores. How should specific learning disabilities be defined? In the most widely used approach, a specific learning disability is defined by large discrepancies among subscales of an IQ test—for example, high scores on verbal and low scores on quantitative subtests—with corresponding patterns of school performance. Children may have patterns corresponding to dyslexia (difficulty learning to read), dyscalculia (difficulty with quantitative tasks), or dysgraphia (difficulty learning to write). Dyslexia is the most frequently encountered learning disability. While there are several reasons why dyslexic children may have trouble reading, difficulties with phonological processing is among the most important. Phonological processing can be tested using "pseudowords." Linda Siegel and her colleagues found that, by 9 years of age, normal readers were proficient in reading pseudowords; disabled readers, on the other hand, were no better at 14 years of age than normal readers were at 7. Dyslexia is assumed to involve some kind of anomaly in brain development, but specific difficulties in reading have not been linked to abnormalities in specific areas of the brain. Paula Tallal and her colleagues discovered the possibility that, at least for those dyslexic children with oral-language impairment, there is a difference in the part of the brain that is active when children are, for example, asked to identify rhyming and nonrhyming letter names; this is the part of the auditory cortex specialized for language. They may have difficulty in processing stimuli that presented rapidly, in any sensory modality. Tallal has developed computer games to help language impaired children practice making discriminations among rapidly presented speech sounds; children who are not language delayed often are assigned to remedial programs focusing on improving phonemic awareness.

B. Motivation to Learn

An aspect of formal schooling is that children need to pay attention and try hard even though the material may be uninteresting, or difficult; they must also cope with the fact that they will not always be successful. Yet children may lose their *academic motivation*—the ability to persist and try hard at school tasks even in the face of difficulties. There are two patterns of motivation displayed by children that become prominent once they enter school: a "mastery orientation," in which they are motivated to learn, to try hard, and a "performance motivation," in which children are motivated by their level of performance, ability, and incentives for trying. Those with a mastery orientation tend to do better in the long run; those with a performance orientation may become discouraged when they fail at a task, and may give up trying altogether. Interestingly, Carol Dweck and her colleagues found that these patterns are not related to IQ scores or to academic achievement. But these different motivational patterns relate to children's conceptions of ability. While even 2½-year-olds can become discouraged and unmotivated after failure of their problem-solving attempts, it is during formal schooling that children are directly compared with one another through grading practices. During elementary school, children begin increasingly to view ability as a fixed characteristic of people. Some children have an "entity" model of intelligence (everyone has a fixed amount); others have an "incremental" model (intelligence grows as one learns and has more experiences). Some children believe that success depends on ability; others believe that it depends more on effort and that, by expending effort, one can develop greater intelligence. Not surprisingly, children who adopt an entity model tend to have a performance orientation, while those who adopt an incremental model tend to have a mastery orientation. This becomes important once children make the transition from elementary to middle school. Children who believe that intelligence is a fixed entity may believe that they fail because of lack of ability; they may develop a helpless motivational pattern and avoid situations that put them at risk of failure. One way of avoiding this problem is for teachers to provide feedback in ways that foster a mastery orientation; another way is to retrain children themselves, so that they attribute failure to lack of effort rather than lack of ability.

C. Mismatches between Home and School Cultures

Cultural and economic circumstances also structure children's experience of schooling. For example, as described in the box "Comparing Mathematics Instruction across Cultures," differences in mathematics achievement among U.S. schoolchildren and their counterparts in other countries, for example, Japan and China, reflect variations in classroom practices that are deeply rooted in their respective cultures.

It has been suggested that each culture has a particular *cultural style,* a dominant way of thinking about and relating to the world that comes from a people's common historical experience; for example, some cultures place more emphasis on fostering independence (an individualistic orientation), while others consider interdependence a more important value (a collectivist orientation). Patricia Greenfield and her colleagues believe that children from cultures that value interdependence may be at a disadvantage in U.S. schools. Other researchers point out that children from cultures valuing interdependence—for example, Southeast Asian cultures—are often quite successful in school, perhaps because their parents are supportive and committed to education.

There are other dimensions along which to define cultural style. Wade Boykin conducted studies in which African American children were given stories to remember and problems to solve under conditions that allowed them to run, jump, and dance; other children were given the same materials in a more "school-like" setting. The children who were allowed to express themselves physically outperformed those in the other group. According to Boykin, this reflects the importance of expressive movement as part of the everyday communicative behavior of African Americans.

Clearly, cultural values and modes of behaviors are important influences on children's success in school; however, there is no one "right way" to incorporate these factors into classroom activities.

- Shirley Heath has studied the way oral and written language in the home differs from that associated with school success. She found that one of the groups she studied—children of European American teachers—performed better in school that children from the other groups—children of European American textile workers and African Americans with farming and textile jobs. The relative success of the three groups was correlated with the degree to which the language they were exposed to in the home matched the way language was used in school settings.

D. Schooling in a Second Language

Some schoolchildren, especially recent immigrants, have not mastered the language in which school instruction takes place. School districts, acting in accordance with a 1974

Supreme Court ruling, attempt to remedy this situation by giving children a variety of types of special help. There is disagreement as to what form this help should, ideally, take. Some believe that children should be "immersed" in English quickly, so that they can begin to participate in all aspects of the curriculum as soon as possible; others feel that children should receive a firm grounding in literacy and numeracy in their native language ("bilingual education") before moving on to courses taught exclusively in English. It has not been possible to conduct true experiments to settle this issue, so investigators have had to do "quasi-experiments" using naturally occurring differences in language programs. After reviewing 72 studies, Christine Rossell and Keith Baker concluded that there was no evidence that bilingual education was superior to English immersion. Stephen Krashen, on the other hand, has argued that the studies providing the best evidence show bilingual programs to be more effective; this conclusion was also reached by a panel of the National Research Council. According to Krashen, an effective environment for immigrant children to learn English includes: easy-to-understand lessons in English; teachers who have command of their subject matter and can teach in the child's language when appropriate; literacy development in the child's native language; and continued development in the child's native language for cognitive and economic advantages. It is also necessary to give the process sufficient time, according to Kenji Hakuta; while minority-language children usually are reasonably fluent in English with 2 or 3 years, they may need as many as 4 to 5 years to master the language skills they will need for academic success. A major obstacle to successfully implementing bilingual programs is a shortage of bilingual teachers, especially in places in which many different languages are spoken in the same school.

VI. CULTURALLY RESPONSIVE CLASSROOM STRATEGIES

Schools are important contexts for development during middle childhood; however, they are also problematic contexts for children whose home cultures differ from that of the school. Studies conducted in diverse cultures demonstrate that teachers who make their classroom procedures congruent with the cultural practices of their students can help their students to be more successful. For example, in one influential example of a culturally responsive approach to teaching, an expert teacher of the Odawa Indian tribe in Canada, while following the usual recitation-script approach used in schools, employed language and feedback in ways that were consistent with Odawa cultural practices. In another example, Carol Lee drew upon African American students' familiarity with the linguistic form called "signifying" to promote higher levels of literary understanding and interpretation. Of course, culturally specific strategies are likely to be most applicable in culturally homogenous classrooms.

A. Neighborhoods Matter

The neighborhoods children come from also have an impact on their academic achievement. In a "natural experiment" in Chicago, mainly African American families living in high-rise housing projects had the opportunity to move to other housing; they were assigned either to middle-class suburban neighborhoods or to other urban neighborhoods. When researchers compared the academic performance of children of the two groups, they found that the children who had been relocated to the suburbs did better academically, had lower dropout rates, and higher college attendance compared with the children who remained in the city.

VII. OUTSIDE THE SCHOOL

Although schooling is an important part of middle childhood, it does not represent all of children's lives. Chapter 14 examines the characteristics of children's peer groups and the effects of peer interaction on development.

Key Terms

Following are important terms introduced in Chapter 13. Match the term with the letter of the example that best illustrates the term.

1. ______ academic motivation
2. ______ apprenticeship
3. ______ conceptual knowledge
4. ______ cultural style
5. ______ decoding
6. ______ education
7. ______ environmentalist hypothesis of intelligence
8. ______ initiation-reply-feedback sequence
9. ______ innatist hypothesis of intelligence
10. ______ instructional discourse
11. ______ intelligence quotient (IQ)
12. ______ mental age (MA)
13. ______ phonemic awareness
14. ______ procedural knowledge
15. ______ reciprocal teaching
16. ______ schooling
17. ______ school-cutoff strategy
18. ______ specific learning disabilities
19. ______ utilization knowledge

a. A kind of verbal exchange frequent in schools, in which a teacher asks a question, a student answers, and the teacher provides feedback.
b. This would be equal to 8 for a child who can answer questions on an intelligence test as well as the average 8-year-old.
c. These are characterized by large differences among the subscales on IQ tests.
d. This helps keep children working in school even when things are going badly.
e. This is an application of Vygotsky's idea of a "zone of proximal development."
f. This form of deliberate teaching is not characteristic of hunter-gatherer societies.
g. A kind of language used in schools that varies in important ways from everyday language.
h. A child knows that, to determine how many more candies Amy has than he has, he should subtract his number of candies from hers.
i. According to this idea, one would expect people's intelligence scores to be more highly similar the more closely related they are.
j In this kind of job training, the participant often lives in the master's house.
k. When applied to inversion, an example is knowing that, if you add three cards to your pile and put three cards back, you will have the same number you started with.
l. A number used to compare the intelligence of different people.
m. An example is realizing that the word "cat" begins with /c/.
n. This idea is supported by evidence that IQ scores have been improving over the years.
o. Knowing, for example, how to add two numbers to get their sum.
p. This is one way to assess the effects of formal education on cognitive development.
q. Learning this is the major task of beginning readers.
r. A form of education with characteristic forms of motivation, social relations, and social organization.
s. Examples of this are "individualistic" and "collectivist."

Multiple-Choice Practice Questions

Circle the letter of the word or phrase that correctly completes each statement.

1. In which way is apprenticeship training different from formal schooling?
   a. In apprenticeship training, relatively little explicit instruction is given.
   b. In apprenticeship training, knowledge is immediately put to practical use.
   c. The shop in which an apprentice works is likely to contain people of diverse ages and skill levels.
   d. All of the above.

2. The symbols in the alphabet represent
   a. phonemes.
   b. morphemes.
   c. basic concepts.
   d. syllables.

3. Computers in schools are
   a. are greatly increasing in number.
   b. are usually connected to the Internet.
   c. both a and b are true.
   d. are able to present lessons as well as a skilled teacher.

4. Which curriculum was specifically developed in order to promote a "zone of proximal development" in reading instruction?
   a. the look-say method
   b. learning letter-sound correspondences
   c. the whole-language approach
   d. reciprocal teaching

5. The school-cutoff strategy allows researchers to investigate
   a. the problem-solving abilities of children who drop out of school.
   b. the effect of schooling on children's cognitive abilities.
   c. differences in IQ among ethnic groups.
   d. the effect of teacher expectations on achievement.

6. Which is an example of instructional discourse?
   a. On the first day of school, the teacher asks a child, "What is your name?"
   b. The teacher asks the class, "Has anyone seen my red pencil?"
   c. After writing a word on the blackboard, the teacher asks, "What does this say?"
   d. All of the above are examples.

7. Schooling affects children's performance on which of the following?
   a. memory for items connected by an everyday script
   b. concrete operations in everyday contexts
   c. ability to describe their mental activities
   d. all of the above

8. A 9-year-old child with a mental age of 10 has an IQ of
   a. 100.
   b. 90.
   c. 119.
   d. 111.

9. Intelligence tests are composed of questions that
   a. are ordered from least to most difficult.
   b. are culture-free.
   c. can be answered equally well by all children of the same age.
   d. are selected to be unrelated to school performance.

10. Studies of heritability of intelligence have shown that
    a. differences in IQ scores within cultural groups is attributable, to some extent, to genetic factors.
    b. differences in IQ scores between cultural groups are largely attributable to genetic factors.
    c. about 50 percent of each person's IQ score is attributable to genetic factors.
    d. all of the above are true.

11. A major problem with bilingual education is that
    a. it results in significantly lower achievement than English immersion.
    b. it is difficult to find a sufficient number of bilingual teachers.
    c. teachers in bilingual programs have low expectations for their students.
    d. all of the above are true.

12. Researchers studying children's academic motivation have found that
    a. children who adopt a mastery orientation are more likely to succeed in the long run.
    b. children who adopt a performance orientation may become discouraged when they fail at a task.
    c. both b and c are true.
    d. children who adopt a mastery orientation tend to be those who are less able to begin with.

13. Which of the following is true of intelligence?
    a. Only modern, industrialized countries describe people's abilities in ways that can be called "intelligence."
    b. The meaning of intelligence is the same in all cultures.
    c. With modern testing methods, intelligence can be measured precisely.
    d. The concept of intelligence is used to explain differences in school performance.

14. Children are demonstrating their _________ knowledge when they correctly solve simple division problems.
    a. procedural
    b. conceptual
    c. utilization
    d. logical

15. Learning to speak "Pig Latin" is helpful to which aspect of learning to read?
    a. decoding
    b. reading for meaning
    c. phonemic awareness
    d. all of the above

16. Nunes and her colleagues found that Brazilian schoolchildren working as street vendors solved mathematical problems
    a. much better in school than they did in work-related contexts.
    b. much better in everyday contexts than as strictly mathematical operations.
    c. equally well in everyday contexts and in school.
    d. only when they were presented as strictly mathematical operations.

17. Differences in mathematics achievement between U.S. children and children in Japan and China are most likely due to
    a. the fact that Asian students spend much more time in school studying mathematics than American students do.
    b. genetic superiority of Asian students in mathematics ability.
    c. the fact that American students use more manipulable objects in learning mathematics.
    d. the fact that Asian classrooms are organized in a more decentralized way.

18. Which pattern of IQ test subscale scores might predict that a child has dyslexia?
    a. low scores on all subscales
    b. low scores on verbal subscales and high scores on quantitative ones
    c. high scores on all subscales
    d. none of these; there is no relation between IQ subscale scores and dyslexia.

Short-Answer Practice Questions

1. Discuss the differences between apprenticeship education and school learning.

2. What differences have been found between the performance of schooled and unschooled children on cognitive tasks?

3. Describe the basic elements of standardized intelligence testing.

4. What evidence is there for the importance of genetic factors in determining children's IQs? What evidence is there for the importance of environmental factors?

5. Discuss the contribution children's families make to their success in school.

6. What role do teachers' expectations play in children's school success?

7. What evidence is there that parents' use of "school language" in the home benefits children's school performance?

8. Make up your own definition of "intelligence." Describe how this type of intelligence might be affected by genetic, environmental, and/or cultural factors.

Putting It All Together

Look back at the information on gene–environment interactions in Chapter 2. On the basis of what you have learned from Chapter 2 and from Chapter 13, discuss why it is difficult to assess the role of genetic factors in intelligence.

Sources of More Information

Baumeister, A. A. (1987). Mental retardation: Some conceptions and dilemmas. *American Psychologist, 42*(8), 796–800.
This discussion of mental retardation touches on some of the issues involved in the use of standardized tests to measure intelligence.

Bissex, G. L. (1985). *Gnys at work: A child learns to write and read.* Cambridge, MA: Harvard University Press.
This case study follows one child from age 5 to age 11 as he learns to read and write.

Copeland, R. (1984). *How children learn mathematics: Teaching implications of Piaget's research* (4th ed.). New York: Macmillan.
This describes a Piagetian approach to the learning of mathematics in the elementary classroom. There are good descriptions of the many numerical concepts children acquire as they learn to manipulate numbers.

Eisenstein, E. L. (1985). On the printing press as an agent of change. In D. Olson, N. Torrance, & A. Hildyard (Eds.), *Literacy, language and learning: The nature and consequences of reading and writing*. New York: Cambridge University Press.
This is a discussion of social change as related to the invention of literacy.

Gardner, H. (1999). *Intelligence reframed: Multiple intelligences for the 21st century.* New York: Basic Books.
This book presents Gardner's theory that every person has a unique set of competencies that together comprise his or her intelligence. Gardner describes how his theory has evolved and been revised since it was first introduced in 1983.

Nichols, R. C. (1975). Schools and the disadvantaged (A summary of the Coleman Report). In U. Bronfenbrenner and M. Mahony (Eds.), *Influences on human development* (2nd ed.). Austin, TX: Holt, Rinehart, & Winston.
A discussion of how the environment of education affects children's academic achievement.

Saxe, G. B. (1999). Selling candy: A study of cognition in context. In M. Cole & Y. Engestroem, et al. (Eds.), *Mind, culture & activity: Seminal papers from the Laboratory of Comparative Human Cognition.* New York: Cambridge University Press.
This book describes a series of studies of the development of mathematical thinking among children who sell candy on the street in Recife, Brazil.

Trotter, R. J. (1986, August). Three heads are better than one. *Psychology Today,* 56–62.
This article presents Robert Sternberg's triarchic theory, which hypothesizes componential, experiential, and contextual aspects of intelligence.

Answer Key

Answers to Key Terms: 1.d, 2.j, 3.k, 4.s, 5.q, 6.f, 7.n, 8.a, 9.i, 10.g, 11.l, 12.b, 13.m, 14.o, 15.e, 16.r, 17.p, 18.c, 19.h.

Answers to Multiple-Choice Questions: 1.d, 2.a, 3.c, 4.d, 5.b, 6.c, 7.c, 8.d, 9.a, 10.a, 11.b, 12.c, 13.d, 14.a, 15.c, 16.b, 17.a, 18.b.

Social Development in Middle Childhood

chapter 14

Although the changes that usher in the period called middle childhood are biological, behavioral, and social, it is in the social domain that the greatest changes arise as children move from the shelter of parental supervision to new contexts and challenges. Six- to 12-year-olds are more often left to the company of their peers than they were during the preschool period. They are expected to take responsibility for their activities during this time, get along with other children, and follow the social rules of their society even when no one is watching. They are also expected to take on personal responsibilities, such as completing homework, practicing musical instruments, feeding pets, and regulating their own behavior in numerous other ways. Their play begins to include more complex and competitive games, and the role-playing of early childhood gives way to Scrabble and Monopoly.

These changes in social behavior depend to some extent on the cognitive abilities that children are developing. At the same time, new opportunities for interaction with other children serve in turn as stimuli for further cognitive development. Parents and teachers recognize children's greater competencies and adjust their expectations accordingly. And cultural variations in behavior become more pronounced as the adults in children's environments push them toward the kinds of skills and social interactions that are valued and useful in their particular societies.

Learning Objectives

Keep these questions in mind while studying Chapter 14.

1. In what ways does children's play change as they enter middle childhood? In what ways do games serve them as a model of society?
2. What changes take place in children's thinking about moral rules and social conventions? Is their behavior related to their reasoning about these things?
3. What factors cause children to be accepted or rejected by peers? How does acceptance or rejection influence their later lives?
4. How do children's relationships with their parents change as the children get older?

5. How do the ways children describe themselves change over time? What influences them to develop a positive or negative image of themselves and their abilities?

Chapter Summary

During middle childhood, children spend more time than before with peers, children of their own age and status, and less time with parents. When playing with *peers,* children engage in different activities than they do when adults are present; also, their behavior is regulated by different forms of social control. Children's sense of themselves and their relations with others changes as they come to inhabit new contexts, and parental socialization techniques shift from physically removing them from danger to explanation and discussion. Because children spend more time away from adult supervision, it is also more difficult for developmentalists to study their behavior in contexts outside of school.

I. GAMES AND GROUP REGULATION

It appears that game-playing is an important area in which children develop the ability to regulate their social interactions when adults are not present.

A. Games and Rules

In middle childhood, children continue the fantasy play, based on roles, begun in the preschool period; starting at 7 or 8 years of age, however, games based upon rules move into a position of prominence. Piaget's ideas about how children's play and their social interactions affect one another have proved interesting to developmentalists. Piaget studied children's ideas about rules by observing them playing the game of marbles. Six- to 8-year-old children had "mystical respect" for the rules—that is, they would not agree to any alterations in the rules, believing that they had been handed down by authority figures and could not be changed (as in the heteronomous morality discussed in Chapter 10). At 10 to 12 years of age, they began to treat the rules as social conventions that could be changed if the other players agreed (as in autonomous morality). Interestingly, children's conceptions of God change during this period, as discussed in the box "Children's Ideas about God."

Rule-based games require the same kinds of concrete operational abilities that are also required by the new tasks and responsibilities typically assigned to 6- and 7-year-olds. That is, they require children to pursue goals while keeping a set of overall task conditions in mind, to engage in social perspective-taking, and to coordinate their own actions with those that other players may be planning. Rule-based games often involve large groups of children and typically last longer than preschoolers' interactions do.

B. Games and Life

According to Piaget, rule-based games are models of society; he linked the ability to play within a system of rules to children's development of respect for rules and to their having reached a new level of moral understanding. Through playing games, children come to understand that social rules make cooperation with others possible; this allows peer groups to be self-governing.

Other developmentalists are interested in the nature of children's social interactions during play. Gary Fine's study of Little League baseball examined how participants struggled with moral themes such as controlling aggression and keeping their bond of unity.

II. REASONING ABOUT SOCIAL AND MORAL ISSUES

As discussed in Chapter 10, internalization of social and moral rules occurs with the development of the superego; now, children's behavior becomes less dependent on external rewards and punishments and more dependent on an internal, personal sense of right and wrong. Much research in this area has examined the relationship between children's moral reasoning and their moral behavior.

A. Reasoning about Harm and Justice

Lawrence Kohlberg modified and elaborated on Piaget's ideas about moral reasoning. Based on subjects' responses to a series of story-dilemmas, Kohlberg classified moral reasoning into six stages—two stages at each of three levels—representing people's thinking from 3 years of age through adulthood. Kohlberg found that children at Stage 1 (coinciding with the preschool period and the beginning of middle childhood) adopt an egocentric point of view and base their judgments on objective outcome. Stage 2 reasoning appears at around 7–8 years of age. Children's viewpoints are still egocentric, and their judgments are characterized by *instrumental morality* (the idea that it is okay to use others for one's own interest). In Stage 3 at 10 or 11 years of age, children's moral judgments are made on the basis of a social-relational perspective; agreement with others is seen as important and reasoning is similar to the Golden Rule. The characteristics of each of Kohlberg's six stages are outlined in Table 14.1.

Most contemporary research in moral development is based, like Kohlberg's work, on presenting children with hypothetical moral dilemmas. An example is work in the area of prosocial moral reasoning.

B. Prosocial Moral Reasoning

Prosocial moral reasoning, the thinking that is involved in deciding to share with others or to help them when doing so may prove costly to oneself, also undergoes stagelike developmental changes, according to Nancy Eisenberg. Presenting children with story-dilemmas, she found that, while younger children's reasoning is focused on themselves and what they will gain from a situation, older children express more empathy for a person in trouble and a greater consideration of social norms. High levels of prosocial moral reasoning are positively related to high levels of prosocial behavior; however, being capable of prosocial behavior does not guarantee that a person will engage in such behavior.

C. Reasoning about Moral Rules versus Social Conventions

Children exhibit a sense of justice and fairness even earlier than developmentalists once thought. For example, 5- and 6-year-olds will question the legitimacy of an authority figure who, in a hypothetical situation, allows children to fight with one another. Thus, Elliot Turiel and his colleagues concluded that children's reasoning about moral issues is different from their reasoning about authority and social conventions. Turiel found that children judge behavior such as hitting as moral rules; to violate these rules is always wrong, even if someone in authority says that it is okay to do so. On the other hand, children's reasoning about social conventions takes into account rules, authority, and custom; whether a person has authority to issue directives concerning social rules depends on the situation. Cross-cultural studies have found similar results in many societies; however, according to some researchers, there are cultures in which breaches of social conventions are considered more like moral violations than they are in the United States. This topic will be considered further in Chapter 16.

D. Moral Reasoning and Theories of Mind

Research indicates that how children judge someone's moral behavior may depend on their ability to understand the person's mental state (theory of mind). Michael Chandler and his colleagues used a Punch and Judy puppet show in order to investigate this. Children rated the "badness" of Punch's behavior in a scenario in which he tries to knock Judy off the stage (but does not succeed) and in a scenario in which Punch tries to rescue Judy, but accidentally knocks her off the stage. The youngest children maintained what Chandler described as an *objective view of responsibility,* rating Punch's behavior according to its consequences; older children and adults demonstrated a *subjective view of responsibility,* evaluating his behavior according to his intentions.

III. THE INDIVIDUAL'S PLACE IN THE GROUP

During middle childhood, children need more than ever to be able to make places for themselves within the social group.

A. Peer Relations and Social Status

When a group of children exists over a period of time, a *social structure*—a complex organization of relationships between individuals—emerges. As is true for other species, dominance hierarchies develop. Those children who are dominant are those who control resources such as toys, play space, and the determination of group activities. A crucial moment in development for children is the transition from elementary school to middle school, when new social groupings are being formed. Bullying reaches a peak in sixth grade, then diminishes during seventh grade, once dominance patterns have been formed. Bullying is discussed in the box "Bullies and Their Victims: The Darker Side of Children's Relationships." Among girls, *relational aggression*—-actions that threaten the relationships and social standing of peers—occurs, taking the forms of derogatory comments, rumor spreading, and gossip intended to tarnish the reputation of others. Like other forms of bullying, it peaks during the sixth and seventh grades.

The relative popularity of children in a group can be studied using the nomination procedure (asking children whom they would like to sit near or play with) or asking children to rank every child in the group using a rating scale. With this information, researchers are able to construct a sociogram showing how all the children in the group feel about one another. The children named as friends by the most people are assumed to be the most popular. Using such data, developmentalists have identified the following categorizes of children: popular, rejected, neglected, and controversial.

B. Factors Relating to Sociometric Status

Many studies have found that popularity is related to physical attractiveness; attractiveness and popularity are correlated among both boys and girls. Popular children are skilled at maintaining positive relationships, compromising, and negotiating. Rejection appears to be a more complicated issue. Some children are rejected because they are shy and withdrawn; they tend to be aware of their social failure and lonelier than other children. Children who are aggressive are likely to be rejected by peers, especially if they also have lower levels of sociability and cognitive ability. Aggression is associated with a variety of negative outcomes such as academic problems, low achievement, delinquency, health problems, and later unemployment.

Unfortunately, once children have been rejected, their reputations may persist even if they change their behavior. Shelley Hymel and her colleagues found that other children may even provoke the behavior that led a child to be rejected in the first place.

Neglected children are less sociable than others but are not aggressive or extremely shy. They are also better able to improve their social status than are rejected children, tend to perform better academically, and are better liked by teachers.

Controversial children are both highly accepted and highly rejected. They may be aggressive but have compensating cognitive and social skills; neglected and controversial children tend not to be distressed by their lack of social success and to have at least one friend. Children without best friends are lonelier than children with best friends, regardless of how well they are accepted by classmates.

A number of traits are associated with children's *social competence*—the set of skills that result in successful social functioning. These include: athletic ability, academic success, leadership ability and confidence, cooperativeness and helpfulness, competence in entering peer activities, physical attractiveness, nonaggressiveness, positive affect during social interactions, and skills in problem solving, role taking, and understanding nonverbal emotional information.

C. Peer Relations and Children's Development

Does children's experience with peer interactions have an important effect on their later adjustment? Researchers study this question using *retrospective studies,* starting with developmental outcomes in later childhood or adulthood and looking back at the individual's early life for predictive signs of those outcomes. Emory Cowen and his colleagues, studying the long-term consequences of children's social status, found that people who had come into contact with a psychiatric facility were likely to have been labeled in a less desirable way by classmates ten years earlier. Researchers also conduct *prospective studies,* in which children are studied as they grow older. John Coie and his colleagues found, in a 3-year prospective study, that children who were rejected by peers in elementary school were reported by their junior high school teachers to be more likely to misbehave in class, have short attention spans, and be physically uncontrolled. Eventually, 25 percent of these children dropped out of school, compared with 8 percent of the children who were not rejected by their peers. Rejected children show higher levels of delinquency, substance abuse, and psychological disturbance; they are almost twice as likely to be arrested. However, this is not true of all rejected children; rejected aggressive children are the ones most likely to have problems with delinquency or need psychiatric treatment. And, interestingly, bullies have been found to be four times as likely as other children to have criminal records as young adults.

IV. GETTING ALONG WITH OTHERS

How do competition, cooperation, and gender affect children's group relationships?

A. Competition and Cooperation Among Peers

As children spend more time with peers during middle childhood, they must learn to balance competition and cooperation. Muzafer and Carolyn Sherif, in a summer camp experiment, found that intergroup competition can lead to conflict and hostility. Simply getting the members of two feuding groups together under pleasant circumstances did nothing to reduce hostility, the Sherifs found. Mutual respect replaced dislike only when members of both groups had to cooperate to solve problems affecting everyone's welfare.

The Sherifs' experiment showed that cooperation and competition are both highly influenced by social context. As other researchers have found, they also vary according to cultural context. For example, studies by Millard Madsen and his colleagues have explored the way that groups choose cooperation or competition to solve problems. They found that Israeli kibbutz children, socialized to cooperate, performed significantly better on a task requiring cooperation than did urban Israeli children. Research in other countries supports the finding that culture influences group interaction. For example, Madsen and his colleagues found that urban European American children were far more competitive than children of the same age from rural Mexico. George Domino found a similar result when he compared European American and Chinese children. A possible explanation for these findings is that societies that value interdependence over independence also foster collaboration over competition. However, the fact that urban-rural differences have been found in a variety of diverse societies suggests an effect of local cultural factors as well. Most educational practice in the United States are based on individual performance and competition; there is some evidence that more cooperative learning has a beneficial effect on achievement, especially in classrooms of children with diverse cultural origins and ability levels.

B. Relations Between Boys and Girls

During middle childhood, children tend to segregate themselves by sex, although they may make "raids" into one another's territory. In the United States, 68 percent of 6-year-old children were found to have a best friend of the same sex; this number had risen to 90 percent for 12-year-olds. Sex segregation is not complete; boys and girls participate in joint activities on occasion, and they are more likely to mix in their own neighborhoods than in school, as discussed in the box "Gender Politics on the Playground: Defining a Moral Order." Boys tend to play in larger groups; girls are more likely to congregate in groups of two or three. While not all children follow the pattern of keeping with others of their own sex, it is the most common social pattern in all cultures during middle childhood.

C. Friendship: A Special Type of Relationship

According to Willard Hartup and other researchers, friendships serve four main functions: they allow children to develop and practice social skills; they provide children with information about themselves, others and the world; they provide fun and relieve stress; and they provide models of intimate relationships. As shown in Table 14.3, children consider that friends make each other feel good about themselves, are easy to get along with, and provide mutual assistance and companionship. Psychiatrist Harry Stack Sullivan believed the experience of friendship during middle childhood to be a necessary precursor of interpersonal intimacy during adulthood.

- Proximity is an important factor in determining who children become friends with. Friends are also likely to be of the same age, race, and sex and to be at the same skill level in various activities. In a study by John Gottman, pairs of 3- to 9-year-olds were given several opportunities to play together. Those that became friendly tended to have interactions characterized by: common-ground activity; clear communication; exchange of information; resolution of conflicts; and reciprocity. Those who became friends were also more attentive, emotionally positive, vocal, active, involved, relaxed, and playful with each other.
- Why do some children have an easier time making friends than others? According to Robert Selman, social perspective taking is a key to successful relationships. Table 14.4 shows how Selman relates children's levels of perspective taking to developmental levels of friendship. Selman has proposed that there are three spheres of influence that are affected by the development of perspective taking: friendship understanding (the child's developing knowledge of the nature of friendship), friendship skills (specific action strategies that children use in developing their relationships), and friendship valuing (the child's personal motivation and emotional involvement in the relationship). All three are necessary for the maintenance of friendships and each takes its own developmental course. Greater social competence provides children with a greater variety of resources for dealing with their social environment, especially when conflicts arise. Brett Laursen and his colleagues found that, during middle childhood, children are more aware of *social repair mechanisms*—strategies that allow them to remain friends when serious differences temporarily drive them apart. In practice, however, coercion

continues to be the method used by children in conflict interactions throughout middle childhood.

V. THE INFLUENCE OF PARENTS

Middle childhood is a time of significant change in the relationship between children and their parents; the effects of this are evident in other areas as well, including children's relationships with their peers.

A. Changing Relations with Parents

As children get older, their parents are less overtly affectionate and more critical of mistakes children make. They expect more responsible behavior from their children and adopt different strategies for correcting misbehavior when it occurs. There are cultural differences in the ages at which children are expected to display various behavioral competencies, as shown in Table 14.5. During middle childhood, the issues that arise between parents and children change; now, parents worry more about children's schoolwork, how to deal with school behavior problems, what chores children should be required to do, and to what extent parents should monitor their children's social lives. They attempt to influence their children's behavior through appealing to reason, humor, self-esteem, or guilt. Eleanor Maccoby has given the name *coregulation* to this sharing of responsibility between parents and children.

B. Parental Influences on Children's Peer Relations

Family life influences children's peer interactions in two ways: first, patterns of parent–child interaction serve as working models for interaction with others; second, the way parents organize children's interactions with peers has an affect on their peer relations. There is evidence that secure attachment in infancy is helpful to peer relations in early childhood and leads to better personal relationships in later life—what Alan Sroufe calls the "cascade effect." The cascade effect also applies to negative forms of attachment, which can lead to poor peer relations. Whether this effect occurs depends on the stability of environmental conditions. Also, because children's behavior has considerable influence on the behavior of their parents, a transactional model is more useful for understanding how the characteristics of the child and the characteristics of the child's environment interact than is a more simple assumption that children's behavior is caused by how they were raised by their parents.

Current parent–child interactions also influence peer relations. For example, Thomas Dishion found that socially rejected boys were exposed to more coercive family experiences and were judged more aggressive than their peers. Poverty acted as an indirect cause by increasing family stress, making coercive discipline more likely. Similar results have been found in a study carried out in the People's Republic of China. Maltreated children have also been found to be more likely to be rejected by peers; in this case, rejection seems to be related to the mediating effect of aggression. Maltreated children are at greater risk of becoming aggressive.

Parents also influence children's peer relations by their influence over how children spend their time and the neighborhood in which they live; they also exert influence by monitoring their children's behavior. Children whose parents are not aware of where they are or what they are doing may be more likely to be engaged in antisocial activity and to be rejected by peers.

VI. A NEW SENSE OF SELF

Changes in children's social lives during middle childhood are accompanied by changes in the ways they think about themselves.

A. Changing Conceptions of the Self

William Damon and Daniel Hart asked 4- to 15-year-old children to describe themselves. They found that children of all ages referred to their appearance, activities, relations to others, and psychological characteristics. However, while children between the ages of 4 and 7 tended to make categorical statements about themselves that placed them in socially recognized categories and seldom made comparative judgments, children between 8 and 11 began to relate their characteristics to those of others—a process called *social comparison.* After spending a great deal of time with peers, children realize that questions such as "Am I good at math"? have no absolute answers; success is measured in terms of the social group. Around 7 or 8 years of age, children change from describing themselves in terms of more general, stable traits (for example, "I am a good student" rather than "I can spell lots of words."). At this time, they also begin to assume that other people have stable traits that can be used to predict their behavior.

B. Self-Esteem

The new expectations faced by children during middle childhood are challenges to their *self-esteem*—their evaluations of their own self-worth. Susan Harter and Robin Pike found a change in the basis of children's self-evaluations as they made the transition to middle childhood. In a study of 4- through 7-year-olds, they found that children lumped physical and cognitive competence together into a dimension of "competence" and combined peer and maternal acceptance into a single dimension of "acceptance"; the self-ratings of children who had been held back in school reflected self-evaluation of low competence, while those children who were newcomers to their school reflected low acceptance. In another study, they found that older children (8 to 12 years of age) made more differentiated self-evaluations, distinguishing between cognitive, social, and physical competence. During middle childhood, children also begin to form ideas about the person they would like to be—their "ideal self"—and to measure their actual self against it. This can become a source of motivation or a source of distress. Around the time they are 8 years old, children's evaluations of their cognitive, social, and physical competence also begin to agree with the judgments of their peers and teachers.

- Stanley Coopersmith discovered that 10- to 12-year-old boys with high self-esteem had parents whose style of child-rearing included acceptance, clearly defined limits, and respect for individuality; the key to high self-esteem seems to be a feeling of control over oneself and one's environment. According to Coopersmith, children with high self-esteem know their boundaries; however, this does not detract from their feelings of effectiveness.
- While self-esteem has a prominent place in the beliefs of American mothers of European descent, it may be a culture-specific concept. In a study of Taiwanese mothers, it was rarely mentioned; a study of European American and Mexican American families found a strong relationship between parenting practices and children's self-esteem among the European Americans but a comparatively weak relationship among the Mexican Americans studied. While the authoritative parenting style has been associated with positive social and intellectual outcomes for European American children, families from other cultures can often not be classified according to Baumrind's categories.

VII. RECONSIDERING MIDDLE CHILDHOOD

Is middle childhood a stage of development characterized by a common set of features in every culture? Table 14.8 summarizes the changes that distinguish middle childhood from early childhood. In the social domain, adults in all cultures appear to assign 6- and 7-year-olds to a different category than younger children and to require them to carry out new roles and duties. Peer groups also become more important. In the cognitive domain, children's thought process become more logical and consistent; they can keep in mind more than one point of view in a greater variety of contexts, and they can moderate their emotional reactions, which is helpful to their relations with adults and peers. In the biological domain, there are increases in size and strength, changing relations between different kinds of brain-wave activity and greater influence of the frontal lobes of the brain. When the biological, behavioral, and social components of middle childhood are considered separately, development appears relatively continuous with that of early childhood. However, the consequence of changes in all of these domains is a pattern of changes that suggests a bio-social-behavioral shift.

Key Terms

Following are important terms introduced in Chapter 14. Match the term with the letter of the example that best illustrates the term.

1. ______ coregulation
2. ______ objective view of responsibility
3. ______ peers
4. ______ prosocial moral reasoning
5. ______ prospective study
6. ______ relational aggression
7. ______ retrospective study
8. ______ self-esteem

9. ______ social comparison

10. ______ social competence

11. ______ social repair mechanisms

12. ______ social structure

13. ______ subjective view of responsibility

a. Judging the wrongness of an action on the basis of the outcome.
b. A collection of skills that help along children's relationships with their peers.
c. Without these, it is difficult to keep a friendship intact in the face of disagreements.
d. For a child in the third grade, these would be other third-graders.
e. One example of this is spreading rumors about another child.
f. This might involve doing something to help someone even at a cost to oneself.
g. This is an indication of how children evaluate their self-worth.
h. A child describes herself as "the best reader in the class."
i. Judging the wrongness of an act according to the protagonist's motivation.
j. An example of this is a dominance hierarchy.
k. A researcher follows a group of children to see how their social behavior now will relate to their behavior later on.
l. This involves sharing responsibility for children's behavior between children and parents.
m. Researchers search back to earlier in childhood to find clues to children's current problems.

Multiple-Choice Practice Questions

Circle the letter of the word or phrase that correctly completes each statement.

1. Compared with parents of younger children, parents of children in middle childhood are more likely to
   a. restrict the time children spend with peers.
   b. use physical force to control their children.
   c. rely on coregulation in controlling their children's behavior.
   d. supervise their children closely.

2. During middle childhood, ________ become(s) more important in children's play.
   a. rule-based games
   b. role-playing
   c. props such as blocks and dolls
   d. fantasy

3. During middle childhood, girls and boys are more likely to play together
   a. at no time.
   b. on the school playground.
   c. in their neighborhoods.
   d. during organized sports.

4. ________, which include prohibitions against killing and stealing, are found in all societies.
   a. Social conventions
   b. Social repair mechanisms
   c. Group norms
   d. Moral rules

5. Which is true about children's reasoning about social conventions?
   a. They do not distinguish them from moral rules.
   b. Their judgments depend on context and on "who is in charge."
   c. Their reasoning does not change with age.
   d. All of the above are true.

6. Lawrence Kohlberg studied children's moral reasoning by
   a. observing their behavior on the playground.
   b. asking them to react to moral dilemmas presented in stories.
   c. asking them about the morality of their own behavior.
   d. exposing them to real moral dilemmas and observing their responses.

7. According to Robert Selman, children's increasing ability to ________ leads to changes in their conceptions of friendship.
   a. conserve
   b. remember lists of unrelated materials
   c. take another person's perspective
   d. engage in logical classification

8. Shapira and Madsen found that __________ children performed best on a task requiring cooperation.
   a. middle-class urban Israeli
   b. suburban U.S.
   c. U.S. farm
   d. Israeli kibbutz

9. Children whose self-esteem is high tend to have parents who
   a. are accepting of them.
   b. set clearly defined limits for them.
   c. have respect for their individuality.
   d. are all of the above.

10. During middle childhood, the child who has the most influence over the activities of a group of children playing together is
    a. the most dominant child.
    b. the most controversial child.
    c. the most aggressive child.
    d. a bully.

11. Children who respond to the "Heinz dilemma" by saying "He should steal the drug because someday he might be sick and need someone to steal it for him" are demonstrating
    a. an understanding of social rules.
    b. concrete operations.
    c. instrumental morality.
    d. positive justice.

12. Children who are rejected by their peers
    a. are sometimes very shy children.
    b. are often children who are aggressive.
    c. are both a and b.
    d. receive little attention, positive or negative, from peers.

13. Which is an example of a "prospective study" of sociometric status?
    a. Researchers measure the sociometric status of children in third grade and in middle school and later compare it with measures of adjustment in high school.
    b. Researchers compare children's sociometric status in third grade with measures of their adjustment in third grade.
    c. Researchers observe children who have poor adjustment in high school and examine their elementary school and middle school records for signs of social problems.
    d. All of the above are correct.

14. Children who are bullies during middle childhood
    a. are aggressive because of a deficit in social information processing.
    b. are aggressive because their behavior is instrumental.
    c. are aggressive because they are afraid of other children.
    d. are no more likely to have long-term problems with aggression than children who do not engage in bullying.

15. According to research by the Sherifs, which is true about conflict between groups of children?
    a. Competition between groups does not lead to conflict between the groups.
    b. Participation in pleasant joint activities is effective in reducing conflict between groups.
    c. Requiring the groups to work together to solve a common problem is effective in reducing conflict between groups.
    d. Requiring one group to share resources with the other group is effective in reducing conflict between groups.

16. Which are more likely to be issues between parents and children once children reach middle childhood?
    a. schoolwork and household chores
    b. temper tantrums and fights
    c. establishing daily routines
    d. All of the above are likely.

17. When asked to define themselves, 8- to 11-year-old children would be most likely to say which of the following?
    a. I play baseball.
    b. I am a good athlete.
    c. I play sports, which makes me popular with other kids.
    d. All of the above are correct.

18. Susan Harter has found that the self-evaluations of 8- to 12-year-old children
    a. are more differentiated (cognitive, social, physical) than those of younger children.
    b. reveal that children are forming ideas of their ideal selves.
    c. correlate relatively well with the judgments of peers and teachers.
    d. All of the above are correct.

Short-Answer Practice Questions

1. Why did Piaget feel that rule-based games were an important part of development during middle childhood?

2. Give examples of the kinds of moral reasoning typical of children in Lawrence Kohlberg's stages 1, 2, and 3.

3. What factors influence children's popularity within a group? What relationship exists between social status and level of social competence?

4. Discuss how the "two-sidedness" of thought during middle childhood helps facilitate children's social relations.

5. What are some differences between boys and girls during middle childhood in preferred activities, play, and social relations?

6. What major changes occur in children's sense of themselves during the years of middle childhood?

Putting It All Together

Look back at the material on play in previous chapters for help in completing this assignment.

I. Match each of the following examples of play to the developmental period of which it is most characteristic.

______ 1. Stirring a cup of sand "coffee" with a twig.

______ 2. Playing "parents and children."

______ 3. Playing kickball.

______ 4. Banging a hammer on the table.

______ 5. Jumping rope.

______ 6. Cooking a meal on a play stove.

______ 7. Dressing up in sex-stereotyped clothes.

a. Early infancy (less than 18 months)
b. Late infancy (18–30 months)
c. The preschool period
d. Middle childhood

II. Using an example from each period, show how children's play during infancy, the preschool period, and middle childhood reflects their increasing cognitive skills and how play, in turn, promotes further cognitive development.

Sources of More Information

Chance, P. (1982, January). Your child's self-esteem. *Parents Magazine.*
This article discusses the advantages of strong parent–child relationships and early experiences of mastery for children's development.

Durojaiye, S. M. (1977). Children's traditional games and rhymes in three cultures. *Educational Research, 19*(3), 223–226.
This article compares games enjoyed by children in Great Britain, Nigeria, and Uganda.

Furth, H. G. (1981). *The world of grown-ups: Children's conceptions of society.* Westport: Greenwood.
This book, based on interviews with British children, aged 5 to 11, applies Piaget's developmental model to children's understanding of society and its institutions.

Gilligan, C. (1993). *In a different voice: Psychological theory and women's development.* Cambridge, MA: Harvard University Press.
Studies of moral development in women are presented along with a critique of traditional psychological theories of moral development.

Kindlon, D., & Thompson, M. (2000). *Raising Cain: Protecting the emotional lives of boys.* New York: Ballantine.
The authors suggest that society gives today's boys destructive emotional training; in this book, they suggest ways of helping them cultivate emotional awareness and empathy.

Piaget, J. (1997). *The moral judgment of the child.* New York: Free Press.
Piaget's report of his original work on the development of moral reasoning.

Power, C. F., Higgens, A., & Kohlberg, L. (1991). *Lawrence Kohlberg's approach to moral education.* New York: Columbia University Press.
This book describes how schools act as communities and proposes that school culture should become the focus of moral education.

Rubin, Z. (1980). *Children's friendships*. Cambridge, MA: Harvard University Press.
This book describes the evolution of children's friendships, with a special emphasis on middle childhood.

Sernaque, V. (1988). *Classic children's games*. New York: Dell.
This book contains descriptions of games appropriate for 2- to 4-year-olds, 4- to 6-year-olds, 6- to 8-year-olds, and 8- to 10-year-olds.

Soyinka, W. (1981). *Ake, the years of childhood*. New York: Vintage Books.
An autobiographical account of growing up in an African village by a Nobel Prize-winning playwright, poet, and novelist.

Answer Key

Answers to Key Terms: 1.l, 2.a, 3.d, 4.f, 5.k, 6.e, 7.m, 8.g, 9.h, 10.b, 11.c, 12.j, 13.i, 14.c, 15.m.

Answers to Multiple-Choice Questions: 1.c, 2.a, 3.c, 4.d, 5.b, 6.b, 7.c, 8.d, 9.d, 10.a, 11.c, 12.c, 13.c, 14.b, 15.c, 16.a, 17.b, 18.d.

Answers to Putting It All Together I: 1.b, 2.c, 3.d, 4.a, 5.d, 6.c, 7.c.

Biological and Social Foundations of Adolescence

chapter 15

The end of middle childhood is announced by radical biological changes. During puberty, young people's bodies become adult, both in size and in their capacity for biological reproduction. In industrialized nations, the age at which puberty occurs has gradually fallen over the last 200 years; at the same time, technological developments have increased the amount of education young people need in order to become independent members of society. The result has been a shortening of middle childhood and a lengthening of adolescence—the transitional stage between biological maturity and the full independence of adulthood.

According to many theorists, adolescence is a time of emotional upheaval caused both by hormonal changes and by new social arrangements that characterize this stage. After a long period of relative segregation, boys and girls develop an interest in one another, and peer groups support them in establishing attachments with members of the opposite sex. Relations with parents are also in transition, as adolescents move from positions of dependence to more egalitarian relationships. Many adolescents hold paying jobs, contributing to their feeling of independence. Still, according to our society, adolescents are not ready for adult privileges and need to be protected from adult responsibilities. The results of these biological, behavioral, and social aspects of development give adolescence its unique character.

Learning Objectives

Keep these questions in mind while studying Chapter 15.

1. Why have theorists historically viewed adolescence as a time of conflict and instability?
2. What biological changes occur during puberty? What impact do these changes, the timing of the changes, have on adolescents' adjustment?
3. How do young people's social lives change during adolescence? What qualities are important to them in their friends?
4. To what extent are adolescents at risk for engaging in risky or socially disapproved behavior? Is such behavior really the result of peer pressure?

5. How do young people make the transition to associating with members of the opposite sex? In what ways is sexual activity a scripted activity?
6. In what ways do parents continue to influence the behavior of their adolescent children? Which parenting practices are most effective?
7. How do adolescents enter the world of work? How does this affect their lives in other areas, for example, school performance?

Chapter Summary

The bio-social-behavioral shift that marks the end of middle childhood includes major changes: the greatest biological transition since birth results in reproductive capability; boys and girls begin to interact in new social configurations; and children's relationships with their parents change as they become more independent.

The nature of adolescence is shaped by the views of a society about what rights and responsibilities adolescents should have. In modern industrialized societies, it is also complicated by two trends: 1) earlier onset of puberty combined with an increasingly longer period of education, which prolongs adolescence; and 2) separation of adolescents and adults during schooling and work, which increases the influence of peers.

I. CONCEPTIONS OF ADOLESCENCE

The characteristics associated with adolescence are rooted in history and culture.

A. Philosophical Precursors

Accounts of adolescents from the time of Plato and Aristotle, and continuing through the Middle Ages and beyond, portray adolescents as impulsive, sensual, and passionate, due to excessive emotions brought on by puberty.

B. Modern Approaches

According to Jean-Jacques Rousseau, adolescents are characterized by heightened emotional instability brought about by biological maturation; at the same time, their cognitive processes undergo a change to self-conscious thought and logical reasoning ability. During the late eighteenth and early nineteenth centuries, interest in adolescence increased due both to the migration of adolescents to cities in search of work and also to the recognition of the need for a more educated citizenry. Two theorists have especially influenced modern thinking and research on adolescence.

- G. Stanley Hall, like Rousseau, considered adolescence to be a time of storm and stress. He also embraced the idea that "ontogeny recapitulates phylogeny"—that is, the evolutionary history of the species is repeated in the development of the individual child. Therefore, he saw adolescents as the future of the human species.

- In Sigmund Freud's theory, adolescence corresponds to the genital stage of development. The reawakening of primitive instincts upsets the adolescent's psychological balance, producing conflict and erratic behavior, and young people must reintegrate their psychological forces in a mature way that is compatible with their new sexual capacities.
- Some researchers have applied theories and methods from ethology to the study of adolescence. For example, research in this tradition has targeted social hierarchies and aggressive behavior among teenagers. Barry Bogin has pointed out that humans are the only primates to undergo a growth spurt as part of puberty; he argues that adolescence conveys reproductive advantage by allowing adolescents to learn adult economic and social behavior before they begin reproducing.

II. PUBERTY

Puberty is a series of biological events that transform individuals from physical immaturity to physical and reproductive maturity. In the brain, the hypothalamus begins the process by signaling the pituitary gland to produce greater amounts of growth hormones and to produce hormones that will stimulate the gonads. The testes and adrenals of boys will produce testosterone and the ovaries of girls will produce estrogen and progesterone; these, in turn, trigger the physical changes that accompany puberty.

A. The Growth Spurt

One of the first signs of puberty is a growth spurt during which boys and girls grow faster than at any time since infancy and reach 98 percent of their adult height. Different parts of the body develop at different rates: leg length typically reaches a peak first, followed by trunk length, and shoulder and chest width. The brain grows little, although the head increases in size as the skull bones thicken. Girls' hips widen and their breasts develop, while boys develop broader shoulders and thicker necks. Puberty also leads to differences in strength. Boys develop greater strength and greater capacity for exercise; girls, however, will on average live longer and be better able to tolerate long-term stress.

B. Brain Development

While the brain grows little overall during adolescence, there are changes in its organization, especially in the frontal lobes. White matter, an indication of myelination, increases steadily. Gray matter increases rapidly in early adolescence, an indication of a new period of synaptogenesis; it then declines, an indication of another period of synaptic pruning.

C. Sexual Development

The *primary sexual organs,* those involved in reproduction, become mature during puberty. In males, this means the production of sperm cells and semen; in females, it means that mature ova are released and menstruation occurs. During this time, the *secondary sex characteristics*—outward signs that distinguish males from females—appear. A milestone for boys is *semenarche*—the first ejaculation—which often occurs spontaneously during sleep. Girls experience *menarche,* the first menstrual period, about 18 months after the growth spurt reaches its peak. Ovulation typically begins 12 to 18 months after menarche.

D. The Timing of Puberty

There is wide variation among children in the age at which puberty begins. Both genetics and environment play a part in this. Identical twin girls reach menarche much closer in time than do fraternal twins, illustrating the role of genetics. Further evidence of the role of genetics is the observation that African American children reach puberty at earlier ages compared to European American children. The role of the environment can be seen in the effects of caloric intake and exercise on age of menarche. Dancers and other girls who participate in a high level of physical activity reach menarche later than average. Children who live in stressful family environments also reach puberty earlier. In addition, a look at historical trends shows that in industrialized countries and some developing countries the age of menarche has been gradually declining during the last 150 years. Girls in the United States reach menarche an average of two years earlier than they did in 1890, and the trend toward earlier puberty continues today. Boys also pass through puberty earlier than they did before.

E. The Developmental Impact of Puberty

The changes associated with puberty are perceived in varying ways by different individuals and by different cultural groups.

- Individual children vary in their reactions to the events of puberty. Jeanne Brooks-Gunn and her colleagues have studied girls' reactions to their first menstruation. They found that girls' attitudes and beliefs about menstruation are influenced by expectations, attitudes, and beliefs of those around them as well as by their own direct experiences. Boys' responses to semenarche depend on the context in which it occurs. *Emotional tone*—the degree to which a person experiences a sense of well-being versus depression and anxiety—is different on average for boys and girls during adolescence. While boys experience an increase in positive emotional tone during adolescence, positive emotional tone plateaus for girls after early adolescence. This may be a product of the tendency for girls' bodies to be viewed as sexual objects to a greater extent than boys'. Another physical change during adolescence is an increase in weight. For boys, this comes from increased muscle mass; for girls, it comes mainly from the accumulation of subcutaneous fat. This is normal for girls; however, because of cultural ideals emphasizing extreme thinness, adolescent girls may be dissatisfied with their new, mature bodies. This is especially true of American girls of European descent. In some cases, girls (and occasionally boys) develop eating disorders such as anorexia nervosa or bulimia nervosa, both of which are discussed in the box "Eating Disorders." A prospective study found a higher incidence of eating disorders among girls who earlier had reported that thinness was important to their peers. African American and Mexican American girls are less likely to consider themselves overweight than are European American girls. Research in Asian countries has reported lower incidences of eating disorders, although there are indications that this is changing.

- Does the fact that an individual matures sexually earlier or later than his or her peers influence social adjustment, personality, or peer relations? While early maturation may increase girls' popularity with boys, they may experience a decline in academic performance, and may engage in a variety of problem behaviors. This is due partly to associating with older peers and with boys, who tend to be the instigators of girls' problem behaviors. It is, therefore, not surprising that Avshalom Caspi and his colleagues found that early-maturing girls in New Zealand who attended an all-girls secondary school experienced higher academic performance and lower rates of delinquency than those attending a coeducational school.

  Both boys and girls who reach puberty relatively early are more likely to smoke, use alcohol and illegal drugs, and get in trouble with the law than are later-maturers; they are also likely to have lower self-control and less emotional stability. However, adolescents who engage in physical activity, for example, sports, have lower rates of depression and drug use and have higher academic performance and more confidence.

III. THE REORGANIZATION OF SOCIAL LIFE

The biological changes that mark the end of childhood are associated with changes in their interactions with their families and peers.

A. A New Relationship with Peers

Relationships with peers also change during adolescence. U.S. teenagers spend more time with peers and less time with their families. Peer interaction is less under the guidance and control of adults than it was before. Peer groups become larger and increasingly heterosexual. At the same time that peer groups increase in size, friendships and other relationships increase in intimacy. The three primary types of peer relationships seen among adolescents center on: *dyadic friendships* (close relationships between two individuals); cliques; and crowds.

- Adolescents' friendships are distinguished by their reliance on: reciprocity (the give and take of close relationships); commitment (loyalty and trust between friends); and equality (equal distribution of power). They serve at least two developmental functions—intimacy and autonomy. Intimacy—a connection among individuals through shared feelings, thoughts, and activities—is what comes to mind when reflecting on friendship. However, autonomy—the ability to assert one's own needs—is necessary in order to avoid bowing to peer pressure to engage in risky behaviors. Adolescent girls' friendships tend to be more intense than friendships among boys; this results, in middle adolescence, in friendships having a jealous quality which eases later in adolescence when girls are more tolerant of their friends' differences and their relationships with others. Fourteen- to 16-year-old boys form friendships that are less close and more numerous that those of girls. Various explanations have been suggested to account for this difference, for example, that boys' friendships tend to be based more on activities than on disclosure of personal thoughts and feelings. Gender differences are less apparent when a range of ethnic groups are included in studies. Ethnicity, family values, gender, and socioeconomic status interact in complex ways to affect adolescents' friendships.

Friends serve adolescents of both sexes as a "secure base" that supports them as they confront and deal with anxiety-provoking situations. As more situations are negotiated successfully, dependence on friends lessens. Studies show that close friendships are beneficial for adolescents' social and personality development.

- New kinds of peer groups make an appearance during adolescence. Family-sized *cliques* are small enough to serve as the primary peer group. Adolescents may be members of several cliques that meet in different settings; this sets them apart from friendships. Another type of peer group is large mixed-gender *crowd*. One type of crowd arises from preexisting cliques and friendship groups. Another type, the "reputation-based collective" ("jocks," "brains," or "druggies"), is most likely to be seen on high school campuses; its members may or may not be friends. Crowds influence adolescents' social lives by helping them learn about alternative social identities, helping to determine whom they are likely to meet, and by shaping members' interpersonal relations. Being considered a member of a particular crowd reflects on adolescents' social status, according to a study by James S. Coleman. The popularity of different crowds varies according to a school's social climate. For example, in some schools "brains" occupy an intermediate status between elite and disparaged groups; in other schools—for example, in working-class African American communities—"brains" may be ostracized, leading young people to mask their abilities.
- While adolescents now have more opportunities to meet people from different backgrounds, their friends tend to be even more similar to them than they were in elementary school. The degree to which friends are similar to each other is called *homophilia*. Denise Kandil and her colleagues found that adolescents seek out others who are similar to themselves on important dimensions, especially those relevant to social reputation; this is called *selection*. Next, a process of socialization occurs; socially significant behaviors are modeled and reinforced in the course of interactions. Thus, friends become increasingly alike. In this way, children who are friends with delinquent peers are likely to become delinquent themselves.

Adults worry about adolescents spending too much time with their peers; left to themselves, they may engage in antisocial behavior. This can, in fact, be a problem. For example, a questionnaire study by Thomas Berndt and Keunho Keefe found that seventh- and eighth-graders whose friends were reported to have engaged in disruptive behavior reported engaging in such behavior themselves when re-questioned later in the year; girls were more susceptible to this influence. Other studies show that when an adolescent's friends engage in behaviors considered antisocial—for example, smoking, using alcohol or illegal drugs, being sexually active, or breaking the law—he or she will eventually do these things as well. The box "Risk Taking and Social Deviance during Adolescence" discusses possible explanations for adolescents' increased likelihood of engaging in risky behaviors. An interesting observation is that these behaviors are not characteristic of adolescence in all cultures. It is difficult to determine whether the conformity that often occurs during adolescence is a result of peer pressure or whether it follows from mutual influence. However, when Thomas Berndt presented third- through twelfth-grade students with various situations and asked whether they would go along with the crowd, he found that conformity to peer pressure increased between the third and ninth grades, declining thereafter.

It has been suggested that *deviancy training*—that is, positive reactions to discussion of rule breaking—contributes to antisocial behavior among adolescents. Perhaps for this reason, Dishion and his colleagues found that group counseling and therapy for delinquent adolescents may do more harm than good, actually increasing the participants' problem behaviors.

Some behaviors considered antisocial in adolescence—smoking and drinking, for example—are considered acceptable for adults, raising the possibility that adolescents may simply be modeling adult behavior when they engage in these activities.

- In many cultures, a function of peer groups is to aid adolescents in making the transition to romantic and sexual relationships. Dexter Dunphy studied this transition among Australian adolescents in the late 1950s. He discovered that, during early adolescence, young people tended to gather in same-sex cliques. Cliques became part of a larger mixed-sex crowd. Eventually, the crowd dissolved into loosely associated groups of couples. Today, this pattern still occurs in some cultures; however, in comtemporary industrialized societies, marriage is delayed longer than it was at the time of his study. Also, there are subgroups within contemporary societies in which involvement in romantic relationships may be discouraged.

B. Sexual Activity

Adolescent sexual activity varies according to cultural and historical patterns. In the contemporary United States, the official position is that adolescent sexual activity is undesirable; at the same time, the mass media make it appear desirable and common. As discussed in the box "Teenage Pregnancy," adolescent sexual behavior can lead to unplanned pregnancy; about 1 million U.S. teenagers become pregnant each year. Despite the availability of contraception, U.S. teens use it far less often than teens in other developed countries. According to current statistics, most 15-year-olds have not yet had sexual intercourse; however, by 17 years of age, more than fifty percent have had intercourse. Learning is important in sexual activity; the appropriate behaviors vary according to such factors as culture, historical circumstances, and social class. For example, the differing prevalence of oral sex among different cultural groups highlights the role of learning in sexual activity. There are also cultural differences in communication about sexual matters, including health topics related to sexuality, such as AIDS.

- Sexual behavior can be thought of as a scripted activity progressing from kissing through intermediate steps to sexual intercourse, although the script is somewhat variable across cultures. Their scripted knowledge gives young people engaging in sexual activity for the first time an idea of the roles they are supposed to play. A script also gives sexual meaning to activities, such as holding hands and kissing, that also occur in nonsexual contexts. Scripted activities are not organized in the same way in all cultures. For example, in Kenya at the turn of the century, the traditional Kikuyu script for adolescent sexual behavior included "ngweko," a culturally sanctioned kind of lovemaking that did not involve direct genital contact.

- Males and females initiate sexual activity for different reasons. To some extent, these differences are biological, resulting from the fact that sexual arousal in males is more straightforward and boys are more likely to have had experience with masturbation. Because of these differences, boys are more likely to say that their first sexual experience was the result of curiosity, and only secondarily the result of affection for their partner. Girls are more likely to report affection as the most important motive, with curiosity a secondary reason. Boys and girls respond differently to their first sexual intercourse. Boys are likely to report that their first intercourse was a positive experience; girls are likely to report feeling ambivalent. This may be because many girls are coerced into having sex; in one study, about 60% of girls who had intercourse before 15 years of age reported being coerced.

C. Changing Parent–Child Relations

During adolescence, young people's changing relations with their peers are accompanied by changes in their relationships with their parents.

- Brett Laursen and his colleagues, reviewing a large number of studies carried out over several decades, found that patterns of conflict between parents and children change over adolescence. The frequency and intensity of disagreements increase in early adolescence and then decrease, perhaps because older adolescents spend less time at home. During this time, adolescents are switching their emotional attachment more to their peers. What are the subjects of adolescent–parent conflict? Mihaly Csikszentmihalyi and Reed Larson conducted a study in which adolescents carried beepers and filled out reports on what they were doing and experiencing at each time they were "beeped." They found that many parent–child conflicts center around matters of personal preference, such as the cleanliness of the teenager's room. Often, arguments involve disputes about the boundaries of teens' "personal space." These seemingly trivial conflicts, however, may actually be expressions of larger conflicts over independence and responsibility.
- During adolescence, parents continue to play an important role; in addition to providing food, clothing, and shelter, they exert influence over who their children interact with, and the extent and timing of those interactions, including what crowds their children are likely to become involved with. According to a study by Andrew Fuligni and Jacqueline Eccles, there is an interaction between the influences of peers and parents on adolescents' behavior. When parents include their children in decisions and enforce rules firmly but not coercively, adolescents retain a closer relationship with them and orient themselves less to peers. In studies of the family dynamics of normally developing and

troubled adolescents, Hausser and his colleagues found two main patterns of interaction: *constraining interactions* that limit and restrict communications; and *enabling interactions* that facilitate communication. The researchers argue that enabling interactions promote healthy psychological and identity development by making it safe for adolescents to try out new ideas and perspectives and to express new feelings. Parallel studies of parenting style have found that children of authoritative parents are more competent in school and less likely to get into trouble than children of authoritarian or rejecting-neglecting parents; their friends also benefit from interactions with these authoritative parents. In general, the most common pattern of child–parent adjustment during adolescence is for children and parents to negotiate a new form of interdependence in which the adolescent is granted an increasingly equal role and more nearly equal responsibilities.

D. Work and Leisure

In the United States, children's first work experience comes from doing the household tasks, perhaps followed by neighborhood jobs such as babysitting and newspaper delivery. By age 15, many adolescents have regular part-time jobs. Each successive job that adolescents hold tends to be more responsible and substantial. By their mid-twenties, young people are generally working in adult careers. According to official counts, one-third of 16- to 19-year-olds work at least part-time, although the proportion varies with race (European American teens are more likely to be employed). There are striking cross-national differences in adolescent employment; more U.S. teens work than those in other countries.

Adolescents who work spend less time doing homework compared with those who are not employed; they are also less involved in school than their classmates. There are some indications—for example, a study by Jeylan Mortimer and her colleagues—that many students who work long hours and do poorly in school were less committed to school even before they began working. Employment during adolescents does not usually provide on-the-job training that will be useful during adulthood, nor do adolescents interact much with adults in work settings. Most adolescents spend the money they earn on "personal items" rather than on education or family expenses. Extensive part-time employment is associated with higher rates of various problems, including drug and alcohol use, psychological distress, poor health, and delinquency.

How do adolescents spend their leisure time? According to a study by Flammer and his colleagues, watching television accounts for more than a third of leisure time for U.S. teens; other favorite activities are hanging out with friends and playing sports. Adolescents' increasing cognitive abilities allow them to take on a more active role in organizing their own activities and experiences.

Key Terms

Following are important terms introduced in Chapter 15. Match each term with the letter of the example that best illustrates the term.

1. ______ clique
2. ______ constraining interactions
3. ______ crowd
4. ______ deviancy training
5. ______ dyadic friendships
6. ______ emotional tone
7. ______ enabling interactions
8. ______ gonads
9. ______ homophily
10. ______ menarche
11 ______ primary sex organs
12. ______ puberty
13. ______ secondary sex characteristics
14. ______ selection
15. ______ semenarche

a. These are directly involved in reproduction.
b. The age at which girls reach this developmental milestone has declined by more than a year since the turn of the century.
c. These outward signs of being male or female develop as a result of hormonal changes during adolescence.
d. This series of biological changes constitutes the most radical change in physical development since birth.
e. These have a tendency to inhibit parent–adolescent communication.
f. A boy's reaction to this event depends on the context in which it occurs.
g. These produce testosterone or estrogen and progesterone.
h. This results in friends being quite similar to one another.
j. Examples of these are "jocks," "nerds," and "brains."
k. This can undermine the effectiveness of group therapy sessions for adolescents.
l. These involve close relationships between two people.
m. For boys, at least, this becomes more positive as adolescence progresses.
n. These are beneficial to adolescents by allowing them to try out new ideas.
o. The tendency for adolescents to like others who have the same values, opinions, and preferences.

Multiple-Choice Practice Questions

Circle the letter of the word or phrase that correctly completes each statement.

1. G. Stanley Hall believed that adolescents
   a. are not qualitatively different from younger children.
   b. recapitulate earlier stages of development.
   c. are subject to emotional ups and downs.
   d. Both b and c are correct.

2. In Freud's theory of development, the period of adolescence corresponds to the ______ stage.
   a. latency
   b. oedipal
   c. phallic
   d. genital

3. During adolescence, what events occur in the brain?
   a. synaptogenesis
   b. synaptic pruning
   c. both a and b
   d. no particular changes

4. The _______ produce(s) the hormone that is responsible for the adolescent growth spurt.
   a. hypothalamus
   b. adrenal cortex
   c. pituitary gland
   d. ovaries and testes

5. Which is correct about the physiological differences between males and females in adolescence and adulthood?
   a. Males are stronger, healthier, and better able to tolerate long-term stress.
   b. Males have greater capacity for physical exercise but females are healthier and longer lived.
   c. Females have larger hearts and lower resting heart rates and can exercise for longer periods.
   d. There are no appreciable differences between males' and females' capacities for exercise and athletic performance.

6. The timing of the events of puberty
   a. is the same, on the average, in all cultures.
   b. is later in children from families undergoing stress than in children from more harmonious families.
   c. is earlier in many societies than it was 100 years ago.
   d. is equally similar for identical and fraternal twins.

7. Adolescents tend to choose friends
   a. who live close by.
   b. with similar values and attitudes.
   c. who are several years younger.
   d. from a different socioeconomic background.

8. Which describes an adolescent clique?
   a. a group of 15 to 30 boys and girls
   b. a loosely associated group of couples
   c. a small group of friends, usually of the same sex
   d. any of the above

9. Cross-cultural studies of sexual behavior indicate that
   a. adolescents in many cultures do not yet have sexual feelings.
   b. traditional societies are generally less restrictive about premarital intercourse than industrialized societies.
   c. the standards for adolescent sexual behavior is the same in all cultures.
   d. different cultures may have very different scripts for learning sexual behavior.

10. During the adolescent growth spurt,
    a. the legs lengthen first, followed by the trunk, and the shoulders widen last.
    b. the trunk lengthens first, then the shoulders widen, and the legs lengthen last.
    c. the chest widens first, then the legs lengthen, and the trunk lengthens last.
    d. the legs and trunk lengthen and the shoulders widen all at about the same time.

11. Which are secondary sex characteristics?
    a. the testes in boys and the ovaries in girls
    b. testosterone in boys and estrogen and progesterone in girls
    c. facial hair in boys and breasts in girls
    d. All of these are characteristics.

12. Adolescents reach ________ percent of their adult height by the end of the growth spurt of puberty.
    a. 78
    b. 85
    c. 98
    d. 100

13. Studies have found early physical maturation to be _______ for girls.
    a. an academic advantage
    b. a risk factor
    c. a protective factor
    d. neither advantageous nor disadvantageous

14. Teenagers who become pregnant
    a. are more likely to keep their babies than place them for adoption.
    b. are more likely to decide to terminate their pregnancies if they are doing well in school.
    c. are more likely to carry their pregnancies to term if they have strong religious convictions.
    d. All of the above are true.

15. About 60 percent of girls under 15 years of age who have had sexual intercourse report that during their first sexual experience they were
    a. very satisfied.
    b. motivated by curiosity.
    c. coerced.
    d. protected by contraception.

16. During adolescence, children of _________ parents are less likely to get into trouble than those whose parents use other styles of interaction.
    a. authoritative
    b. authoritarian
    c. permissive
    d. None of these—adolescents are equally likely to get into trouble regardless of parenting style.

17. Much of the time, adolescents' jobs
    a. compete with their schoolwork.
    b. prepare them for future careers.
    c. result in contact with many adults.
    d. offer good opportunities for advancement.

18. U.S. teens spend the largest amount of their leisure time in which activity?
    a. participating in sports
    b. reading
    c. watching television
    d. hanging out with friends

Short-Answer Practice Questions

1. Discuss the interpretations Rousseau, Hall, and Freud have given to the changes that occur during adolescence.

2. What advantages and disadvantages are there to early maturation? In what way do these differ for male and female adolescents?

3. What factors are associated with the development of eating disorders during adolescence? What factors help prevent these problems?

4. How do peer groups help adolescents make the transition from associating primarily in small, same-sex groups to having romantic relationships?

5. What kinds of conflicts do adolescents have with their parents? How does parenting style affect teens' behavior?

6. Discuss the advantages and disadvantages of adolescents holding jobs outside school hours.

Sources of More Information

Berndt, T. J. (1982). The features and effects of friendship in early adolescence. *Child Development, 53*(6),1447–1460.
The author examines the literature on childhood and adolescent friendship and discusses major findings in this area of study.

Cole, S. (1980). *Working kids on working*. New York: Lothrop, Lee, & Shepard.
The author interviewed more than two dozen working children about why they work. The book also deals with questions about working and the law.

Feldman, S. S., & Elliott, G. R. (Eds.). (1993). *At the threshold: The developing adolescent.* Cambridge, MA: Harvard University Press.
A broad summary of research on adolescence written by outstanding scholars in the field.

Hofer, M., Youniss, J., & Noack, P. (1998). *Verbal interaction and development in families with adolescents.* Stamford, CT: Ablex.
This book discusses issues relevant to the communication between adolescents and their parents; much of the work was done with German families.

Malinowski, B. (1972). The social and sexual life of Trobriand children. In Wayne Dennis (Ed.), *Historical readings in developmental psychology.* New York: Appleton-Century-Crofts.
This observation, first published in 1929, describes the coming of age of children in a society very different from our own.

Ruble, D. N., & Brooks-Gunn, J. (1982). The experience of menarche. *Child Development, 53*(6),1557–1566.
This article reports the attitudes and emotional reactions of adolescents and preadolescents to menarche.

Savin-Williams, R. C. (1987). *Adolescence: An ethological perspective.* New York: Springer-Verlag.
This book describes a naturalistic study of adolescents at a summer camp. A good illustration of the way psychological processes are manifested in social interactions.

Smolak, L., Levine, M., & Striegel-Moore, R. (Eds.). (1996). *The developmental psychopathology of eating disorders: Implications of research, prevention and treatment.* Mahwah, NJ: Lawrence Erlbaum.
The chapters in this book cover many aspects of eating disorders, including roles of the media, sense of self, and social support.

Youniss, J., & Smollar, J. (1985). *Adolescent relations with mothers, fathers, and friends.* Chicago: University of Chicago Press.
This book uses interviews to provide a picture of the social reorganization that occurs during adolescence.

Answer Key

Answers to Key Terms: 1.h, 2.e, 3.j, 4.k, 5.e, 6.m, 7.n, 8.g, 9.o, 10.b, 11.a, 12.d, 13.c, 14.i, 15.f.

Answers to Multiple-Choice Questions: 1.d, 2.d, 3.c, 4.c, 5.b, 6.c, 7.b, 8.c, 9.d, 10.a, 11.c, 12.c, 13.b, 14.d, 15.c, 16.a, 17.a, 18.c.

The Cognitive and Psychological Achievements of Adolescence

chapter 16

Psychologists from various theoretical orientations agree that adolescents' thought processes are more sophisticated than those of younger children. Piaget felt that adolescence was characterized by the emergence of formal operations, a type of systematic, logical thinking, while other investigators feel that the characteristics of adolescent cognition can be accounted for by the development of more advanced problem-solving rules and strategies. Cross-cultural differences complicate the matter, but thinking skills that resemble formal operations appear in people of all cultures, applied in specific contexts in which they are appropriate.

Adolescents' improved thinking skills are applied to social, political, and moral as well as academic problems. Capable of seeing the faults in existing systems, they may feel frustrated by the seeming impossibility of social change. Young people also face important personal tasks during adolescence. They must loosen their attachments to their parents and look outside their families for someone to love. At the same time, they must establish identities, developing and committing themselves to their own points of view in many domains, including sexual and ethnic identity, occupational choice, and friendship as well as political and religious orientation.

Adolescence exists because, at least in industrialized nations, there are delays in some components of the bio-social-behavioral shift that mark the end of childhood. It is not surprising, therefore, that the existence of adolescence as a separate, unified stage of development depends on the cultural context in which it occurs.

Learning Objectives

Keep these questions in mind while studying Chapter 16.

1. What characteristics of thought make their appearance in adolescence?
2. To what extent is formal operational thought seen in all people?
3. In what ways are adolescents' thoughts about moral and social issues different from those of younger children?
4. What steps must adolescents go through in the process of forming an identity? How does this process differ according to gender, sexual orientation, minority group membership, and culture?

5. Is adolescence truly a separate stage of development? How does it different from previous stages?

Chapter Summary

The physical and social changes of adolescence are accompanied by the development of a new quality of mind, characterized by the ability to think systematically, logically, and hypothetically.

I. RESEARCH ON ADOLESCENT THOUGHT

Developmentalists suggest that adolescent thinking is characterized by the following: reasoning hypothetically (thinking about possibilities contrary to fact); thinking about thinking (during adolescence, metacognitive thought processes become more complex); planning ahead, rather than considering only the present; and thinking beyond conventional limits about such topics as politics, morality, and religion. While there is evidence for these characteristics of adolescent thought, psychologists now acknowledge that adolescents' thinking is variable according to content and context. Therefore, there is disagreement as to whether adolescence brings stagelike changes in cognition.

A. Formal Operations

Piaget felt that changes in the way adolescents think about themselves, their social relationships, and their society have their source in the development of *formal operations,* a new level of logical thought. In contrast to concrete operations, formal operations involve, he believed, the ability to think systematically about aspects of a problem. Formal operations are also called *second-order operations* because they involve applying operations to operations.

- Analyzing the performance of children and adolescents on tasks such as the "combination of chemicals" problem, Piaget found that adolescents' reasoning could be described as a "structured psychological whole"—a system of relationships—while younger children's reasoning was unsystematic. Adolescents solve the combination of chemicals problem by trying all the combinations of chemicals—systematically—until they discover the combination that produces a yellow color.
- A consequence of formal operational thinking is the ability to reason by *logical necessity,* in which the conclusion of reasoning is set entirely by the rules of logic. Logical necessity underlies *hypothetico-deductive reasoning,* in which, if the premises are true, the conclusion must be true. Formal deductive reasoning is rare before 11 to 12 years of age; it becomes more likely as children grow older.

  In Piaget's theory, development occurs through the conflict of assimilation and accommodation, as children struggle to reach an equilibrium between current levels of understanding and new ideas encountered in their interactions with the physical and social environment. Piaget considered *sociocognitive conflict*—cognitive conflict rooted in social experience—to be important in reaching new levels of understanding. Evidence for this idea comes from a study by Rose Dimant and David Bearson, who had college students work through problems similar to the combination of liquids task, either alone or in pairs. They found that the students benefited from sessions in which they worked collaboratively with another student on a series of increasingly difficult problems; sessions that included disagreements, contradictions, and alternative solutions were particularly effective. Students who worked alone or did not collaborate made smaller gains.

B. Alternative Approaches to Explaining Adolescent Thought

Information-processing theorists focus on the way that changing memory capacities and expanding knowledge bases allow adolescents to demonstrate more effective problem-solving strategies and metacognitive understanding. Cultural-context theorists have concentrated on the ways in which specialized practice in particular domains give rise to the systematic thought processes that characterize adolescent cognition.

- According to information-processing theorists, when adolescents solve problems they benefit from larger working memories and the ability to apply more powerful strategies. These are viewed as being gradual acquisitions rather than resulting from global, qualitative change in the quality of thought. Researchers have explored adolescents' problem solving by examining how they make decisions.

  The quality of adolescent decision-making is important in terms of their health and well-being and also to questions about whether they are capable of giving informed consent to, for example, medical procedures, independent of their parents' input. In a study by Bonnie Halpern-Felsher and Elizabeth Cauffman, sixth- to twelfth-graders and young adults were presented with dilemmas involving the domains of medical procedures, the family, and informed consent, and were invited to respond with advice. The researchers found that the adults demonstrated higher levels of decision-making competence compared with the adolescents, especially the sixth- to eighth-graders. Adults were more likely to consider options, risks, long-term consequences, benefits, and advice from others. However, many adolescents displayed high levels of competence, making it difficult to generalize with respect to policy regarding about when they should be allowed to make important decisions for themselves.
- There is a great deal more variability in adolescent reasoning—both within individuals and across groups—than occurs in the stages that precede it. Studies find that only 30 to 40 percent of well-educated Americans in their late teens solve the combination of chemicals problem and other formal operational tasks. Adults may apply formal operational reasoning in some domains but not in others, and experts routinely take short cuts in reasoning rather than exhaustively considering all options. In contrast to Piaget's idea of a new logic underlying adult thought, cultural-context theorists emphasize the differences that occur as a result of the variation in contexts of adult activity. An example of the effect of culture was demonstrated by a review of studies that revealed a decline in

gender differences in formal operational reasoning over the 20-year period in which the studies were conducted. Today, as girls and women are encouraged to participate in math and science, differences in formal operational thinking, if they occur, are minimal.

Cross-cultural work indicates that uneducated people, from small societies that are not technologically advanced, rarely demonstrate formal operations when tested with Piagetian methods. Apparently, the type of experience obtained in formal educational settings is a precondition for the development of formal thought. Taken together, these findings suggest that improvements in cognitive ability during adolescence can appear continuous or discontinuous, depending on a person's depth of knowledge about the content or context. It is necessary to examine many different contexts to assess whether the cognitive changes from middle childhood to adolescence represent continuity or a stagelike change.

II. ADOLESCENT THINKING ABOUT MORAL ISSUES

There is some evidence that, like thinking about politics or scientific problems, reasoning about moral issues undergoes development during adolescence.

A. Kohlberg's Theory of Moral Reasoning

According to Lawrence Kohlberg's theory, Stage 3 is based on relations between individuals and appears toward the end of middle childhood. Stage 4 reasoning, based on relations between the individual and the group, makes its appearance during adolescence. Moral behavior is, therefore, behavior that maintains the existing social order. Stage 3 and stage 4 reasoning depend on partially attaining formal operational thought, according to Kohlberg. Thinking in stages 3 and 4 depends on being able to consider all the existing factors relevant to a moral decision; thinking is still concrete insofar as it does not yet consider all the *possible* relevant factors. Stage 5 reasoning in Kohlberg's system generally does not appear until early in adulthood and is rarely seen even then. Rather than focusing on maintaining the existing social order, stage 5 thinkers seek possibilities for improving it. Stage 6 reasoning is even rarer and involves placing certain universal ethical principles above the rules of society. Stages 5 and 6 represent a "postconventional" level or moral reasoning. The characteristics of all six stages are summarized in Table 16.3.

B. Evaluating Kohlberg's Theory of Moral Reasoning

A common criticism of Kohlberg's theory is that children are able to understand the difference between social conventions and moral issues earlier than estimated by Kohlberg. Melanie Killen and her colleagues argue that social-conventional beliefs are not stepping stones to higher moral beliefs; instead, both moral and social-conventional reasoning are important to children's reasoning about moral issues; social-conventional reasoning increases throughout middle childhood and adolescence.

Carol Gilligan and her colleagues have argued that Kohlberg's approach reflects a *morality of justice* that emphasizes issues of fairness, rightness and equality, while neglecting another important domain—the *morality of care,* that stresses relationships, compassion, and social obligations. Gilligan asserts that girls and women are oriented to the morality of care, while boys and men are oriented to the morality of justice; however, there is little evidence for gender differences in levels of moral reasoning. Nonetheless, Gilligan's view of the development of moral reasoning covers broader issues than that of Kohlberg.

C. Cultural Variations in Moral Reasoning

Cross-cultural studies reveal that people from small, technologically unsophisticated societies rarely reason beyond Kohlberg's stage 3, and often reason at stage 1 or 2. Kohlberg explained this as the result of differences in social stimulation. Other investigators, such as anthropologist Richard Shweder, have pointed out that Kohlberg's stage sequence itself contains value judgments specific to Western traditions of liberal democracy. In any case, using other approaches to measuring moral reasoning yields different results from Kohlberg's; the shift to postconventional reasoning in adulthood appears quite widespread. What differences do appear across cultures seem to be related to level of education. According to Elliot Turiel and his colleagues, there is agreement across cultures on issues of morality; where differences occur, they tend to involve social conventions and personal choice, the importance of obedience to authority, and the nature of interpersonal relations. An example is provided by Cecilia Wainryb's work with 9- to 17-year-old Jewish and Druze children in Israel. When asked to make judgments on questions of justice, there was little difference between the groups; the only significant difference was that Jewish children were more likely than Druze children to assert personal rights over obedience to authority. Some differences between societies take the form of what distinctions are drawn between moral rules, social conventions, and matters of personal preference. However, all societies make these distinctions. For example, a study by Joan Miller and her colleagues showed that both Indian and American subjects judged violation of dress codes in terms of social convention and theft as a moral issue.

D. The Relation between Moral Reasoning and Moral Action

What relationship is there between adolescents' moral reasoning and their behavior? As in middle childhood, there is a moderate relation between the two; adolescents who score higher on moral reasoning tests are also less likely to do things such as cheat in school and more likely to perform prosocial acts such as helping a person in distress. However, there is also evidence that, in many cases, the links between moral judgments and moral action are not especially close. Many competing factors enter into moral choices. For example, cheating is widespread in many high schools; it is especially likely to occur when there is little chance of being caught and punished. A factor that helps adolescents to act morally is their increasing ability to consider the points of view of others and to reason prosocially; studies of Brazilian and North American adolescents have found strong correlations between sympathy, perspective-taking skills, and prosocial reasoning. One factor affecting the relationship between adolescents' moral reasoning skills and their behavior, as well as conflicts with their parents, is where they place the boundary between the moral and the personal domains. For example, Tara Kuther and Ann Higgins-D'Alessandro found that adolescents reporting higher levels of drug and alcohol use were likely to see these behaviors as personal decisions rather than as moral or conventional decisions.

E. Parent and Peer Contributions to Moral Development

According to Kohlberg, interaction with peers should have greater effect than interaction with parents on the development of higher levels of moral reasoning; he felt that adolescents are more likely to take seriously contrasting points of view when they are expressed by peers. In fact, both quantity and quality of peer relationships are related to moral reasoning in adolescence. However, it has also been found that responsive, authoritative parenting is associated with higher levels of moral maturity in adolescents. Lawrence Walker and his colleagues conducted a longitudinal study that found parents provided a higher level of cognitive functioning during discussions, especially when a "gentle Socratic method" was used; with respect to peer interactions, those that were more turbulent and conflict-ridden were associated with development of higher moral levels.

III. INTEGRATION OF THE SELF

It is widely believed that adolescence is the period during which an individual forms the basis of a stable adult personality.

A. The Puzzle of Identity

According to William James, a major puzzle of identity was to determine how the self could get outside of itself in order to reflect on its own qualities; this is called recursion. James defined two components of the self: the *me-self,* or object-self (including all the things people know about themselves); and the *I-self,* or subject-self (the part of the system that guides and reflects on the self). The I-self has the attributes of self-awareness, self-agency, self-continuity, and self-coherence. Modern theorists are preoccupied with additional puzzles; according to Kenneth Gergen, modern society has resulted in a *saturated self,* with multiple "me's," in response to a wide range of social roles and relationships. Adolescents must be different people in different contexts; this is reflected in the appearance of "multiple selves" in their self-descriptions. Michael Chandler and his colleagues argue that a major task of adolescence is to understand self-continuity, the fact that selves persist in time even though they change in obvious ways, as do the environments in which they live; this can be difficult for adolescents who live under conditions of dramatic social upheaval.

B. Resolving the Identity Crisis

Erik Erikson viewed the need to create a uniform identity as the final developmental crisis before adulthood. Adolescents must resolve the crisis by achieving a secure sense of personal identity or face psychological problems in later life. Adolescents must resolve their identities in both the individual and the social spheres and establish "the identity of these two identities," according to Erikson.

James Marcia developed an assessment method to examine the process of identity formation (for another method, see the box "From Diaries to Blogs: Personal Documents in Developmental Research). He used interviews to elicit information about the degree to which young people have adopted and committed themselves to well-thought-out views on politics, religion, occupation, friendship, dating, and sex roles. Marcia focused on two factors identified by Erikson as being especially important for achieving mature identity: 1) crisis/exploration, a stage in identity formation during which adolescents actively examine their opportunities, reexamine their parents' choices, and begin to search for alternatives they find personally satisfying; and 2) commitment, the final phase in identity formation during which individuals commit to the goals, values, beliefs, and future occupations that they have chosen for themselves. On the basis of subjects' responses, four patterns of coping with identity formation were identified: identity achievement, in which young people had experienced a decision-making period and decided on their own views; foreclosure, in which they had not gone through an identity crisis but had simply adopted their parents' identity patterns; moratorium, in which young people were experiencing an identity crisis at the time of the interview; and identity diffusions, in which they had tried on several identities but had not settled on one. Many studies have indicated that, as they grow older, more and more adolescents can be classified in the identity achievement category and fewer in the identity diffusion category, a trend that continues into adulthood.

Studies of the relationship of exploration to identity achievement have found that childhood exploration, as indicated by participation in a wide variety of activities, predicted adolescent exploration, which in turn predicted identity achievement. However, while exploration is important in identity formation, commitment seems to contribute to adolescents' satisfaction with themselves and their lives. For example, a study of more than 1500 Dutch adolescents by Meeus and his colleagues found that both identity achievement and foreclosure were associated with a sense of well-being.

- Adolescents' family and peer relations influence the process of identity formation. Harke Bosma and Saskia Kunnen suggested that conflicts arising in the course of adolescents' social relationships trigger higher levels of self-development; the most fertile contexts for identity development are those that promote openness to change and provide a high level of support. Harold Grotevant and Catherine Cooper examined the relation between identity achievement scores and family interaction; they found that family systems which offer support and security while allowing adolescents to create distinct identities are the most effective in promoting identity achievement. Recent work has shown that secure attachment is positively related to identity achievement, while insecure attachment is related to identity diffusion.

  In a study by Wim Meeus and Maja Dekovic of more than 3000 Dutch subjects between 12 and 24 years of age, the support of classmates and friends was rated more important than the support of family members in promoting identity achievement.

C. Gender Differences in Identity Formation

Erikson believed that girls and boys tend to follow different paths to identity achievement; girls, he felt, did not complete the process until they married and became mothers. This view is not relevant in today's North American culture. Recent studies have found little evidence of gender differences in identity formation. However, some studies have shown gender differences in the domains in which young people first achieve identity; for example, a study by Meeus and Dekovic reported that adolescent girls score at higher levels than boys in the domain of friendship, and several theorists have suggested that personal relationships are more important to self-definition for females than for males. The bulk of the evidence indicates that adolescent girls and boys go though similar processes, with some variation in the domains that are most important to them.

D. The Formation of a Sexual Identity

Formation of a sexual identity answers the question "Who am I as a sexual being?" The formation of sexual identity may involve exploration and commitment; like personal identity formation, it occurs against a background of sociopolitical and historical traditions, power relations, and stereotypes. Unlike some other domains of identity formation, it is not a frequent topic of conversation between adolescents and their parents, peers, and counselors.

- In Freud's theory, adolescence is a time when young people must reexperience, in new forms, the conflicts of earlier stages. For example, reworking the Oedipus conflict results in seeking love outside the family, "one of the most painful psychical achievements of the pubertal period," according to Freud.
- Power relations among child, parents, and society are important in Freud's theory; they are also emphasized in modern work on sexual identity development.

  In modern society, women continue to face limitations; research has focused on how the "patriarchal belief system" is expressed in the sexual identity development of adolescent girls. An analysis by Erica Van Roosmalen of letters written to a magazine by teenage girls seeking advice revealed that male dominance and gender-based stereotypes were core issues. Many girls felt caught between conflicting expectations as to how they should behave toward boys. Meenakshi Thapan examined similar issues of conflicting expectations in the society of contemporary India, where more Westernized views of women's roles are becoming popular. She found that adolescent girls spoke of conflict between traditional and modern expectations in balancing work and education with family obligations. The Indian girls also expressed some of the same dissatisfaction with their appearance that has been associated with growing up in Europe or North America.

  While most adolescents will have a heterosexual *sexual orientation* (that is, they have erotic feelings for members of the opposite sex), there are still a substantial number who have homosexual preferences. While between 7 and 8 percent of a representative sample of American adults reported feeling a same-sex desire at least once, only 1½ to 3 percent identified themselves as gay, lesbian, or bisexual.

Richard Troiden has proposed a stage model of sexual identity development for sexual minority youth that fits the experience of many North American gay men in recent decades. It includes the following stages: Stage 1, sensitization, feeling different (during middle childhood the individual feels different from other children); Stage 2, self-recognition, identity confusion (at puberty, the individual realizes an attraction to the same sex and labels such feelings as homosexual); Stage 3, identity assumption (the individual moves from private acknowledgement of homosexual preference to admitting it openly); Stage 4, commitment, identity integration (the stage reached by those who adopt homosexuality as a way of life). Commitment to a homosexual identity may be weak or strong. Table 16.6 shows milestones of sexual orientation, including the average age of disclosure of sexual orientation to other people; this usually occurs only after a person has been able to understand how he or she is different from others and how this relates to sexual orientation identity. There is some indication that women's sexuality is more fluid than men's. For example, lesbians are more likely than gay men to report that their first sexual contacts were with the opposite sex and to report sexual contacts with both men and women. In any case, this sequence of stages is not universal across cultures. In other societies and historical periods, same-sex sexual behavior has served other functions and has not necessarily been viewed as an expression of a life-long sexual identity.

Some scholars such as Ritch Savin-Williams, point out that sexual-minority youth are similar to all youths and that there is a great deal of diversity among them in the origin and development of sexual orientation and identity.

E. Identity Formation in Ethnic Minority and Immigrant Youths

Identity formation is especially complicated for minority and immigrant children in the United States. Adolescents from minority groups face the task of reconciling two different identities, one based on the culture of the majority group and one based on their own cultural heritage; they have twice as much psychological work to do. Ethnic minority children may also face prejudice and discrimination, further complicating identity formation. Also, with the increase in multiracial births, it is important to learn how multiracial children establish ethnic identities.

Children entering middle childhood already know the labels and attributes that apply to their own ethnic groups and have developed basic attitudes about their ethnicity. During middle childhood and adolescence, they undergo three stages in the formation of ethnic identity.

- In the initial stage, unexamined ethnic identity, children still show preference for the values of the majority culture; this may include a negative evaluation of their own group.
- In stage 2, ethnic identity search, young people show a concern for the personal implications of their ethnicity. This stage may be initiated by a shocking experience in which the young person is rejected or humiliated because of his or her ethnicity. In this stage,

young people often engage in an active search for information about their own group; they may also experience anger at the majority group. In some cases, this involves forming an *oppositional identity* in rejection of the dominant group.

- Stage 3, ethnic identity achievement, is characterized by acceptance of ethnicity and a positive self-concept.

  Ethnic identity is positively related to psychological variables such as self-esteem, personal identity, and school involvement. It may be protective in other ways. For example, a study of seventh-grade students who identified themselves as American Indian found that those who had a greater sense of ethnic pride also had stronger antidrug norms compared with their peers. The box "Suicide among Native American Adolescents" discusses challenges to ethnic identity formation. Jean Phinney and her colleagues studied immigrant Armenian, Vietnamese, and Mexican families to identify factors that may facilitate ethnic identity formation. They found that when the native language is used in the home, when adolescents spend time with peers who share their ethnic heritage, and when parents instruct their children in cultural traditions, identity formation is strongest. Adolescents who immigrate into established communities of their ethnic heritage find it easier to develop a shared sense of ethnic identity. Others use art and music in the process of identity formation. For example, see the box "The Hip-Hop Generation: Keeping It Real and Disturbing the Peace."

F. Cross-Cultural Variations in Identity Formation

Identity formation can differ profoundly between cultures. For example, Hazel Marcus and Shinobu Kitayama describe differences between cultures with an independent sense of self—in which individuals are oriented to being unique, expressing their own thoughts and opinions, and pursuing their own goals—and those with an interdependent sense of self (collectivist cultures)—in which individuals seek to fit into groups and to promote the goals of others. Adolescents in different types of societies need to resolve different sets of problems in developing a unified sense of identity. In addition, not all societies require the full range of decisions and choices—related to work, marriage, and ideology—that are faced by young people in North America.

Elliot Turiel argues against grouping cultures into two broad categories, on the grounds that cultures are much more diverse than is accurately described by a two-category system. In fact, there is little research on identity formation in nonindustrialized, hunter-gatherer or agricultural societies. As reported by anthropologists, the transition to adult identity in such societies is characterized by *rites of passage*—cultural ceremonies and events that mark a transition in status from child to adult. According to Arnold van Gennep, these share a three-part structure: separation from old ways of being; transition to new practices and knowledge; and incorporation into the new role.

In the United States, various rites of passage are performed, including confirmations, bar and bat mitzvahs, and high school graduations.

IV. SELF AND SOCIETY

Despite the fact that adolescents all over the world are witnessing shifts in the cultural, political, and economic structures of their communities and societies, most adolescents show little interest in news and political affairs.

A. Adolescents' Subjective Well-Being

Subjective well-being is a concept that includes self-esteem and satisfaction with one's life. Developmentalists are interested in the relationship between adolescents' subjective well-being and the broader contexts of their lives. According to cross-national studies, most adolescents have a positive sense of subjective well-being and are satisfied and optimistic. As shown in Table 16.8, sociohistorical conditions, for example, greater security and economic stability, affect the sense of well-being; everyday stress and a sense of personal control are also important.

B. Thinking about Politics and the Political Process

According to existing evidence, adolescents' reasoning about political issues is, for the most part, immature. However, based on interviews with adolescents from several countries, Joseph Adelson and his colleagues concluded that around 14 years of age a major change occurs in adolescents' reasoning about politics. For example, in answering questions about society and its laws, 12- to 13-year-olds answered in terms of concrete people and events ("If we had no laws, people would go around killing people") while 15- to 16-year-olds were more abstract ("They limit what people can do."). Twelve- to 13-year-olds also tended to give authoritarian answers when asked, for example, what should be done if a person breaks the law. The shift in reasoning corresponds to changes in mid-adolescence noted by Inhelder and Piaget in their studies of scientific problem solving.

C. Sociopolitical Identity Development

Recent work focuses on how identity processes affect adolescents' reasoning about and response to sociopolitical events that affect their lives. For example, how have young people in Eastern Europe responded to the radical shifts in regimes and policies that have occurred in their countries? An international team of researchers invited adolescents to discuss their knowledge, concerns, values, and experiences in the sociopolitical arena; consistent with results of previous studies of adolescents, most participants believed that the changes in their countries had little significant impact on their lives. Like their North American peers, as their reasoning became more complex with age, their interest in politics waned. Because the adolescents tended to define themselves in terms of their relationships with their families, when their families diluted the significance of sociopolitical issues—perhaps in an attempt to shield their children from the effects of the transitions—the adolescents were less likely to link their own experiences to the broader social system.

D. Fostering Sociopolitical Engagement

Out of concern that many adolescents reach adulthood uninterested in sociopolitical issues or unable to reason about them effectively, some developmentalists have urged schools to offer *service-learning classes*—classes that allow young people to confront social problems through personal experience, for example, by helping out in a soup kitchen for the homeless. James Youniss and Miranda Yates found that such experiences stimulated students to think more deeply about social problems and also resulted in the development of more complex reasoning about the relevant issues. Other researchers found that participating in a course focused on how environmental factors contribute to social problems resulted in greater community activism by adolescents in low-income neighborhoods; the adolescents' efforts led to a number of important changes in their schools and neighborhoods.

According to Erik Erikson, successful historical change requires a realignment of self and society. Adolescents are prepared to contribute to this process, given support from the adults in their lives.

V. RECONSIDERING ADOLESCENCE

The period between middle childhood and adulthood does not entirely fit the pattern of earlier stages. In some societies, puberty begins later than it does in industrialized countries and coincides closely with marriage and taking on adult responsibilities.

A. Adolescence in Modern Societies

In societies such as that of the United States and other industrialized nations, with a long delay between puberty and adult status, biological, social, and behavioral changes are not coordinated in the same way as in earlier stages. Some developmentalists have proposed new labels, such as "youth," or "emerging adulthood" to describe the development of individuals between 18 and 25 years of age in rapidly changing societies. Under such circumstances, as a result of fast-paced technological, social, and political changes, young people may turn to each other, rather than to their elders, to sort out issues of identity. Whether the transition to adulthood is prolonged or abrupt, it reflects a special relationship between young people and their cultures.

Key Terms

Following are important terms introduced in Chapter 16. Match the term with the letter of the example that best illustrates the term.

1. ______ emerging adulthood
2. ______ formal operations
3. ______ hypothetico-deductive reasoning
4. ______ I-self
5. ______ logical necessity
6. ______ me-self
7. ______ morality of care
8. ______ morality of justice
9. ______ oppositional identity formation
10. ______ rites of passage
11. ______ saturated self
12. ______ second-order operation
13. ______ service-learning classes
14. ______ sexual orientation
15. ______ sociocognitive conflict
16. ______ subjective well-being

a. A label applied to 15- to 25-year-olds in modern industrialized societies.
b. This can be heterosexual, homosexual, or bisexual.
c. This develops in response to the need to act differently in many different situations.
d. A kind of systematic logical thinking on which adolescent thought is structured, according to Piaget.
e. An example would be categorizing categories.
f. According to many developmentalists, this helps power development of the ability to consider many sides of a problem.
g. Reasoning according to this is one of the characteristics of adolescent thought.
h. An example is "Dolphins are mammals; Flip is a dolphin; therefore, Flip is a mammal."
i. According to Carol Gilligan, Kohlberg's theory is based too strongly on this aspect of moral reasoning.
j. When this applies to an African American adolescent, everything about "white" culture may seem wrong.
k. In U.S. culture, confirmations and bar mitzvahs are examples.
l. According to Carol Gilligan, this is more characteristic of girls and women.
m. This includes such things as self-esteem and satisfaction with one's life.
n. The part of the self that includes all the things people know about themselves.
o. These might include participation in community service activities.
p. If a person's life were a story, this would be the protagonist.

Multiple-Choice Practice Questions

Circle the letter of the word or phrase that correctly completes each statement.

1. Which of the following are characteristics of adolescent thinking?
   a. planning ahead
   b. formulating hypotheses
   c. thinking about one's own thought processes
   d. all of the above

2. According to information-processing theorists, differences between the performance of adolescents and younger children on Piaget's balance task are due to adolescents'
   a. ability to balance assimilation and accommodation.
   b. ability to apply more power problem-solving strategies.
   c. increased working memory.
   d. both b and c are true.

3. Research on adolescent decision making about important issues such as medical treatments has shown that
   a. adolescents can make decisions just as effectively as adults.
   b. adolescents were no more effective at decision making than were younger children.
   c. adolescents were less likely than adults to consider options, risks, and long-term consequences and benefits.
   d. adolescents were more likely than adults to consider options, risks, and long-term consequences and benefits.

4. People from which age group tend to be most authoritarian in their views on social control and the appropriate punishment for breaking the law?
   a. 12- to 13-year-olds
   b. 15- to 16-year-olds
   c. college-age young people
   d. adults

5. The most common mode of moral reasoning during adolescence is Kohlberg's
   a. stage 2.
   b. stage 3.
   c. stage 4.
   d. stage 5.

6. Which of Kohlberg's stages of moral reasoning is based on maintaining the existing social order and is sometimes called the "law and order" stage?
   a. stage 2
   b. stage 3
   c. stage 4
   d. stage 5

7. Which is Carol Gilligan's objection to Kohlberg's theory of moral development?
   a. It is biased toward the morality of justice and neglects the morality of care.
   b. The method of scoring answers can be difficult to use.
   c. The relationship between moral reasoning and moral behavior is unreliable.
   d. It does not include a separate scale for moral reasoning in traditional, nonindustrialized cultures.

8. Freud believed that adolescents need to _______ earlier conflicts; for example, the Oedipal conflict.
   a. rework
   b. repress
   c. succumb to
   d. recognize

9. According to Erik Erikson, establishing _______ is the fundamental task of adolescence.
   a. intimacy
   b. identity
   c. autonomy
   d. foreclosure

10. Studies have shown that there is a ________ relationship between the level of adolescents' moral reasoning and their behavior.
    a. nonexistent
    b. small, positive
    c. strong, positive
    d. moderate, negative

11. ________ is a term applied to adolescents who have tried out several identities but have not been able to settle on one.
    a. Foreclosure
    b. Identity diffusion
    c. Moratorium
    d. Identity achievement

12. ________ may be the response of minority young people to a shocking experience of being rejected because of ethnic background.
    a. Ethnic identity search
    b. Internalization of ethnic identity
    c. Developing an interdependent sense of self
    d. Indifference to ethnic identity

13. Young people in hunter-gatherer or small agricultural societies
    a. often undergo initiation rites at puberty.
    b. have fewer decisions to make about occupation and marriage than those in industrial societies.
    c. have not been extensively studied with respect to identity formation.
    d. are all of the above.

14. Young people who are immigrants to the United States have fewer difficulties in formulating an ethnic identity when
    a. their native language is used in the home.
    b. they relocate to areas where there is a preexisting community of people from their ethnic group.
    c. they have many friends of their own ethnic group.
    d. all of the above are true.

15. Research on the political interests of adolescents has shown that most adolescents
    a. are unable to reason logically about political issues.
    b. are not especially interested in politics.
    c. are extremely interested in politics but not especially active.
    d. are very active in politics.

Short-Answer Practice Questions

1. Discuss the differences between adolescents' thinking and the thinking of younger children. How are these differences explained by Piaget? By information-processing theorists?

2. How does sociocognitive conflict affect performance on measures of formal operational reasoning? How does it affect performance on moral reasoning tasks?

3. Discuss the important developmental tasks of adolescence according to Freud and Erikson.

4. What position have Kohlberg and other developmentalists taken with respect to applying his theory of the development of moral reasoning to a variety of cultures?

5. How might identity formation in sexual minority youth and ethnic minority youth vary from that of youth from the majority culture? In what ways is it the same?

6. Discuss the rites of passage that occur in North American society. In what ways are they similar to and different from the rites of passage characteristic of traditional societies?

Putting It All Together

Match each example with the stage of which it is most characteristic:

a. infancy
b. the preschool period
c. middle childhood
d. adolescence

_____ 1. Lisa is developing scripts that help her get through activities such as birthday parties, visits to the dentist, and meals in restaurants.

_____ 2. Anne has an authoritarian view with regard to laws and punishment.

_____ 3. When asked to figure out what combination of paints produces a particular color, Frank uses pencil and paper to keep track of the combinations he has tried.

_____ 4. Children of Janet's age are learning that other people have feelings that may not always show in their behavior.

_____ 5. Luke's major tasks in personality formation involve establishing first trust, then autonomy.

_____ 6. Games with rules are now important in Jonathan's play with his friends.

_____ 7. Michael no longer automatically accepts his parents' view of the world and is formulating his own opinions about politics, religion, and occupational choices.

_____ 8. Susan likes to engage in pretend play with her friends—other children in the neighborhood whom she sees frequently.

______ 9. Richard's reasoning can be primitive or fairly logical, depending on his familiarity with the task and on whether he has scripted knowledge about the situation.

______ 10. Sara needs a best friend to supply feedback about her behavior and her feelings about boys.

Sources of More Information

Bem, D. J. (1996). Exotic becomes erotic: A developmental theory of sexual orientation. *Psychological Review, 103*(2), 320–335.
This article presents a theory of the development of sexual identity that attempts to explain same- and opposite-sex desire in both males and females.

Erikson, E. (1994). *Identity: Youth and crisis.* New York: Norton.
In this book, first published several decades ago, the author discusses adolescent identity formation and some of the difficulties involved in this process.

Keating, D. P. (1980). Thinking processes in adolescence. In J. Adelson (Ed.), *Handbook of adolescent psychology.* New York: Wiley.
In this chapter, the author describes the characteristics of adolescent thought and takes up problems of stage versus continuity and competence versus performance.

Kohlberg, L. (1984). *The psychology of moral development: The nature and validity of moral stages.* New York: Harper & Row.
This volume brings together many of Kohlberg's most influential papers on moral development.

Kroger, J. (1996). *Identity in adolescence: The balance between self and other.* New York: Routledge.
This book pays careful attention to each of the major theories of identity formation. The biographical accounts of the theorists place their work in a cultural-historical context.

Linn, M., Clement, C., & Pulos, S. (1983). Is it formal if it's not physics? (The influence of content on formal reasoning). *Journal of Research in Science Teaching, 20*(8), 755–770.
This article examine the effects of content and subjects' expectations on performance on tests of formal operational reasoning.

Marcia, J. E. (1980). Identity in adolescence. In J. Adelson (Ed.), *Handbook of adolescent psychology.* New York: Wiley.
In this chapter, the author discusses his findings on adolescents' identity statuses.

Piaget, J., & Inhelder, B. (1975). *The origin of the idea of chance in children.* New York: Norton.
Reasoning about chance and probability are examples of logical thought. Piaget and Inhelder report on their studies of the development of these concepts in children with reasoning levels from preoperational through formal operational.

Pipher, M. (1994). *Reviving Ophelia: Saving the selves of adolescent girls.* New York: Putnam.
The author, a psychologist with extensive experience working with adolescents, suggests ways to prevent problems caused by aspects of contemporary culture that are destructive to girls.

Siegler, R. S. (1976). Three aspects of cognitive development. *Cognitive Psychology, 8,* 481–520.
This article describes the author's information-processing approach to Inhelder and Piaget's balance beam problem.

Youniss, J., & Yates, M. (1997). *Community service and social responsibility in youth.* Chicago: University of Chicago Press.
This book describes the authors' work with African American teens who were given hands-on experience working to help alleviate social problems.

Answer Key

Answers to Key Terms: 1.a, 2.d, 3.h, 4.p, 5.g, 6.n, 7.l, 8.i, 9.j, 10.k, 11.c, 12.e, 13.o, 14.b, 15.f, 16.m.

Answers to Multiple-Choice Questions: 1.d, 2.d, 3.c, 4.a, 5.b, 6.c, 7.a, 8.a, 9.b, 10.b, 11.b, 12.a, 13.d, 14.d, 15.b.

Answers to Putting It All Together: 1.b, 2.c, 3.d, 4.c, 5.a, 6.c, 7.d, 8.b, 9.b, 10.d.